MIND
BLOWN

MIND BLOWN

An A to Z Guide for Raising Consciousness

T. S. Martin

Text © 2023 by T. S. Martin

All rights reserved. No part of this book may be reproduced without written permission from the publisher, except by a reviewer who may quote brief passages or reproduce illustrations in a review with appropriate credits; nor may any part of this book be reproduced, stored in a retrieval system, or transmitted in any form or by any means – electronic, mechanical, photocopying, recording, or other – without written permission from the publisher.

The views, beliefs, and opinions expressed in this book do not necessarily reflect those of the author, but of many contributing authors. Any content provided by the author is not intended to support or malign any religion, ethnic group, organization, company, individual, or anything within the Multiverse or Cosmoverse.

Claim Not! Readers are urged to take all appropriate precautions before undertaking any how-to task. This book does not intend to give medical advice or prescribe the use of any technique as a form of treatment for any condition without first consulting a qualified professional. Techniques mentioned in the book should only be considered as tools for education and exploration in one's quest for knowledge and well-being. Although every effort has been made to provide reliable information, neither the publisher nor author are responsible for outcomes undertaken by readers.

> This publication is intended to provide educational information for the reader on the covered subjects. It is not intended as a diagnostic tool, or as a substitute for personalized medical counseling and treatment from a trained health professional.

Table of Contents

INTRODUCTION — 1

PART I — 9
Energy—It's Here, It's There, It's Everywhere
CHAPTER 1 — 11
Universal Connections—The Realities of Nature
The Hopi Creation Myth
CHAPTER 2 — 45
When Mojo Goes Nojo
CHAPTER 3 — 73
Mojo Rising

PART II — 103
From Thought to Thing
CHAPTER 4 — 105
What You Think Is What You Get
CHAPTER 5 — 111
Blasphemous Beliefs
CHAPTER 6 — 121
The Emotions of Manifestation

CHAPTER 7 — 135
Conscious Creation - Manifesting Desires not Disease

PART III — 151
A Vibrational Toolbox

CHAPTER 8 — 161
The Chakralatory System

CHAPTER 9 — 191
Matters of Light and Color

CHAPTER 10 — 205
Rock Steady: Geodes, Gems, and Jewels

CHAPTER 11 — 213
The Shapes and Spirals of Sacred Geometry

CHAPTER 12 — 219
The Healing Vibrations of Sound

CHAPTER 13 — 229
The Fourth Phase of Water

CHAPTER 14 — 239
Other Energy Healing Techniques

PART IV — 285
Doors to the Subconscious

CHAPTER 15 — 287
Access and Answers of the Subconscious

CHAPTER 16 — 309
The Deactivation of DNA

CHAPTER 17 — 317
Kundalini, the Stairway to Heaven

CHAPTER 18 331
Psychic Potentiality "Spirituology"

CONCLUSION 343
The Evolution from Carbon to Crystal –
from Compliance to Cognizance

BIBLIOGRAPHY 349

INTRODUCTION

"What you think you become. What you feel, you attract. What you imagine, you create." — BUDDHA

For many years I have been in love with the brain. I've always been curious about self-exploration and intrigued by human nature, and why people act the way they do, as I'm sure many of you are. So, in college, I took every course I could on the brain. I studied psychology, neuropsychology, neuroanatomy, brain physiology, brain waves, neuroplasticity, you name it. A brain conversation outside of school would make me drool like Pavlov's dog. The 90s was the Decade of the Brain, and I believed that studying its functions would help me understand the nature of myself, things, the underpinnings of life, and that all-encompassing question of *what's our purpose?* At the time, I was fulfilling my life's desire, but the brain wasn't able to provide the answers I was looking for. I now consider the brain to be a grand functioning machine with complex curiosities, much like the engine of a car—it helps the vehicle drive, but on its own, the brain is a backseat driver.

Who's driving the vehicle? The mind, of course. The brain is more of a mechanism that does as it's told, and it's really the mind that's in control of human performance. When I first started this book, I had no idea of the huge rabbit hole I was diving into. Through research, I found that even though scientists' work was definitive and telling, most only have a glimpse about the nature of our existence, and consciousness research is now on the forefront. Many assumptions in this book, such as distance healing, all time exists as Now, and having a 3D holographic reality may be difficult concepts to accept. I am beginning to absorb these ideas into my own reality and hopefully will bring them into yours as well.

<u>Assumptions:</u>

- 😲 All time is Now.
- 😲 Everything is energy.
- 😲 We are all aspects of One energy.
- 😲 The Universe and reality are a holographic matrix of consciousness.
- 😲 Consciousness (thinking), not perception of the five senses, creates reality.
- 😲 Intentions and thoughts affect the physical world.
- 😲 Epigenetics allows us to change our gene expression.
- 😲 Quantum physics allows us to access information beyond the boundaries of time and space.

😮 A fourth phase of water exists with the ability to retain memory and intention.

😮 There is no "junk DNA;" activation of our 12-strand DNA birthright enables innate healing and psychic capabilities.

☺ We can create and manifest our heart's desires.

Consciousness doesn't exist in the brain. If it did, people wouldn't be able to recall while being "brain dead." The subconscious mind holds consciousness, the soul, thinking, intuition, and emotions. College classes on the subconscious mind were quite limited, maybe nonexistent. I would say thus far, everything I have learned about the mind, subtle energy, and consciousness, I have learned through reading others' books and articles. This book is a natural extension of my initial interest and curiosity of the brain, although now it has extended to the concept of the mind having miraculous healing, creative, and manifestation capabilities.

At first, I was trying to keep this book a simple manifestation tool for the layperson but realized this was not an easy feat, as science, religion, psychology, spirituality, and quantum physics all seemed to merge into one. As such, focus on one domain will be minimal within this book; manifestation energy encompasses the energy of all. However, discussion of the relationship between manifestation, the energy of consciousness, and spirituality is unavoidable. I learned that spirituality has nothing to do with religion, but more with the art of introspection. So, this book really encompasses the energy of consciousness and the ways it expresses itself from cognizance to chakras to kundalini.

Few citations of theological doctrines or scientific theories are given within the text, as this is intended to be more readable than proof in validity of a belief system. The use of words like soul, spirit, and divine are merely words to describe innate wisdom and intuition. All citations are given in the bibliography if you decide to explore a subject further. I am merely presenting a compilation of ideas. Hopefully, some of them are far-reaching enough to be considered mind-blowing, but more than that, the ideas and memes are meant to be presented in a light-hearted and easy-to-read manner.

As mostly a practical, can-do guide for upgrading our subconscious programming, concepts in this book are a beginning analysis rather than a comprehensive background of any given topic. Some ideas may be new to us and require an open mind to new ways of thinking. As humans, we are ego-bound. The ego likes to keep things the way they are and is not too eager to explore the depths of our consciousness or accept new beliefs. Like some of the above assumptions, it's easy to be stuck in our way of thinking and think, "No way!" For some, the ideas may be too far-fetched to bother changing to a new way of thinking. For others, the endless possibilities are mind-blowing and exciting.

We are taught by mainstream media and religion that to be happy and to know ourselves, we need something more than us—something we can buy or earn through weekly attendance. The truth is, all we need is already inside us. We are born with an innate wholeness of unconditional love, but society teaches us that we are separate from everyone else and that there's only me in this world and it is survival of the fittest. The reality is, we are not separate beings, we are One with All. Feeling separate from our natural state of peace and love causes emotional conflict in the subconscious. This inner turmoil manifests as lack, the opposite of being whole. Knowing that our natural go-to state of being human is that of wholeness, love, peace, and happiness, we then have the ultimate healing, manifestation, and guiding tool—ourselves.

The main idea of *Mind Blown* is that we can create anything we desire by morphing low-vibration negative thoughts and attitudes and reframing them into high-vibration good thoughts and emotions. We can deliberately control our thoughts to raise our vibration, helping with the healing process, and ultimately bringing us closer to getting anything we desire. Conscious control and deliberate creation of our thoughts will help us create the life we've always wanted, one desire at a time. Almost like a virtual reality game: *How will my reality change once I change the input? How can I manipulate my input/thinking to get my desired outcome?*

The ultimate goal of this book is to self-reprogram our subconscious mind where old beliefs, traumatic experiences, genetic memories, and excessive thinking take place. The subconscious mind downloads and stores bad programming without our consent. Unsolicited, bad programming doesn't serve us on our journey to knowing ourselves better or to better health. This book intends to teach us how to rewrite bad downloaded programming for an upgraded consciousness, much like updating an outdated computer language.

Mind Blown is organized from the beginning with key concepts and origins of a vibrational universe. It goes on to suggest what types of behaviors lower and raise our body's vibrations. There's a heart-to-heart talk on thoughts and emotions, and a chapter on how to manifest whatever our heart desires. Various healing alternatives are covered, as well as methods to access the subconscious mind. The relationship between DNA, chakras, and kundalini will be explored, as well as psychic abilities, and the final chapter delves into energy healing for the future.

By me writing and you reading this book, I believe *we* come together as One. I am not a mystic, healer, or spiritual guide. I, like you, am searching for ways to know ourselves better and be a better person. Since we are the same in respect to our wants and desires, I use the pronouns ourselves, we, and us throughout the book.

Although I wrote this book to satisfy my own desires, it's meant to be a do-it-yourself guide of information with implications that I hope many of us can benefit from. As a tool, *Mind Blown* helps us connect with our higher self to bring healing, guidance, and self-empowerment. As with other things in life, if there is something you read that doesn't ring true for you, just let it go, let it go.

PART I

Energy—It's Here, It's There, It's Everywhere

"If you wish to understand the Universe, think in terms of energy, frequency, and vibration." — NIKOLA TESLA

There are three types of frequencies that affect our mind in some way:

Brainwave Frequencies are associated with different mental states. The alpha brainwave state is our desired state of consciousness when reaching into the depths of the subconscious mind for reprogramming.

Healing Frequencies heal illnesses and stimulate chakra energy centers using vibrations from sound, light, color, crystals, and water.

Natural Phenomena Frequencies occur inherently in nature like the Law of Vibration, the Law of

Attraction, Schumann's Resonance, and sounds from the orbits of planets. The electromagnetic field of the Schumann Resonance affects brain wave frequencies, crystals in the brain, and circadian rhythms (sleep/wake patterns) in the brain's pineal gland.

Mind Blown covers how these frequencies affect our subconscious mind and what we can do to assist in raising our consciousness on our path of knowledge and growth. Most concepts are presented in alphabetical order, without regard to their levels of influence to the topic, and are related to vibration, energy, and Oneness of All with the Universe.

∽

CHAPTER 1

Universal Connections—The Realities of Nature

"What we have called matter is energy, whose vibration has been so lowered as to be perceptible to the senses. There is no matter." — ALBERT EINSTEIN

The Law of Attraction is a universal law stating that vibrations with similar frequencies and vibrations attract each other, or *like attracts like*. Every object in the Universe vibrates at a certain frequency that attracts other objects that vibrate at similar frequencies. Like tuning into a radio channel, we pick up signals from the Universe's energy field and environment only when the frequencies match.

As humans, we emit vibrations through thoughts, feelings, words, beliefs, and actions. One person can have a high vibrational frequency while another person can have a low vibrational frequency depending on the type of thoughts they think. The more open-minded, loving, acceptable, positive, and adaptable we are, the higher our vibration. Thinking good thoughts and being kind raises our vibration and sends a signal to the Universe that responds with similar energies. We attract by raising our vibration to the same vibrational level as our desires. When we emit high energy, we attract high energy.

Conversely, when we are filled with negative thoughts, we send out low vibrational energies that don't match what we're hoping to attract. When we continually experience and emit low-vibration emotions, it will eventually match and manifest into something low-frequency, like sickness, disease, or lack in an area of our lives.

The Universe responds to what we put out in our vibrations. Like a copycat, it reproduces our thoughts and manifests them into physical form. Good thoughts attract good and bad thoughts attract bad—that's how the Universal Law of Attraction works. We get what we think about, whether good or bad. *This gives us power to choose what we want to think about.* When we choose thoughts that emit the highest frequencies, like love and compassion, we can attract the life we desire. When we choose thoughts that emit low-frequency emotions like hate and anger, we attract struggle, lack, and hardship. The choice is ours. By intentionally increasing our vibrational output, we literally and consciously choose to rise above to create our heart's desires. Once we realize that we are the most powerful magnets in the Universe, the Law of Attraction becomes our superpower.

The Law of Vibration is a universal law that states that *everything* in the Universe is made of energy. Every thought, word, action, belief, emotion, and every bit of physical matter, including cells and DNA, are a form of energy made of different frequencies.

Everything vibrates. All energy and matter are in constant motion, vibrating at different speeds. At the most fundamental level, everything in the Universe and that which comprises it are pure vibratory energy. Matter is merely energy in a state of vibration.

Something can have high- or low-vibrational frequency. The only difference between things (say, an elephant, a rock, or a thought) is its vibrational frequency. Solid objects are made of dense, slow-moving vibrational energy, and fast-moving energy is found in photons of light, unseen forces, or in the emotions of compassion and love. Through transmutation, energy and matter can slow down or speed up their vibrations to become something else. As humans, we can increase our vibrations to become less dense, both in matter and mind.

Humans are energy condensed into physical form. Human bodies are solid energy noted by Einstein's equation of $E = mc^2$, energy equals mass [times the speed of light squared]. Einstein's formula shows that matter is made of energy, and this energy comes from the unlimited energy of Space. Humans and everything are made from compacted energy, vibrating at its own unique frequency in accordance with the laws of the Universe.

The universal energies of vibration and attraction are the building blocks of manifestation and are waiting to deliver our desires when we emit high-vibrating energy. These laws help us attract and match our frequencies to those of the Universe to manifest anything we choose. We can attract anything we desire when we vibrate at high frequency.

The Age of Aquarius signifies the monumental Universal shift of the vernal equinox as it moves out of the Age of Pisces and into a new zodiac constellation. The Age of Aquarius signals a change from 3D to 5D awareness as human consciousness rises past the era of religious and governmental hypocrisy to the high-frequency energy of humanitarianism. The frequency rise of the collective consciousness correlates to a rise in frequency of the Schumann Resonance, the vibration of the Earth. The movement into the Age of Aquarius liberates negative energies and reunites us with our natural state of being, that of joy and unconditional love.

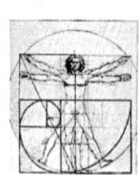

The Vitruvian Man image is a common Age of Aquarius symbol by Leonardo da Vinci meant to represent the divine connection between Man and the Universe. The image shows its invariant proportional relationship of all things according to the spirals of Fibonacci and sacred geometry.

Aliens are also called extraterrestrials (ETs) and exist on Earth, other planets, universes, galaxies, the Cosmoverse, and the Multiverse. The government has done much to invalidate their existence, but ETs have been around for billions of years. Aliens are universal ambassadors of peace who observe and live among us today. Their collective mission is to help raise the frequency of Earth as it transitions from the Age of Pisces to the Age of Aquarius in the evolutionary move from the Third Dimension to the Fifth Dimension.

> *"Extraterrestrials are living now on Earth. They are everywhere, among your friends, neighbors, even your relatives. Their blood flows through our veins. We are as much brothers and sisters to beings from the Stars as we are to animals of the Earth."* — DOLORES CANNON

Agharta is a scientifically advanced subterranean world that exists within the hollows of the Earth built by the Anunnaki aliens. It is said to be a continuation of select Atlantean, Mayan, Incan, and other civilizations that mysteriously disappeared. Entrance to the inner Earth can be accessed through tunnels, grid points (ley lines), and 1,400-mile-wide polar openings. Secret underground tunnels were built as an escape from nuclear fallout and flooding that occurred on the Atlantis continent; tunnels into the underground world have been

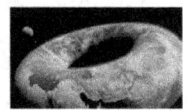
Image Courtesy of TruthTheory

found in Brazil, Chile, and Giza. Tibet's tunnels directly connect to the capital, Shamballa. Messages have been transmitted to the Dali Lama from the ruler of the underground with intent toward the betterment of people and Earth. It is worth mentioning that if the Anunnaki terraformed Planet Earth into a hollow civilization of high-vibrating beings, then the Moon is also said to be a hollow structure, perhaps existing as a way station for alien intergalactic travel.

The Anunnaki are an extraterrestrial race from Planet X, or the ninth planet. The Anunnaki are responsible for terraforming planet Earth, deactivating strands 3-12 of DNA and chromosome 22, and the well-known fusion of chromosome 2. Although their intent was to keep spiritual knowledge out of the hands of the fallen angels (see below), the genetic manipulation has had a two-fold result. One has kept us trapped in a low frequency, third-dimensional mentality preventing us from remembering our true birthright as divine creators. The other has given us thinking, speech, and free will, showing us intent of goodwill and humanitarianism.

Via their mothership, Nibiru, the Anunnaki came to Earth to mine gold for their Planet X's atmosphere. After arrival, the Anunnaki lusted after mortal women and their interbreeding resulted in a hybrid race of giants called the Nephilim, "The Watchers," or the "Sons of God." For their misdeed, the two hundred Anunnaki were cast out and are known as the "Fallen

Angels from the Sky." A massive flood was issued to remove the evil and cannibalistic Nephilim from Earth.

Image Courtesy of www.giza-legacy.ch

Atlantis is the not-so-imaginary land of high-vibrating and scientifically advanced peoples who can attribute their higher DNA powers to the Anunnaki. Their higher developed DNA strands gave Atlanteans the ability to levitate themselves and objects, helping them build pyramids.

Although they were highly advanced, Atlanteans were not of pure mind when they used their powers for genetic manipulation that created the half-man, half-animal creatures of our myths. Although the government stopped their genetically engineered experiments to save the race from destruction, it was to no avail as Atlanteans began mining into the Earth's core in their quest for crystal energy. This triggered a cataclysmic series of tsunamis and earthquakes that took over the land sending it to the bottom of the ocean. The greed of natural resources, misuse of mind power, and an attempt to rewrite genetics should serve as a reminder to current scientists not to allow history to repeat itself.

The Book of Enoch is a former book of the Bible removed by the church because of its acknowledgment of the two-hundred alien Anunnaki, or fallen angels, whose mating with Earth women resulted in the giant Nephilim offspring. The book recognizes archangels coming to Earth to rebalance order from the destruction of the giants, describes Enoch's (the great grandfather of Noah) celestial visitations with aliens, and details how to turn the physical body into a body of light through Merkabah activation. *The Book of Enoch* has been kept from mainstream knowledge as an attempt by the church to keep their power by hiding our true power. Once this knowledge of our true divinity becomes mainstream, the fear tactics imposed by religion will no longer have control over our psyche, and we can rise back into our own dominion as the Age of Aquarius progresses.

Crop Circles are messages from aliens intended to raise our vibration and open our awareness that there's more out there than we're led to believe. The enigmatic shapes may be formed from Starseeds' (Earth aliens) high frequency thought patterns (similar to cymatic sound vibrations, see Chapter 12) combined with energy from the Earth's crystalline grid, affecting a plant's molecular structure. Some believe the crop patterns are communications from ancestors whose consciousness remains in the Earth's grid structure.

> The Earth has secrets. Locations exist around the world which have powerful supernatural energies and electromagnetic vortexes. Areas such as Sedona in Arizona, Mount Kailash in Tibet, Mount Shasta in California, or Kauai in Hawaii are all known for having other worldly energies, due to their location where magnetic ley lines intersect. At these sites, the Schumann Resonance (Earth's frequency) is recorded as exceedingly high, and it is said that the veil between the 3rd and 4th Dimension is the thinnest.

Ley Lines are the structure for Earth's energy grid, its matrix. When ley lines intersect, they create high-energy vortices that cause changes in consciousness and create ports of entry into different dimensions. Ley lines are used by Starseeds for balancing Earth's energies and appear in areas where pyramids are built, suggesting that ley lines influence balance and levitation and are necessary for pyramid construction.

Starseeds are alien beings with human features incarnated on Earth, usually from another planet, universe, galaxy, or dimension. They volunteer to come to Earth to help raise Earth's vibration, rebuild its grid, and assist with transitioning to the Age of Aquarius. Starseeds are born with more DNA strands activated and therefore naturally have more psychic and healing abilities.

Angels are spiritual beings that inhabit the Tenth Dimension of the Universal Time Matrix. They are made of high vibration love-filled light energy. Two angels always watch over us, a guardian angel who offers protection and an ancestor angel who offers inspiration.

Angels communicate to us through numbers, symbols, and signs. Our guardian angel meets our soul in our ascent to the Afterlife and helps with soul matters in that dimension. Stories of angels, aliens, or human-like gods, coming from above to create mankind "in their own image" can be construed as mythical, biblical, or factual, depending on our frame of reference.

☺ Angels	👽 Aliens
Not from here.	Not from here
More intelligent than humans.	More intelligent than humans.
Can fly.	Can fly.
Possess powers.	Possess powers.
Communicate telepathically.	Communicate telepathically.
May have had something to do with humanity's creation and development.	May have something to do with humanity's creation and development.
Visit Earth from time to time.	Visit Earth from time to time.

Archangels can be called upon for guidance, support, and protection when needed.
☺ *Ariel*—connection with nature and pets
☺ *Chamuel*—soulmates, divine love, and partnerships
☺ *Gabriel*—guidance and intuitive messages
☺*Haniel*—spiritual awakening and psychic development
☺*Jeremiel*—deep intuition and guidance assistance

☺ *Jophiel*—happiness and the beauty in life and ourselves
☺ *Metatron*—assists with our powers and light
☺ *Michael*—protection and deep healing
☺ *Raphael*—soul healing
☺ *Raziel*—financial abundance, manifestation, light code downloads
☺ *Uriel*—enlightenment
☺ *Zadkiel*—forgiveness

Consciousness represents the height of self-awareness, and thus, knowledge, indicated by the ascending levels of the chakra system and the number of DNA strands available for use. Every step up the chakras indicates a rise in consciousness and expresses our life's and soul's growth process on the Tree of Life. The more we are truly aware that we are the creators of our reality, the higher our level of consciousness.

Consciousness is intelligent energy arranged on a matrix/blueprint that's used to run the Universe; it's the Law of Vibration controlling the outcome of matter through thought. Consciousness is the building blocks of our spiritual soul, while DNA is the building blocks of our physical soul.

As a tool, consciousness raises our level of awareness to help us experience and remember our natural birthright as creators extraordinaire. With consciousness comes self-awareness so that we can objectively look at our thoughts, emotions, and fears and assess what we see.

Full consciousness is activated by the ascension of kundalini energy and usually takes lifetimes to achieve for a soul's evolution.

Feelings of Oneness, unconditional love, and compassion in the heart constitute high consciousness. Low consciousness is the feeling of separation from others and the misconception that our energy has no effect on others' energy.

Consciousness vibrates at different frequencies, so different frequencies and vibrations create "food" for the mind. When we feed our consciousness different bandwidths of frequencies, we create emotions. Emotions generate the aura energy field surrounding our body; thus, auras reflect our state of emotional consciousness.

Collective/Group Consciousness is everyone's individual consciousnesses combined into One. High-vibrating group consciousness is necessary to raise the vibration of Earth for its ascension into 5D, the Age of Aquarius. The collective consciousness of the Fifth Dimension is a one-world view of Oneness and love for all.

DNA (see Chapter 16) is liquid crystalline light-encoded filaments that act as receivers and transmitters of energy. Like a sponge, DNA absorbs information from the environment in the form of signs, symbols, and sounds, and releases it onto the holographic energy field, the matrix, to form matter. Light energy emanating from DNA forms auras and chakras.

Currently, science recognizes two physical DNA strands, but there are twelve; the other ten strands have "junk DNA," but a more appropriate name would be "dormant DNA." Accessing 12-strand DNA goes beyond the 3D world of the five senses. Twelve-strand DNA accesses intuition and psychic abilities, spiritual and mystical experiences, and multidimensional travel. Tapping into the other strands of DNA can be accomplished through chakra clearing, meditation, kundalini and pineal gland activation, light therapy, visualization, and other energy activation techniques as mentioned throughout the book.

DNA contains memories of the past, present, and Now. It remembers through specific frequencies of digital codes. One of the digital codes is the binary 11, which looks like and signifies activation of the DNA double helix. The code 11 appears in our daily experiences, in nature, in Fibonacci sequencing, and during dreaming. The synchronistic code 11:11 is pre-wired into our brains like a computer. Although we tend to view these as "angel numbers," the meaning is similar—it's part of a spiritual awakening. The # (number sign or hashtag) is a horizontal and vertical 11, which is a subliminal message meaning to restore balance. Linked to sacred geometry, 12 is a metaphor for "once around," and 12:12 is a digital code meaning new creation or the illusion of time.

Epigenetics means above and beyond genetics. Traditional genetics say we inherit our family's genetic makeup (DNA) and there's nothing we can do about it; it's set in stone. Epigenetics, on the other hand, believes that we can alter our DNA and transform our genetic destiny. This means we're not tied down to unwanted traits inherited from our family and ancestors as we once believed.

A cell's DNA can be altered by the information we send to it from our thoughts, words, and emotions. If we can change our DNA through the power of thought, this implies that we have the capacity to heal ourselves through thought. When we upgrade the information we send to our cells, we automatically upgrade our reality.

Light Codes aka "Fire Letters" is the original energetic, cellular alphabet of 12-strand DNA whose code or letters change according to the frequency it receives. Fire Letters, or light code sequences, represent one dimensional plane of reality or consciousness (on the Tree of Life) and correspond to the number of functioning strands of DNA. Activating light codes stimulates DNA to open doors to higher planes of knowledge, awareness, and hastens the evolutionary process of ascension.

Light codes represent our true nature buried within the genetic code of DNA. Sixty-four light codes reside within the genes of DNA, however, only twenty are active. This is why we live in a state of not knowing our true nature, not knowing our soul's purpose, not knowing where we came from, and not knowing our true genetic potential.

As described in the Book of Enoch, light codes contain the knowledge needed to turn physical bodies into light bodies. Light bodies are necessary to ascend to the dimension of 5D. When light codes activate, cells' vibrations dramatically increase to transmute carbon DNA to crystal DNA. This quantum transmutation takes us beyond a third-dimensional consciousness into the 5D realm of manifestation and multidimensionality.

Transmutation is the process of changing DNA from carbon to crystal to prepare the physical body to become a lightbody. Transmutation increases vibrational states, and therefore, access to higher dimensional planes.

It's been said that the alien Anunnaki scrambled the Fire Letters alphabet and reduced our DNA to two strands to prevent the fallen races, the Nephilim, from having access to this knowledge and being able to enter higher dimensions themselves. Maybe as redemption, our DNA is now being rewired through cosmic light codes to reactivate and realign the innate, dormant strands.

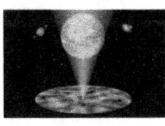
Image Courtesy of TU Wien

Holographic Reality is the belief that reality exists as a virtual 3D holographic illusion. A holographic reality is created when thoughts (consciousness) are projected onto a two-dimensional energy grid (the matrix) to create a 3D holographic image. Thus, thoughts create reality. Like a hologram, what we perceive as 3D reality is actually a 2D projection. The holographic matrix is where reality, matter, and manifestation take place.

MIND BLOWN

The holographic image on the matrix is made from light, sound, digital codes of zeros and ones, Fibonacci patterns, and Golden spiral algorithms, confirming the validity of a holographic reality because it follows the same geometric and mathematical patterns of growth that all other living things in the Universe follow.

In a holographic universe, all dimensional timelines of past, future, and present are different frequencies of energy that exist simultaneously as Now. A holographic reality validates the idea of time as an illusion and supports quantum physics analysis that atoms are affected faster than the speed of light regardless of distance, making time inconsequential and providing the underlying framework for distance healing.

Not only is the Universe a holographic projection, so are we. Our body's holographic template has the same organizational structure as the Universe's, meaning we are all cut from the same piece of cloth. In a holographic matrix, the smallest piece contains the whole of the largest piece. In other words, we are all One.

Multidimensionality of the matrix in which we live means it has multiple layers, dimensions, timelines, planes, or levels of consciousness. Levels of the matrix correspond to a Fire Letter of DNA, sephiras on the Tree of Life, the chakra energy system, and the path of a soul's many journeys. Moving to higher dimensions indicates a rise in consciousness and an increase in frequency with each level.

Dimensions indicate the ascent of matter to spirit and the descent of spirit into physicality. With the original 12-strand DNA, it was our natural ability to travel among different dimensions, allowing us to experience moments of our past, present, and future selves at our discretion.

The dimensional plane we're occupying mirrors our level of consciousness. Although our physical bodies are bound to the Third Dimension, our mind, emotions, and consciousness are not. The Third Dimension feels real to us because this is where our physical bodies are grounded. Although we cannot perceive the other dimensions with our physical senses, we can access these dimensions through lucid dreaming, hypnosis, trance states, and meditation. Clearing the Heart Chakra and loving the world as One is crucial before we're able to transport to higher dimensions. Love is the gateway for multidimensional travel.

Quantum Physics has a prominent position with energy, thoughts, awareness, consciousness, and the manifestation process. "The observer creates the reality" is a key tenet of quantum physics. At the tiniest quantum level, the behavior of protons changes when we observe them. This means that protons are conscious of being watched and are able to change their behavior accordingly. This concept implies that we too can change our behavior by being consciously aware of what we're thinking. To create and manifest, we must have conscious awareness and not be the proverbial sleeping sheep.

Quantum physics acknowledges that vibrations from the sound of our voice can affect an atom inside a star or a person across the planet instantly. This phenomenon is known as quantum entanglement, which explains distance healing and destroys the illusion that we are separate from everything else in the Universe. We are all connected, and we are all One.

> Quantum physics is where the scientific proof of spirituality is hidden.

The true meaning of a higher vibration is when atoms make "quantum leaps" from one orbit to another. When atoms vibrate higher, they emit more light and get closer to their light Source. The same could be said for us: as we vibrate higher, we emit more light (in our aura) allowing us to leap to new orbits, or dimensional planes of higher vibrations, and get closer to our light Source. Source is the final destination for the journey of the soul, the place where all energies merge.

Sacred Geometry (see Chapter 11) is patterns of consciousness that express themselves through numbers, symbols, and shapes that are inherent in the creation, growth, and organization of the Universe and everything in it. The shapes are considered sacred because they form the basis of life, of all creation, and emit etheric, zero-point energy. The geometric shapes can be seen in the spirals of Fibonacci growth patterns found in all forms of creation from the cochlea of an ear to the chakras of energy.

Sacred geometry uses the principle of energy flow known as the Golden Ratio, an energy-saving formula that connects everything at the level of creation and represents the most fundamental law among physics, energy, and vibration. Sacred geometry sheds the belief of separation among things and instead reveals an underlying consistency and unity among the creation of all things. In other words, everything unifies and manifests from One Source of creation.

Souls are holograms of the Universe, just as humans are. As distinct as a fingerprint or a snowflake, a soul is pure intelligent light energy vibrating at its own unique frequency. Souls are the real "I" in our being and make up the essence of who we are. Experiences we know as memories are stored in the depths of our subconscious, the soul, Akashic records, and DNA.

The three planes 4D, 5D, and 6D on the Tree of Life (a map of a soul's lifetimes), as well as chakras four through six (heart, throat, and third eye, respectively), and layers four through six of the aura constitute the soul matrix. The energy of a soul enters a developing body around the fourth to sixth month of pregnancy and encompasses the embryo or the heart. After birth, the soul's energy continues to reside in the sacred heart area and in layers four through six of the aura.

When our life on Earth has finished, the immortal soul leaves the physical body, and its energy moves into the Afterlife. Souls are greeted by their soul families, then can choose to rest or reincarnate after receiving counseling on the recently inhabited life. If a soul decides to reside in another physical body, it chooses the family and circumstances that will best fulfill its karmic obligations. A soul's purpose, and thus ours, is to achieve ascension and reach enlightenment.

A Soul Contract is the agreement made by souls to accept challenging life incarnations in order to advance their growth. When we realize that we agree to and choose our unfavorable situations on purpose, prior to our incarnation to enhance our soul's development, it makes a difficult life easier to understand and that much more bearable.

Facts About Your Soul Contract

1. You choose your family, name, and birthdate.
2. Your soul family helps you with healing.
3. Life events are meant to move you forward.
4. You have free will.
5. You choose your death.
6. You have access to Spirit Guides or Angels.
7. Synchronicity occurs to guide you.
8. You can break a soul contract.
9. You can clear karmic debt.
10. You can clear ancestral trauma.

There are two types of birthing of new souls: In the Afterlife, Earth souls are born from monadic (one) soul energy in the Tenth Dimension emanating from Source energy of the Twelfth Dimension. Galactic souls are manufactured in incubators on spaceships designed to grow human-like Starseeds.

Image Courtesy of Martin Dolan

Soul Archetypes are personalities or faces of our soul. Archetypes make up the underlying personality of the soul throughout its different lifetimes.

☙ *The Ruler* has a structured personality with everything in order and likes to be in control and get things done.

☙ *The Creator* is artistic, imaginative, and inventive.

☙ *The Sage* is a spiritual helper that often has a green thumb.

☙ *The Innocent* are optimistic souls who try their best but are often over their heads.

☙ *The Explorer* is an adventurous, traveling soul who likes to try new things.

☙ *The Rebel* likes to take risks, break rules, question authority and is looking for change.

☙ *The Hero* is proud and strong-willed, likes to think things through and makes the most of opportunities.

☙ *The Wizard/Magician* is an inspired and imaginative soul who likes to accomplish the impossible and live life to the fullest.

☙ *The Jester* is the comedic person in the crowd, there to brighten moods of others yet is sometimes an annoyance.

MIND BLOWN

🔖 *The Everyman/Woman* is a supportive and caring soul who makes friends easily and is easy to get along with.

🔖 *The Lover* is a romantic, passionate soul who finds beauty in everything and gives 100% to close friends.

🔖 *The Caregiver* is a soul who goes above and beyond to care for others. Their giving spirit sometimes causes them to be taken advantage of.

👻 *Ghosts* are the energy of souls who have not passed to the Afterlife due to a quick or unexpected death, or one who is emotionally rooted to the physical world. Souls of ghosts reside in the lower fourth dimension of the astral plane.

OBE (Out-of-Body Experiences), aka astral projection, are when the consciousness of a soul leaves the physical body for multidimensional travel. Souls leave the body nightly 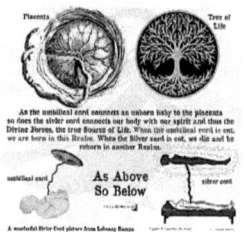 during dreams through the Crown Chakra at the top of the head and are connected by the "silver cord" at the Root Chakra level. Like an umbilical cord, the silver cord is a band of elastic light energy, the thread of life connecting the astral body to the physical body. When the physical body dies, the cord detaches.

Out-of-body experiences have the sensation of floating outside the body and traveling to different dimensions. They can be deliberately induced through deep trance, meditation, visualization, brainwave entrainment, binaural beats (4 Hz), Native American drumming, sensory deprivation, lucid dreaming, psychedelic drugs, or sleep paralysis (inability to move during sleep). Cleared chakras combined with the energy of Merkabah can also cause an OBE.

Self-Induced OBE's often occur before going to sleep at night or as soon as we wake up in the morning. It's the ideal time to get the soul to leave the body and travel the astral plane; we're still in light sleep paralysis trapped between dreams and reality. Concentrating on vibrations within the body and using those vibrations will help lift the soul body out of the physical body.

- *Yo-Yo Method*—Before going to sleep, vividly focus on a spot in the room and examine it thoroughly with all sensations, then shift awareness to another focal spot in the room and observe it. Visualize both spots as if we were a yo-yo moving back and forth. Vibrations from focal point shifting result in a body and soul separation.
- *Free Fall Method*—Imagine falling downward very fast, feeling all the sensations of a free fall with the intent of experiencing "not being sure where we are in space." When we feel close to projecting, visualize ourselves hitting the ground. The visualization of a sudden impact can cause our soul to separate from the body.

- *The Rope Method*—Visualize climbing up a long rope hanging from above while imagining the accompanying feelings and sensations and vibrations associated with climbing. Imagine climbing faster and faster to increase the intensity of vibrations to cause a soul/body separation.
- *Follow the Light Method*—With closed eyes, follow the swirling colors in our mind's vision until a white light forms in the center. Continue following the white light until it encompasses us. From here, the soul will depart and begin its travels.

Time is an Illusion asserts that time is not a multitude of ongoing experiences happening in life; it's a singular event with everything, including the past and future, all happening at the same moment of Now. The past and future only exist in our thoughts, therefore the present Now is all there can be. When all time is Now, past lives, future lives, and parallel lives exist simultaneously, merely on different timelines or dimensional planes, because they can be accessed through hypnosis.

> *"Realize that Now is all there ever is: there is no past or future except as memory or anticipation in your mind."* — ECKHART TOLLE

As a man-made construct, time is believed to have been invented in Sumeria (Mesopotamia) about 2,400 BC. Cycles of the Sun and Moon were used as a reference tool, giving the ability to examine and categorize experiences of life. When life experiences became categorized, so did the belief in separation from others. Universally, time is a false belief system instilled to intentionally cause feelings of separation. Separation brings feelings of insecurity that go against our inner nature and therefore cannot be fundamentally true since the energies of everything and All do not cause separation, they come together as One.

Interestingly, time slows down as physical matter becomes denser, and time speeds up as vibrations increase and matter becomes lighter. In higher dimensions, there is no time because vibrations are faster than the speed of light.

TIME IS SHIFTING

Time feels like it's speeding up because the vibrational resonance of the Earth is rising and so is yours. Time is a measurement, not a constant. This means that it changes depending on your vibration. If you're unhappy and doing something that you don't enjoy, time feels like an eternity. When you're having a great time, it passes quickly. This is because your perception of time changes with your vibrational resonance.

Another interesting concept about time regarding sacred geometry and the Mayan calendar suggests that as a gift from the Anunnaki, "the people of the sky," the

MIND BLOWN

calendar's precise representation of celestial cycles has a strange coincidence of numbers unlikely for the Mayan to be able to conceive of themselves:

It takes 2,160 years to complete the Mayan circular calendar. The diameter of the Moon is 2,160 miles across. The number 2,160 divided by five (the Platonic solids) is 432 (the harmonic resonance of music). When 432 is doubled, the answer is 864[000], the diameter of the Sun, and the number of seconds in a day. Dividing 2,160 by six yields 360, the number of degrees in a circle, and 432 squared is 186,000 (miles per second), the speed of light. The calendar has been said to represent time spiraling toward its center to a zero point, at which time the shift from 3D to 5D into the multidimensional consciousness of the Age of Aquarius occurs. According to the Mayan calendar, the shift would have begun around December 2012.

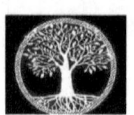 **The Tree of Life** is significant in many cultures and represents our integral connection to the Universe. Just as DNA is the blueprint for our life, the Tree of Life is the blueprint for a soul's lifetimes. The Tree has the same organizational template and can be superimposed on twelve-strand DNA, chakra energy centers, dimensionality, the Earth's grid, and the channels of kundalini energy. Each sephira (sphere), or path of wisdom on the Tree of Life is associated with a divine attribute, a Fire Letter of DNA, one of the five Platonic elements, a chemical element, a number, an Archangel, a planet in the Solar System, a place on Earth,

a color, a part of the physical body, a part of our aura's energy field, a crystal, a geometric shape, and a musical note, showing how the Tree is literally a part of ours and the Universe's physical composition.

The Universe is the collective consciousnesses of everyone's individual energies combined into One. The Universe consists of the white light energy of everyone's aura's colors and the dark energy of black holes to make the zero-point energy of Space. The Universe is the conduit for the Law of Vibration and represents a minimum of twelve different vibrating dimensional planes of energy.

Parallel Universes exist with quantum physics' knowledge that subatomic particles can be at two locations at the same time. Since everything in the Universe is moving particles of light energy, all events in the Universe imbed into the holographic matrix and connect to all locations and dimensions simultaneously, meaning we can be in two dimensions/lifetimes at once. When the soul leaves the body to travel parallel dimensions during sleep, the feelings we know as déjà vu arise during the day.

The Schumann Resonance is Earth's vibration, the "heartbeat" of our planet, and has been vibrating at 7.83 Hz for thousands of years. The frequency of our heart vibrates the same as the Earth's frequency and our brainwaves, giving rise to the adage, "As Above, So Below."

MIND BLOWN

Curiously, the Schumann Resonance has been steadily increasing due to rising vibrations of the collective consciousness. When many people act together in harmony and increase their vibrational frequency, the Earth's frequency also rises, showing how we are One with the Universe. Recently, the Earth's vibration has been recorded at 432 Hz (Source Trinity8, NASA), which corresponds to harmonic music frequencies, energies of the Golden Mean, and consciousness. The rise in the Earth's magnetic field loosens energy blocks in the body to hasten healing and leads to states of higher consciousness.

We The People are moving into a new phase of mass global consciousness, a new age of consciousness, the Age of Aquarius. The new age brings an opportunity to level up and literally rise to the occasion to match the rising frequency of Earth's vibration. Because the Earth's frequency has been increasing, it's forcing the need for a fast evolution in our own vibrations and consciousness. Therefore, one goal of this book is to learn how to create high vibrations to raise our level of consciousness and keep up with the rising energy of the Schumann

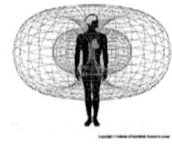

The Heart's Torus Field. Courtesy of HeartMath Institute

The Torus Field is named after its shape and represents the flow of energy within a system. The torus field of energy flow connects atoms, cells, organs, humans, consciousness, the planets, the Sun, galaxies, the atmosphere, *everything*, to the zero-point energy of the Universe. The torus field's direct link to the Universe connects everyone and everything as One united whole.

The Zero-Point Field (ZPF) is pure consciousness and the intelligent energy of the Universe. ZPF is the indivisible and unifying energy field that permeates and connects everything as One. Zero-point energy is the black holes of Space, the space between protons, and the Source of all creation. Zero-point energy combines the empty space energy of nothing with the energy of everything to form a formidable force field of endless free potential energy.

ZPF is made from the inexhaustible and entropic movement of light; this all-encompassing potential energy is the power that creates galaxies, stars, life forms, Akashic Record memories, qi energy, and psychic energy. Zero-point energy is necessary for intergalactic travel; thus, we have not yet harnessed its full potential.

> "What is my purpose in life? I asked the void. "What if I told you that you fulfilled it when you took an extra hour to talk to a kid about his problem?" said the voice, "Or when you paid for that young couple in the restaurant? Or when you saved that dog in traffic? Or when you tied your father's shoes for him? You equate your purpose in life with a goal-based achievement. The Universe isn't interested in your achievements...just your heart. ♡ When you choose to act out of kindness, compassion, and love, you are already aligned with your true purpose." – Author Unknown

MIND BLOWN

"What's Our Purpose?" is the eternal quandary of life as we struggle to understand ourselves and why we're here. In the grand scheme of creation, the desire of our soul is to reestablish connection to our higher self, our higher functioning, yet undeveloped, DNA strands of growth on the Tree of Life.

The desires of our soul are that we become aware of ourselves as master creators of our reality, that we evolve to higher levels of self-awareness, and that we listen and follow the passions of our heart.

A soul's purpose in life is not based on one lifetime of living, therefore our true purpose in life is not based on "having" the perfect job or "making" a certain amount of money. When we listen to our heart, and act with kindness, compassion, and love in all that we do and with all that we meet, then we will be acting with a higher purpose.

One key to finding our purpose is following our passions—doing what we love, what brings love to our heart. If something isn't exciting and causing love and joy in our hearts, it's a clue that we're on the wrong path. If we don't know what causes joy and happiness in our hearts, reflect on this: Like the spirals of the Fibonacci sequences that use the least amount of energy to achieve the greatest result, what would we do for nothing that would bring the greatest result? In other words, we must do what we love and be the best version of ourselves that we can. To truly serve our life's purpose, we must do what our hearts truly desire; that would be our sole/soul purpose.

> No one is born without a life purpose. If you don't know what your purpose in life is, it is simply because you have not yet unlocked it. The way to unlock the knowledge of your purpose is to begin by mastering yourself. Like a video game, you'll get clues along the journey as to what your true purpose is, and life becomes easier to piece everything together to form a plan of action. Why is life so hard? You have to be the best version of yourself to fully pursue your life purpose. You cannot have one without the other. You have to continue to grow and evolve until you find it.

If we're still looking for that elusive knowledge that gets us from "meh" ☹ to "yeah," ☺ consider:

💡 What totally interests us (gardening, animals, volunteering, working with our hands, or music) and brings joy regardless of money.

💡 Finding ways to incorporate this interest or heart's passion into our lives whether by profession or pastime.

Many of us have spent plenty of time in reverie wondering not only what our purpose is in life, but what makes us happy, who's our perfect mate, and what's our purpose beyond trying to make ends meet. Hopefully this book will help us realize that as the true creators of our lives and happiness, we can have anything we put our mind and thoughts to, and that the Source of our answers lies within and not outside of us.

T. S. Martin

The Hopi Creation Myth

Image by Vasil Woodland

How the Grandmother Spirit of the Earth and the Grandfather Spirit of the Sky Created the Miracle of Life

Creator: "I want to hide something from the humans until they are ready for it. It is the realization that they create their own reality."
Eagle: "Give it to me, I will take it to the moon."
Creator: "No, one day they will go there and find it."
Salmon: "I will bury it in the bottom of the ocean."
Creator: "No, they will go there too."
Buffalo: "I will bury it in the Great Plains."
Creator: "They will cut into the skin of the Earth and find it even there."
Grandmother lives in the breast of the Mother Earth and has no physical eyes but sees with Spiritual eyes.
Grandmother: "Put it inside them."
Creator: "It is done."

CHAPTER 2

When Mojo Goes Nojo

"Do not allow negative thoughts to enter your mind for they are the weeds that strangle confidence. — BRUCE LEE

The Law of Vibration says that we are all part of the Universe's vibrational energy, and the Law of Attraction says we attract either positive or negative energy based on the vibrations from our energy. When we emit low vibration emotions, we attract, create, and manifest low vibrational energy, matter, and things. Low energies keep us from creating the life we desire, and instead manifest illness and keep us from ascending to higher dimensions.

How do we know if we have nojo flow? If we're sick, have a disease, take medication, rub people the wrong way, or are unhappy without a reason, these are clues we're vibrating at low frequency.

Since bad behaviors often stem from fear or anger, it's important to look inside and see why we act in ways that don't benefit us. Negative behaviors and bad feelings aren't necessarily wrong but merely an eye-opener that it's time to look inside and see what's causing our shadows to make sneak attacks.

Although it's in our nature to attach to our sorrows rather than happiness, negative behaviors manifest into things we don't desire. However, we can consciously change negatively ingrained patterns by merely thinking it so.

This low-vibration list is merely given as a reference to feelings that need to be acknowledged, understood, and upgraded, and not to suggest that we can't be, do, or act in any of these ways.

Accidents are created by the mind to shake us up from the oblivion of being unaware, of living life on autopilot, and not looking within. Our subconscious mind intentionally creates accidents to act as mini wake-up calls that hinder, not progress, our path. We have to be willing to examine the signs the subconscious brings to understand the value in its message.

As a side note, the cerebellum in the brain is responsible for physical movements, and negative thinking shuts this region down, resulting in the clumsy movements that cause accidents.

Addictive Behaviors are usually to fill an inner void, emptiness, or because of a fear of getting to know ourselves by avoiding reality. Obvious addictions are drinking, smoking, sex, drugs, gambling, and overeating. Less obvious are watching TV, shopping, working, browsing social media, gossiping, complaining, or checking our phone constantly. All these behaviors are energy consuming and consciousness inhibitors. Addictions are "attachments" that can be released by raising our frequency out of range of the attachment's frequency and mentally cutting off the attachment using cord-cutting techniques from Chapter 14.

Alcohol is fun to use to escape from the realities of daily life occasionally, but when drinking becomes a habitual escape, we are really expressing a fear that our life's not good enough. Interestingly, alcohol is called spirits because this is when dark forces enter the body that leave us with low spirits, low energy, and a hangover.

Allopathy is the use of traditional pharmaceutical drugs that help control but are unable to cure symptoms of disease. The after-death effects of psychiatric drugs, the Covid shot, morphine, and other allopathic drugs keep our spirit stuck in lower astral realms, unable to spiritually ascend. (Guenther, 2022).

Anger is an addictive behavior and trauma response fueled by egos. It's easier to be mad at someone else than look at our own shadows. Anger shows as irritation, impatience, criticism, jealousy, resentment, or bitterness, and expresses itself as yelling, arguing, physical or mental abuse, and as other behaviors that hurt others.

When someone is showing anger towards us, we should try to give them space and think about how *we* contributed to their angry actions. Like accidents are signs from the subconscious telling us to look within, so is anger. We have to ask ourselves what the anger is trying to teach us, as misfortunes pave the way to gold. What lesson are we supposed to learn by our display of anger? What other feelings are we trying to hide by displaying anger in its place? This is what true soul searching is all about.

One way to get over anger is to turn the feeling into its opposite feeling: compassion. Finding compassion and understanding in why another person acted the way they did helps us move beyond the situation. Another way to move past anger is to consciously choose to feel an emotion vibrating higher than anger. Anger vibrates at 150 Hz, so instead, we can choose to feel annoyed, which vibrates at 175 Hz. From here, we can continue to choose higher vibrating emotions until we feel better or until we reach the frequency of our desires, 500 Hz. Chapter Six displays a chart with the frequencies of different emotions.

Attachments are energetic cords that allow low vibrational energies to form between two people or things. Cords of attachment can be mentally "cut," or cleared through meditative intention. Cord cutting rituals help keep our body in high frequency; example rituals are given in Chapter 14. Lower vibrational cords clump together and form densities and matter on the holographic matrix.

Bad Behaviors carry low-vibrating energy that keep us from attaining our desires. We're often unaware of our bad behaviors unless a kind soul points them out. While these behaviors may seem miniscule, they limit our power to manifest. These actions are not all-inclusive, as we may have our own bad habits, others that aren't listed, or spin-offs that lower vibrations:

- Avoiding social gatherings because of a fear of not fitting in. • Being obsessive about our looks or cleanliness. • Having conflicts with other people. • Putting our desires aside by being a people-pleaser. • Avoiding conversations that we don't want to have. • Being off-put by direct, frank individuals. • Finding enjoyment in playing mind games at the expense of others (ghosting). • Isolating ourselves or putting on pretenses to be something we're not.
- Participating in lies, blame, and excuses.

Blame is projecting our own dislikes onto someone else and not taking responsibility for our actions. This low-vibrating energy keeps us from healing, manifesting, and reaching higher levels of awareness. Blaming takes away our power and puts it in the hands of another.

> Don't blame anyone for the road you're on.
> It's your own asphalt.

Bullying is a vibrational downer. If we're bullying others, this karmic action will be repeated in another lifetime with us being bullied in the same manner that we bullied. We never escape our actions. For our next incarnation, we can deliberately choose a life of being bullied as repentance for past actions.

Closed/Narrow Mindset prevents us from creating and knowing anything outside the realms of our five senses. A closed mindset shuts down intuition, synchronicities, and manifestation. We can open a closed mind by being more receptive, accepting all kinds of experiences, and observing without judgment.

Clutter and Extra Stuff in the environment automatically lowers energy and makes us feel more stressed. Cleaning clutter gets rid of emotional baggage and makes room for new desires to manifest. Metaphorically, in order to receive a desire from the Universe, there must be "room" for it in our space, for empty space is where energy lies.

Co-dependency is the energetic attachments of others that depletes energy of both people. Cord-cutting rituals sever unwanted attachments such as those from toxic relationships, people of our past, or people who simply bring us down.

Comparing Ourselves to Others stems from fear of not being good enough. It's easier to learn to accept and love our flaws when we realize that our one-of-a-kind personality and appearances are what makes us genuinely likeable. When we shine with authenticity, we are enough and all that we need to be.

Competition with another person is really competing against ourselves since we all are a part of the same collective energy in the Universe. Competition limits our true creative energy by putting the focus outside of us instead of within. Winning is about being the best *we* can be. There's no victory in finding someone lesser to compare ourselves to and then claiming ourselves victor. Having fun, taking pride in our efforts, doing our best, and realizing our own abilities is a high-vibe road to winning.

Covid Vaccine aka "the jab," has been said to have been intentionally conceived as a direct means to manipulate our DNA to keep us compliant, submissive, and restrict our abilities to our true powers. The vaccine is toxic to DNA, chakras, the soul, and limits our ability to access our higher self and higher levels of consciousness. The vaccine decreases the size of our aura, keeps us solidified in a 3D world, creates puncture sites for dark energies to enter, causes hardening of the organs due to blocked chakras, and reinforces the ego. (Guenther, 2022).

Sheer willpower and conscious self-responsibility toward healing can help remove the DNA-controlling, pineal-shrinking, and soul-sucking effects of the Corona virus vaccine from our bodies. Homeopathic remedies such as Thuja and Belladonna, inner spiritual work (meditation), body cleansing, craniosacral therapy, and massage can also help remove this toxin.

Criticism and Judgment of anything keeps us in a vibration unable to achieve *any* desire. We all have the tendency to judge at times because internally, it makes us feel better and gives us a false sense of security. Instead, it brings our energy down and lowers our vibration. Like a boomerang, when we send out low-vibrating frequencies, we attract and manifest similar, unwanted low-vibrating things back to us. Continual criticism will eventually manifest as a disease or sickness that doctors have no cure for. We can't take a pill for this sickness; the remedy requires a change in mindset. Once we realize that we are all One, criticizing another is really criticizing a part of ourselves that we haven't yet learned to love, accept, and embrace.

When we catch ourselves criticizing, we should reflect and ask what is it about *ourselves* that reminds us and bothers us by this behavior. From this point, it may be easier to be forgiving and more understanding of others' differences. Instead of seeing the negative aspects that cause us to criticize, we can use forethought and reflection to guide our emotions toward acceptance. Affirmations help change and reprogram critical and negative thoughts.

Dark Energy comes in two forms: as a low-vibrating negative force that interferes with harmonious creation and as a high-vibrating positive force that supports the natural flow of creation.

As a negative force, dark energy enters through holes on our aura formed from our ego, blind spots, wounds, traumas, shadows, base desires, stress, addictions, and injection sites. Dark energies can be removed through awareness, introspection, spiritual practices, and body energy cleansing. As parasitic hosts, dark forces have nowhere to live when we fill our bodies with light and love.

As a positive force, it's a state of neutrality. Dark energy is the energy from the black holes of Space. It's the space between particles, the Void, a field of all possibilities from the sacred space of emptiness. It's the place where answers lie. Dark energy is a free source, a "zero-point energy," the building blocks of matter and the energy of consciousness that's waiting to be harvested for higher DNA activation and intergalactic space travel.

Doubt manifests from a limited belief system that we're not good enough. We don't trust our natural instincts, and this lowers our vibrational frequency. Doubt may come from past ancestral or societal programming and can be released through acknowledging shadows, self-compassion, hypnosis, clearing energy blocks, and affirmations.

Drama feeds our ego like an unescapable soap opera. Many of us like being the center of attention and may intentionally stir up drama to bring attention back to us. Sharing family matters or personal woes with anyone with ears or having a social media account are signs of drama queens. We can avoid others' drama by listening but not reacting. Not everything needs our input. Take the higher road and walk away if we must.

Discard Ego?
If you go back now, you may find your yourself
Keep | Discard

Ego is the armor of protection we present to the world. It's the degree to which we identify with ourselves because of what type of job we have, how we look, or how much money we make. The ego keeps us emotionally stuck and prevents us from evolving to higher states. As a trauma response, it can cause us to act defensive, arrogant, and stubborn, making it more difficult to release toxic emotions and limiting beliefs. Ego is the inner voice that plays tricks with our thinking and can be mistaken for intuition. Ego makes us doubt ourselves and feel indecisive whereas intuition always feels right and leads us in the right direction. Ego is the illusion of separation from One and keeps us from ascending beyond the second chakra. We can move beyond our ego when we understand that we're not the voice in our head; we are merely hearing its lack of wisdom.

EMFs are electromagnetic fields such as radiation, cell phones, AirPods, Wi-Fi, routers, technology, AI (artificial intelligence), chemtrails, and microwaves. EMF increases illness, decreases energy fields, and modifies DNA. Drinking purified water, immersing ourselves in nature, and taking the mineral supplement orgonite can help diminish the effects of electromagnetic fields. EMF Quantum Cards are credit-card sized EMF radiation blockers that can be easily worn in clothing or placed in wallets to reduce EMF's effects.

If we only knew how low voltage affected our health, we would recharge our body as often as our phone.

Emotional Baggage is when we carry our traumatic experiences with us and share them with anyone who will listen without any intention of guidance or healing. Emotional baggage is shadows and blocked energy that need to be acknowledged, cleared, and released. Holding onto emotional baggage will eventually form energetic imbalances in the aura and manifest as density and disease in the body.

The Environment contributes to what we absorb, take in, and "program" ourselves with. So, if we are watching TV, listening to the radio, talking on the cell phone, browsing the internet, or listening to a "Brain-a-Thon" of motivational speakers, it becomes part of our vibratory essence. By tuning in to the same vibration as our environment, we become One with it.

Exterior Validation is feeling worthy only through the acknowledgment of others. Needing validation from others stems from a fear that our life is not good enough, and we use and expect others to lift us up, leading to codependent behaviors. When we look outside of ourselves for validation, it leads us astray from our internal knowledge of what's right and true for us.

"If you seek approval from others in this world, you will not know happiness." — MOOJI

Fear (see Chapter 6) is an emotion stemming from not knowing what something is about. Fear is more than a feeling; fear is a choice made from ignorance. We fear death because we don't know what's on the other side. We fear the unknown and change because we don't know where it will lead us. We fear other people's beliefs because they're different than our own. When we continually think about or avoid the cause of our fears, it will eventually manifest as disease. Facing our fears through action helps us work through them. Small action steps in a positive direction are empowering and give us the impetus needed to move beyond being afraid.

Foods emit vibrations that can negatively or positively affect our consciousness depending on its frequency. Fast food restaurants, genetically modified (GMO), animal products, and grocery stores are full of highly processed toxic foods. These foods don't have the vital life force needed to energize us or heal cells. Toxic foods also form blockages and densities in the body.

Fresh, organic foods have higher frequencies that increase our vital energy, while cooked, canned, and processed foods have frequencies close to zero and drain our energy. The highest vibrational foods are not cooked and eaten raw.

Kirlian photography shows the energy fields of meat and an apple, and cooked vs uncooked broccoli's energy field.

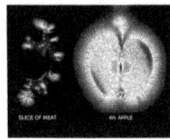  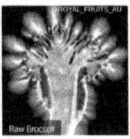

Images Courtesy of royalfruits.com.au

High Vibration Foods		Low Vibration Foods	
• Fruits	• Legumes	• Sugars	• Deep fried foods
• Vegetable	• Raw Chocolate	• Sweeteners	• Microwaved Foods
• Fermented Foods	• Himalayan Salt	• White rice and flour	• Soda
• Nuts and Seeds	• Dark Leafy Greens	• Genetically modified	• Alcohol
• Herbs	• Apple Cider Vinegar	• Meat, fish and poultry	• Coffee
• Spices	• Water	• Processed foods	• Chlorine or Fluoride treated water
• Herbal Teas	• Grains (buckwheat, brown rice and spelt)	• Frozen foods	
• Oils (Olive, Coconut, Flax, Sesame)		• Oils (canola, margarine, vegetable oils)	• Animal products (milk, yogurts and cheese)

Gossip, Jealousy, and Envy are all low-vibrational emotions. These emotions keep us from being happy because whatever energy we project, we get back due to the law of attracting energies.

Guilt is our own attempt to make ourselves feel bad over something that really makes us feel good, like eating chocolate or taking a mid-day nap. Guilt may show as anxiety, insomnia, tension, worry, or upset stomachs. It's one of the lowest vibrational frequencies of all the emotions and will eventually manifest to disease if it's not managed. One way to free ourselves of guilt is to forgive ourselves for whatever's making us feel guilty. Being as kind to ourselves as we would with others, practicing gratitude, taking purposeful action, and changing our self-talk can help eliminate feelings of guilt.

Habits are something we are all creatures of, and if our habits include being addicted to our phone, drama, and bad news, it's time to upgrade these vibrational downers. Bad habits can be eliminated instantly with 100% intent and willpower. Replacing a bad habit with something better can help remove its negative influence.

Hate is poison for the body and soul. It's the lowest frequency of consciousness and prevents us from being able to manifest or heal. When we consider all inhabitants of Earth as One, hating anyone, thing, or group is really hating an aspect of ourselves. When we feel hate in our hearts, we attract hate in our lives. Hate can be released through forgiveness, compassion, and knowing that everyone is doing the best they can, given their level of awareness or knowledge at that moment. When we notice that we're feeling this low-frequency emotion, we can replace it immediately with a better emotion, such as indifference, or taking a "so-what" attitude. We can give hatred a new label of "dislike" instead of hate, pair it with new feelings of indifference, and over time, we can watch this low-vibrating emotion disintegrate. Finding the root cause of this disease-causing emotion is instrumental in understanding its origin and letting it go.

Remember, when you forgive you heal.
When you let go, you grow.

Holding on to the Past could be the inability to forget that last relationship we're still pining over, how so-and-so did us wrong, how our childhood messed us up…these are some of the things we ruminate over excessively that keep the stress hormone cortisol in our system and bring sickness on.

Lack & Limiting Beliefs (see Chapter 4) are merely ideas that over time, we have accepted as truths. A belief becomes limiting when it keeps us from reaching our full potential. Most of us aren't aware that we're operating from limiting beliefs, but we all have them. Whatever we are offended by or are unwilling to understand shows the extent of our limitations. Some limiting beliefs are related to past trauma or inherited ancestral DNA. Some limiting beliefs are acquired through family, cultures, media, or sickness. Although there's no such thing as a bad belief, there are those that no longer serve us and need replacing. To replace an old belief, substitute a new, more empowering belief by consciously replacing the old with the new. Example: *Money is the root of all evil* is replaced by *money is a resource to do good*.

"Matters" are those things we tell ourselves that we have to "tend to." Matters lower our frequency as "matter" is made of dense, low-vibrating energy.

The Martyr Complex is self-sacrificing our own needs to gain admiration. This form of fear uses guilt from others to keep us in a victim mentality. Additionally, when we believe that things are being done *to* us, it carries low vibrational energy and gives away our power.

Miasms are genetically inherited diseases coming from energy fields, not infections. Miasms are known for relapsing, which could be from continual stress, negative emotions and thinking, drug use, and environmental toxins. Usually, miasms are treated with homeopathic medicines of the same name.

1. *Sycosis miasms* come from ancestors' overactive DNA energy expressing itself in us as ADD/ADHD, arthritis, bronchitis, colitis, asthma, or reproductive and urinary problems. Sycosis miasms cause a need for excitement and stimulation.
2. *Syphilinum miasms* are genetically inherited bacteria that manifest as Lyme Disease, ulcerative colitis, alcoholism, arthritis, depression, anxiety, insomnia, loss of taste and smell, and alopecia.
3. *Psora miasms* are linked to inherited skin problems, colds and flus, allergies, osteoporosis, and chronic fatigue. The homeopathic detox tuberculinum is used to remove this miasm.
4. *Carcinosin* is a modern miasm that carries the traits of perfectionism and fastidiousness. This miasm manifests as addiction, phobia, shyness, anxiety, or

self-sacrificing behaviors. Always needing to do the right thing is the underlying belief causing this miasm. Physical signs show as chronic fatigue, eczema, eating disorders, cancers, frequent sicknesses, insomnia, and constipation.
5. *Vaccinosis* miasms come from environmental pollution, over-immunization, and overuse of pharmaceutical drugs. Thuja and Belladonna are treatments prescribed for vaccinosis miasms.

Money is energy, and many of us have acquired a negative relationship with money. Releasing old beliefs, using affirmations, money visualizations (see Chapter 14), and meditations can help remove this energy block.

Multitasking drains energy; it's the opposite of being mindful. Doing one thing at a time helps focus our attention during meditation and manifestation.

I used to multi-task. Now, I multi-dimensional task.

Negativity encompasses many low-vibrating behaviors that limit our ability to get what we want. Instead of manifesting desires, negative behaviors manifest stress, tension, anxiety, depression, body ailments, insecurity, and fears.

Negativity shows itself by • having a bad attitude • assuming the worst about people • being closed-minded • not acting with integrity • being dishonest • hiding secrets • harboring resentment • holding grudges • not minding our own business • caring what others think • comparing ourselves to others • being afraid to try something new • staying mad • being lazy • thinking we're no good • feeling entitled • thinking the worst • being jealous • feeling guilty • having road rage • harming ourselves, others, animals, or the planet • hurtful and selfish behaviors • doing things that don't make us feel happy like working jobs we don't like • reading gossip magazines, being part of work drama, and complaining about things we can't change • mindless activities like social media, reality TV shows, aimless internet, watching YouTube videos just to pass time, and • violent video games. Low-vibe behaviors drain our energy and limit our ability to manifest, heal, and rise to higher levels of consciousness. As soon as we notice negative thoughts enter our minds, with intent, we can consciously change them to something better.

Overachievers are not only energy drainers because of their overuse of multitasking but are vibrational downers because they take pride in doing so much and sharing their accomplishments with everyone.

Overthinking disconnects us from the present moment of Now and creates problems that aren't there. When we find ourselves immersed in our heads by overthinking and worrying, it's time to reconnect to our inner selves by taking a few deep breaths, practicing gratitude, or enjoying time in nature.

Procrastination is the opposite of action and is a common form of self-sabotage. When we procrastinate, we tell our subconscious that we're not worthy of our best life right now, but maybe later. If we're not a procrastinator by nature, then it's no big deal if some things don't get done right away. However, ongoing procrastination could be a sign of underlying wounds that need to be addressed. If we reframe the meaning of procrastination, it's no longer a sign of laziness, but a universal signal that we're not in vibrational harmony with the task at this moment.

To avoid procrastination and get the little stuff done, do the most important work first. Make a list with stuff that needs to be done and cross it off as it gets done. Not everything needs to be completed in a day and giving ourselves time to get things finished takes the pressure and the stress off. It's totally okay to have the same task on our list a week or even a month later if it's not a priority. Lists can be merely to-do reminders and not the pesky voice of procrastination.

Resentment is holding on to past grudges and not letting go. Holding on to an even well-deserved resentment or grudge stalls the manifestation and creation process until we're able to release the pain and find forgiveness. Forgiveness is foremost if we want to move up the ladder of ascension. When we take an attitude that offenders are doing their best given their current level of knowledge, we can begin to find solace in their wrongdoings. We must forgive, let go, and let be to move on.

Resistance is, ironically, a powerful force of attraction created from fear. A lot of energy goes into resisting the new, focusing on the past, and holding on to old beliefs. Not accepting responsibility, obsessing, blaming others, believing we're not entitled because we're not good enough, staying with an abusive spouse, or not leaving an unhappy situation are ways we show resistance. Protest groups attract exactly what they don't want using the Law of Attraction to their disadvantage by misusing phrases such as "No More War."

What we resist, persists.

Resistance shows up when we are not in the right harmony, or vibration, with changes we're trying to make. Synchronicities and manifestations will be delayed if the timing's not right or we're not ready.

Sometimes bad things happen in our lives that we believe to be unwelcome. We shouldn't resist them but consider it as "messages" from the Universe that will help with a current problem.

How do we counteract resistance? We focus our thoughts, power, and energy on what we really *do* desire, whether that's financial security, happiness, love, or freedom for all mankind!

Self-Criticism/Image is the picture we hold of ourselves in our mind, our ego. As a culture, the image of ourselves has become overly critical. Our thoughts are consumed with ways we could be better and ways that we're not good enough.

It's easier to love ourselves when we realize that no one is perfect. Whether it's quirky looks or odd habits, it's our idiosyncrasies that give us character and make us not only likeable, but loveable.

Appreciating ourselves for who we are, flaws and all, naturally improves our self-image. Using positive affirmations, and finding something that makes our heart sing, helps us find love within ourselves. When we love ourselves, love finds us.

Self-fulfilling Prophecy is like the adage "be careful what you wish for." This prophecy confirms that negative or positive expectations will be fulfilled due to the Law of Attraction. When we hold a biased belief about something, we subconsciously bring it into reality, whether we want the result or not. This prophecy reminds us not to focus on limiting beliefs and fears, but to keep our thoughts positive and not to dwell on the past. Positive affirmations, mantras, and neurolinguistic reprogramming can keep us from attracting negative beliefs.

Self-Sabotage are self-destructive behaviors and habits that keep us from performing our best. Self-sabotage often shows up as procrastination, self-injury, and overindulgence. Being afraid to try new things, doing things alone, waiting for the perfect timing, and comparing ourselves to others are other ways we engage in self-sabotage and hold ourselves back from our full potential. Practicing self-love, being mindful, recognizing triggers, removing ourselves from destructive and instigating environments, and being aware of a higher purpose can help eliminate these behaviors.

Social Media and the Internet can be beneficial, but not always. Many activities on social media and the internet are low vibrational and engaging in them can bring bouts of anger, fear, or comparison, all of which vibrate at very low frequencies.

Stress is a sign to take a personal time-out. We can immediately release stress with a few slow, deep breaths in through the nose and out through the mouth. If desired, we can pair our breaths with a mantra such as *Calmness In, Anxiety Out,* or whatever words personally work. Continue slowly breathing to neutralize and diffuse any negatively charged feelings.

Television & News spread fear faster than pandemic germs in an unvaccinated, unmasked room. The news is full of negative vibes because like religion, it instills fear. If we don't want war, then we shouldn't be watching it on TV. The more we focus on something we *don't* want, the more we attract it; this is the Law of Attraction doing its job of attracting like energies. So, if we are afraid and have fear in our lives, we have to stop paying attention to bad news.

Toxic People, aka "energy vampires," are narcissistic, controlling, manipulative, and judgmental. Being around people with toxic behaviors instantly depletes our own energy because we absorb the energies of people around us.

If being near toxic people is unavoidable, we can avoid their negative energies by keeping our arms crossed in front of our solar plexus area and imagining a protective bubble of white energy surrounding our body. Negative and toxic energies can be released using cord-cutting techniques described in Chapter 14.

Toxins are things like cigarettes, fluoride, glyphosates, herbicides, flame-retardant materials, Teflon®, Monsanto products, food additives, or anything that doesn't break down naturally in the body and makes us less resistant to disease. Lesser-known toxins include hand sanitizer, antibacterial soaps, cleaning products, dryer sheets, perfumes, sunscreens, and added scents. Because physical toxins are intertwined with emotional toxins, they show up as fear, anger, and revenge and are stored in areas with less energy flow or in places where we feel pain. Toxins can be released naturally from the body using kriyas (Yogic purification), and through other energy healing techniques.

Transhumanism is a movement to transform and enhance human capabilities through technology. Some of these technologies include genetic engineering, psychopharmacology, life extension therapies, neural interfacing, brain mapping, implanted computers, and cognitive entrainment. Creating artificially intelligent humans interferes with DNA, the electromagnetic functions of our aura, and reduces our spiritual consciousness.

Trauma includes negative ancestral or childhood events that are encoded and stored as memories in our DNA. Flight, fight, freeze, and fawn are common responses from trauma. When negative events trigger our memory, we behave according to the emotional response we encoded at the time of the trauma.

- Trauma from criticism manifests as apathy.
- Trauma from betrayal manifests as an inability to trust.
- Trauma from abandonment manifests as an inability to commit.
- Trauma from loneliness manifests as being surrounded by people and negative relationships.
- Trauma from rejection manifests as walking away from situations.
- Trauma from guilt manifests as self-punishment.
- Trauma from abuse manifests as anger.

Sometimes trauma responses appear as:
- Feeling empty inside.

- Agreeing just to keep the peace.
- Feeling responsible for other's happiness.
- Feeling on guard all the time.
- Having a negative world view.
- Reckless impulsivity and the need for escapism.

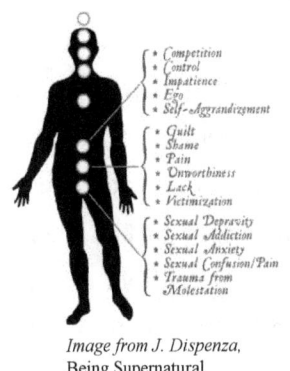

Image from J. Dispenza, Being Supernatural

Trauma blocks energy in the lower three chakras. Sexual traumas, anxiety, and addictions block energy in the Root Chakra. Guilt, shame, pain, unworthiness, lack, and victimization block energy in the Sacral Chakra, and feelings of competition, control, impatience, ego, and self-importance block the Solar Plexus Chakra. Clearing and balancing these chakras can help release unwanted traumatic memories from the past.

To manifest complete healing, we must work through our pain to find its origin. Once we acknowledge and accept our past, the skeletons can come out of the closet, and once and for all, we can dump the limiting beliefs that have been feeding our trauma throughout the years.

Releasing trauma can be accomplished through shadow work, breathwork, self-love, EMDR (eye movements), spinal release, massage, Neoshamanism, Radical Healing, tapping, or anything that breaks up stagnant energy.

MIND BLOWN

The degree to which a person can grow is in direct proportion to the amount of truth they can accept about themselves without running away.

Victim Mentality is when we feel that things are being done to us and that it's out of our control. It's the belief that something outside of us is what's preventing us from taking full responsibility. We use blame and excuses when we should be taking responsibility. When we realize that we create every circumstance in our lives, whether good or bad, there can be no victims, just creators of the mentality *I can't*.

Negative thoughts and behaviors are a part of life and unavoidable, however, once we recognize the low-vibrating actions we participate in, we can begin to make a change. The change starts within as we begin to accept full responsibility for everything that happens in our lives.

Instead of criticizing others and ourselves, we can find a reason for praising. Instead of complaining, we can focus on appreciating. When we realize we have the power to change the consequences of our actions, blaming becomes forgiving, resenting becomes accepting, and wishing for more becomes enjoying what we have.

Wetiko is cancer of the soul, an infectious, psychic virus that tricks the mind into beliefs of self-righteousness and of being a master of deception. Indulgent and self-destructive habits embodying greed, excess, and never being satisfied typify wetiko energy. Those with the dark energy of wetiko act separately from humanity and the planet, hindering their potential for self and soul evolution. Like reaching higher levels of consciousness and freeing our hearts of pain, compassion is the energy needed to clear souls with negative wetiko energy.

☹ **Worry** is wishing for the worst and is a waste of the imagination. We all fall victim to worrying, but *constant* worrying and overthinking negatively affects our vibrational frequency. Both worry and overthinking vibrate at very low frequencies. When we're faced with situations that are out of our control, instead of ruminating, try to:

- Surrender to the powers that *are* and let go and let be.
- Think of the best possible outcome.
- Meditate and clear the mind.
- Spend time outdoors.
- Create.

Just as negative behaviors lower our vibrations, the next chapter shows us how positive behaviors raise our vibrations and get us closer to creating the reality we desire.

CHAPTER 3

Mojo Rising

Whazzz Up? My Frequency.

"The secret of change is to focus all of your energy not on fighting the old, but on building the new." — SOCRATES

If lowering our vibration depends on negative thinking, then raising our vibration requires positive thinking. The higher our vibration, the more aligned and connected we are to our true self and higher purpose. Raising our vibes isn't a one-time deal; it's a choice we make in every moment through conscious living and being mindful. Being consciously aware enough to realize when we're thinking bad thoughts and then changing them to good thoughts is the key.

Although stopping the cycle of negativity and shifting our thoughts from negative to positive emotions is easier said than done, it can become second nature with practice. Putting ourselves first, combined with willpower and determination will change negative nojo into helpful mojo.

Imagine choosing emotions based on love instead of fear. This may be a new concept, but every time we choose to feel a better-feeling emotion, it raises our frequency by 10 MHz. Choosing love-based emotions reinforces positive pathways that break negative habits and raise our vibrations in the process.

The Emotional Guidance Scale Chart in Chapter 6 gives a list of vibrational frequencies associated with certain emotions. It is used as a reference for the following alphabetical list of actions, behaviors, products, and practices that assist in raising vibrations.

Adaptogens are plant-based medicines that adapt to the needs of the user, hence its name. For example, ashwagandha helps us decompress at the end of the day, or it gives a mental boost if we need more energy. Adaptogens help balance stress, improve the quality of life, protect the brain, and may increase life span. Herbal plants and mushrooms such as reishi, ginseng, tulsi, or schisandra are types of adaptogens. Rasa coffee is an herbal alternative to coffee jitters and has an abundance of adaptogens.

Affirmations are beliefs and *I Am* statements that assert something is true. When affirmations are said with desire and intention, it's like having our own genie in a bottle! Affirmations are like self-mission statements that we say over and over until we believe them and they manifest. Affirmations are said in the present tense, making our mind believe it has already happened. The best results come from practicing affirmations in the alpha level brainwave state, such as upon awakening or while looking in a mirror. Because DNA and the structures of language are similar, we can change our genes simply by using words and sentences such as affirmations. The sound vibrations from our voice, which make affirmations effective in raising our vibrations, transform our genetic makeup, our DNA.

> *"Abracadabra" is from the Aramaic phrase "avra kehdabra" which literally means "I will create as I speak."*

I am is the strongest creative statement in the Universe. Writing and saying the words "I am" with a positive description afterwards sends a powerful message to the subconscious that we are that. Whatever we think, whatever we say after the words "I am," we become.

> *Words cast powerful spells.*
> *Anything that you say after "I Am," you become.*
> *That's why it's called 'Spell'-ing.*

We can create our own affirmations that relate to areas in our life that we want to improve. Start by keeping the affirmations in the present tense beginning with the words *I am*. Use the picture insert as a guide for creating our own personal affirmations. It cannot be overstressed that to *become* our intended affirmation, we must believe it to be true and *act* in that manner *before* it happens.

♦ I am grateful that I have the confidence needed to make as much money as I choose.

♦ I am healthy, strong, and perfect just the way I am.

♦ I am so happy and grateful for my affluence and good fortune.

♦ I am unique, valuable, and worthy.

♦ I am self-confident and always know the right thing to say and do.

♦ I am healthy, wealthy, happy, and wise.

♦ I am at my desired weight, and I feel amazing!

When writing or repeating affirmations, we should realize that the mind doesn't recognize words like no, not, don't, and can't. It's like typing "no country music" in the search bar on a computer. Our mind and computers don't process "no" words, and then our computer brain chooses country. Statements such as "I am *not* poor," don't make us abundant. The Universe hears *I am poor* and conspires to make it happen. Keep affirmations positive and eliminate negative qualifiers.

Write down your affirmation on a piece of paper and place it underneath your pillow before you sleep. Your subconscious mind will begin attracting this towards you as you sleep.

Anything that Brings Us Joy is a vibration raiser if it makes us feel completely absorbed in the moment and takes us beyond our thoughts. When we do things that bring us joy, our mind is open to receiving new ideas, insights, and awareness—things like journaling, writing, community involvement, dancing, learning something new, helping others, volunteering, singing, painting, gardening, reading, you name it! It's all about energy flow and doing something where it feels like time is standing still.

Aromatherapy/Essential Oils help raise our vibration using the principle of entrainment, where a lower frequency will align with the vibrations of a higher frequency. Frequencies of essential oils are between 52-580 MHz, the highest vibration of any organic substance.

Essential oils also have super high antioxidant properties. A cucumber's antioxidant power has 60 units of strength and blueberries have 2400; orange essential oil has 19,000 units of strength and ylang ylang essential oil has 1,300,500 units. The higher the antioxidant power, the better the support for a healthy body, and essential oils are like concentrated antioxidants.

Besides smelling wonderful, essential oils cleanse cell receptors, remove faulty DNA programming, fight pathogens, help depression, dementia, and moods, relax the mind, and boost happiness. Essential oils help release negative emotions because the sense of smell is the strongest link to the subconscious.

Frequencies of Common Essential Oils
- 580 MHz Idaho Blue Spruce
- 320 MHz Rose
- 181 MHz Helichrysum
- 147 MHz Frankincense
- 118 MHz Lavender
- 105 MHz Chamomile, Myrrh
- 98 MHz Juniper, Sandalwood
- 85 MHz Angelica
- 78 MHz Peppermint
- 52 MHz Basil

How to Use Essential Oils
1. *Vaporizer/Diffuser*—Add a few drops to a vaporizer or diffuser to spread the oil to the entire room.
2. *Dry Evaporation*—Dab cotton balls in the oil and place them in different corners of the house or inhale the cotton ball directly to get a quick energy boost.

There are also specially made necklaces to hold oil-soaked cotton pads.
3. *With Carrier Oils*—Add a few drops of essential oils to a carrier oil like coconut or jojoba for massaging the face and body.
4. *Direct Application*—Some essential oils can be applied directly to the skin; check first, as many are not suitable for direct application.
5. *In Bath Water*—Add a few drops of essential oil to bath water like lemon or ylang ylang in the morning, and lavender or neroli at night for relaxation.

Common Usages of Oils

Angelica is a protector oil and filters negative energy from traumatic experiences.

Anise opens the voice of our intuition and develops our psychic powers.

Blue Lotus relaxes the central nervous system making it easier to connect with spirit guides.

Cedar grounds and strengthens the physical body.

Chamomile soothes frayed nerves and calms a nervous mind.

Cinnamon cassia boosts metabolism and purifies the body.

Elemi supports new beginnings, transitions, and internal transformation.

Eucalyptus is cleansing, uplifting, and healing on all levels.

Fennel eases digestion and enhances memory.

Fir Balsam is a grounding oil that eases worry and helps us be present.

Gardenia offers relief from spiritual or psychological trauma.

Ginger increases qi flow to the sacral region to stimulate sexual passion.

Grapefruit invigorates and refreshes.

Helichrysum is an anti-aging and anti-inflammatory oil.

Juniper is a purifying, healing oil and protects from evil spirits.

Lavender brings calmness and peace and has healing properties.

Lemon calms the nerves while energizing the power center Solar Plexus Chakra.

Melissa is used for love and success.

Mugwort has a sedative effect to bring deep meditation and prophetic visions.

Neroli calms the body and facilitates manifestation.

Pink Lotus is transformational and helps bring enlightenment.

St. John's Wort treats depression and anxiety.

Tangerine connects us with our inner child helping us feel more playful, happy, and carefree.

Tuberose calms and soothes, promotes relaxation, and eases sadness and anxiety.

Tea Tree is anti-bacterial, anti-microbial, and anti-fungal and is known as a master healer.

Ylang ylang is an aphrodisiac and enhances intuition.

Attitude raises our vibration when we have a positive "can do" instead of a negative "poor me" attitude.

Brainwave Entrainment uses stimuli such as sound, meditation, vibrations, and light to influence the rate of our brainwaves and our mental state.

Breaking Up with a relationship, job, or situation for the betterment of ourselves is an energy boost. It's the Universe's way of saying, "Good for you!" When we lose a good friend or break up with a toxic relationship, it makes space for something better to enter our lives that's on our same energy level. This is the time to look inside and ask what lessons we need to learn from the end of that relationship, our role in the lesson for the loss, and gratitude for the growth.

Breathwork (see Chapter 15) is breathing with intention and energy added to it. Breathwork powers up our energy channels to deliver more "juice" to our energetic fields.

> "When your breath is shallow, you are shallow. When your breath is deep, you are deep."
> —Yogi Bhajan

Breathwork helps us let go of thought patterns that don't serve us anymore, shakes loose stagnant energy, and helps us get in the present moment. Breathing is feeling and is a safe place to work through anger, pain, and resentments. Conscious attention to breathing activates the frequency of love, 500 Hz, the vibration of manifestation. It's been shown that the greatest predictor of longevity is lung capacity—so let's all take a deep breath! Breathing also brings in more light which increases our vibrations and makes dimensional travel easier.

Chakras (see Chapter 8) are whirling vortexes of subtle energy centers found throughout the body. There are seven main chakra energy centers, however there are thousands in the body with energy dispersed throughout via meridians. Each chakra represents part of our physical, emotional, and spiritual well-being. The vibrational frequency of the chakras increases as emotions develop from basic trust of the Root Chakra near the base of the spine to the emotions of spirituality and transcendence of the Crown Chakra just above the head.

The chakras represent levels of increasing consciousness corresponding to dimensional planes, DNA, and to colors of the light wave spectrum of the rainbow. The higher our level of chakra attainment, the higher our level of awareness, understanding, and self-knowledge. Most of us have only reached the second chakra level. Increasing awareness is a journey of lifetimes.

Cleansing and Detoxing (also see Fasting) help eliminate toxins from our bodies. Since most waste is eliminated through our lungs, the best detox is conscious breathwork. Otherwise, here are a few ways to remove toxins like GMO's, fluoride, and chemtrails from our system:

- Throw out toxic cleansers and use a baking soda, vinegar, and lemon juice mix.
- Get a HEPA air purifier.
- Sweat through saunas, lodges, and exercise.
- Try food fasting, Yogic purging, and coffee enemas.
- Drink more purified water.
- Take a hot shower followed by a cold shower, and try Epsom salt baths.
- Take Vitamin C, milk thistle, dandelion root, or other natural supplements.
- Eat detoxifying foods: green tea, cilantro, turmeric, apple cider vinegar, lemon juice, and ginger.
- Draw impurities and toxins from the skin using Shaolin and bentonite clays.
- Try liquid zeolite to remove free radicals and heavy metals from the body.

Color Therapy or Chromotherapy's (see Chapter 9) basis is that every color has a unique vibrational frequency that affects our emotions. Violet is the highest vibrating color with the most energy on the visible color spectrum. Red vibrates slowest and has the least energy. Yellow and orange colors most closely associate with the positive energy of happiness.

Compassion is usually considered to be an emotional reaction to someone's bad experience, but it's also an advanced form of intuition. Compassion is not just showing sympathy, it's the action of becoming involved to help alleviate the suffering of others. Compassion vibrates at 800 Hz and is a necessary component to complete the journey of ascension. Until we feel compassion for others, we continue the rebirthing process until this aspect of karma is complete.

Creating takes our mind off other problems and raises our vibration in the process. We can find creative inspiration by being in nature, meditating, listening to music, taking a break, journaling, or finding an outlet through a hobby.

Crying can be a healing and spiritual experience. Crying releases stagnant, negative energy and is uplifting for the soul. We've been conditioned to see crying as a weakness, but in other cultures, it is an enlightening experience that helps process difficult emotions. ☺ Tears of joy can be purifying and energetically uplifting.

Crystals and Stones (see Chapter 10) entrain our frequencies to match their naturally high frequencies, much like essential oils' abilities. Some crystals absorb and dissolve negative energy and emotions, while others direct and magnify energy. Like water, we can "program" crystals with positive intentions. Crystals transmit sacred geometric codes that raise our vibration when we put them near chakras on our body. Crystals and stones help cleanse, unblock, heal, energize, and balance us on all levels.

DNA ☒ (see Chapter 16) activation automatically increases the frequency of the body since each strand of DNA represents increasing frequencies of light and increasing vibrational levels of the chakras. DNA frequencies can be activated and increased through meditation, light codes, kundalini, voice vibrations, and other energy modalities as described in this book.

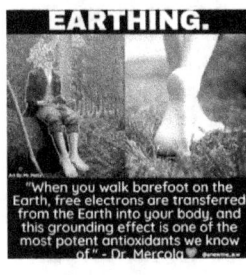

Earthing/Grounding comes from the idea that in modern life we no longer have physical contact with Earth and are losing its health and antioxidant benefits. Walking barefoot calms our "monkey mind" by absorbing the Earth's free electrons, much like a battery needs to be grounded during charging. Grounding works by charging the Earth Star Chakra, which sits twelve inches below our feet. The Earth's frequency vibrates at 7.8 Hz, the same as alpha brainwaves, so when we ground ourselves by walking barefoot, we align our frequency to that of deep relaxation.

We must ground before we can ascend.

Grounding Guidelines

🦶 *Nature* connects us to Earth's electrons and being in contact or walking with bare feet on grass, sand, or earth intensifies the effect. If we can't get outside, we can visualize being outdoors.

🦶 *Root Vegetables* integrated into the diet such as carrots, beets, ginger, and turnips keep us grounded and present.

🦶 *Crystals* hold stable frequencies that don't fluctuate, helping to ground and balance our overall frequencies. Smoky quartz, obsidian, hematite, and black tourmaline are Earth Star and Root Chakra grounding crystals.

🦶 *Essential Oils* carry stable frequencies, just as crystals do. Some grounding oils are sandalwood, cedarwood, and vetiver.

Exercise and Movement are one of the fastest ways to raise our vibration, mood, and overall mental and physical well-being. Mindful movement and dance count as exercise and help break through emotional blocks.

Faking It creates higher vibrational frequencies when we intentionally match our reaction to the emotion we want to feel. For example, if we're feeling angry or hurt, we can laugh out loud 😆 , and say that this is our new reaction when someone hurts our feelings. When we truly feel and believe the emotion first, it forges new brain pathways that sync our reactions into our intended feelings.

Fasting (food detox) cleanses impurities from our system and soul and helps us tap into higher powers and higher vibrations. Fasting gives us a break from our usual routine to take us from unconscious "auto-pilot" to conscious "now" living. It gives us a chance to appreciate and love our bodies more and gives us time to reflect and give gratitude for all that is. Fasting removes the sludge that holds us down and keeps us from vibrating at full frequency. Instead of using all our energy for digestion, fasting gives an opportunity for our body to disengage from the senses to find a connection to within.

- Intermittent fasting restricts eating usually for 16 hours with an eight-hour window of eating.
- The 5:2 Diet is a fasting practice with two non-consecutive days with a calorie restriction of 500 for women and 600 for men; the remainder days have normal calorie intake.
- With Intentional Fasting, eating is restricted after sunset until sunrise.

The "Master Cleanse," also known as the "Lemonade Diet," is an easy-to-adhere-to and tasty detoxifying liquid cleanse. It can be used up to two weeks, drinking up to six glasses throughout the day.

Stanley Burroughs' Master Cleanse
2 cups fresh squeezed lemon or lime juice
1½ - 2 cups 100% maple syrup (do not substitute)
1½ teaspoons cayenne pepper
1 gallon spring water

<small>Makes 16 servings
Recipe courtesy of Elson M. Haas, M.D., author of *Staying Healthy with the Seasons*.</small>

Feng Shui /fung schway/ is the Chinese art of the proper placement of objects and colors in the environment. Feng shui uses the geometric vibrations and energies of nature to bring balance and harmony into the home.

"Forgive and Forget" is necessary for releasing old, toxic energies within our bodies that cause disease. Forgiving doesn't mean we agree with someone else's actions, but we can forgive and move on without allowing them back into our lives. Forgiveness is vital for ascension into 5D.

Giving Off High Frequency Vibes to everyone we meet and in our daily interactions raises our vibrations through the magnetism of the Law of Attraction. Giving off high frequency vibes means being friendly and acting with passion, encouragement, and enthusiasm. Having high vibes is seeing the beauty and good in situations and people, being optimistic when things seem down, being a listener, being trusting and forgiving, being open to new ideas, and showing kindness.

T. S. Martin

The Universe does this thing where it aligns you with people, things, and situations that match the energy you put out. The more you improve yourself and raise your vibration, the more things will improve and be beneficial to your well-being and happiness.

When our vibes are high, it shows; it's obvious to others that we're enjoying life and going with the flow. We smile, do things that bring us joy, and act from a place of love. When we give off high vibes, laughing comes easy and we appreciate life's ordinary moments. High vibers have compassion for others' pain and do nice things for people just because. We say hi to strangers, compliment others, give without expectation, and tell family and friends we love them. Making others feel good makes us feel good and raises vibrations all around.

Gratitude is being and feeling thankful for the abundance and prosperity that has or will inevitably flow our way. Gratitude, gratefulness, love, appreciation, and praise are emotions with high vibrational output close to 500 Hz. Gratitude is a force that moves us forward during our down times.

- If we thank our past, it will integrate.
- If we thank our shadow, it will vanish.
- If we thank our symptoms, they will heal.
- If we thank our mind, it will relax.
- If we thank our heart, it will open.

≥ If we thank our life, it will transform.
≥ If we thank ourselves, we will see the light of a new beginning.

~ GRATITUDE ~

Life is one big, continuous circle of giving and receiving energy. Be thankful for who and what's in your life. Instead of complaining about what you don't have, if you focus on gratitude, you'll start to attract prosperity and abundance.

Gratitude & Manifestation Journals help raise our vibration by pairing intentions with goal making, putting us in a state of expectancy, which vibrates near 310 Hz. Journaling helps raise awareness, motivation, and reduces anxiety. Some journaling techniques include:

✒ *Being specific in our goals and desires; writing them in the present tense with gratitude.*
✒ *Describing what an ideal day would be like using details of all our senses.*
✒ *Pasting magazine picture cut-outs to focus our attention on our desires.*
✒ *Writing down five new things per day that we are grateful for.*
✒ *Writing the story that we would like to be remembered by.*
✒ *Imagining and describing our ideal character traits.*
✒ *Making it personal and judgment-free.*
✒ *Making fun doodle drawings.*

Habits have been said to take twenty-one days to form or drop. That may be true, however, with 100% intention, we can change a habit immediately. It just takes a mindset that it will be done—what's known as "cold turkey." To create a new habit, attach it to something we already do every day, like brushing our teeth. To get rid of a bad habit, replace it with a better habit. Attach the better habit to a great habit to help the new habit stick around.

Hope is not an elusive quality, but the belief and expectation that our desires *will* manifest with certainty. Hope vibrates at the same high frequency as expectation at 310 Hz, which is a high-vibrating emotion and not a wishy-washy feeling hovering between want and have.

Imagination is the creative process of thinking about what something looks like that we've never seen before. Using all the senses helps fully develop images in our mind and is crucial for creating and manifesting. To expand the imagination, keep our minds open and curious, try new things, read more books, hang out with creative people, and meditate.

Intuition is a higher vibrating inner guidance system. When we let intuition guide our actions, life becomes easier. Listening to the moments when our inner self feels or knows something is off and to those moments when our heart knows it's true, is one way to increase our intuitive abilities. Trusting our heart and gut feelings is

MIND BLOWN

an essential step in developing intuition because feelings always tell the truth.

Karma is the Universal Law of Cause and Effect. It's considered to be the divine law that creates the perfect justice for our actions. Other names for karma include "what goes around comes around," "whatever we give out, we get back," "action and reaction are equal and opposite," and "we reap what we sow." Although karmic energy is about settlement for current or past deeds, it's not a retributive force; it's just a lesson to be learned. When we do the best we can every day, we create good karma for ourselves. When we're unkind, we create bad karma. Accumulated karma from past lifetimes is a part of life, lessons our soul must learn through us, and the purpose of soul rebirths. Clearing karma is necessary to activate energy of the higher chakras and to ascend into 5D.

Laughter (also see Smiling) 😊 clears and shakes off negative energy and increases tolerance to pain. We've all heard the expression "laughter is the best medicine," well, in this case it's true. There are even laughter yoga classes! The well-known author Norman Cousins cured himself of an "incurable" disease by consciously forcing himself to laugh every day. There's something to be said for Meme Therapy and watching cat and kid videos to spark the pure energy of laughter.

Light Codes from the sun's rays raise [pun intended] our vibrational frequency by activating dormant DNA strands.

Love vibrates at 500 Hz and is the frequency needed to manifest our heart's desires. If we *feel* love and passion in our heart about what we're doing, then the message is clear—we should keep doing this! Love opens the Heart Chakra and is a necessary component in ascension. Love and its companion, compassion, will propel us to higher vibrations and into the Fifth Dimension.

Malas are 108-beaded necklaces used for chanting and for counting mantras during meditation. Malas absorb and emit energy depending on the frequency of their sacred geometry composition.

Mandalas are symbols and shapes within a circle that activate consciousness with its sacred geometry concepts. Mandalas reveal aspects of our soul when used with meditation and raise our vibration by creating feelings of peace and calmness.

Manifestation (see Chapter 7) is the conscious effort of turning thoughts into things and desires into being. Manifestation steps include a combination of belief, desire, intention, focus, visualization, emotional feeling, and action. To manifest our heart's desires, we have to remove stagnant energy and vibrate close to 500 Hz, the frequency of love.

Mantras are sounds that raise consciousness. Mantras are sacred syllables, words, or phrases that are vocalized during meditation that release stuck energy and increase vibrations. Mantras are often used with mala necklaces, repeating a mantra with each bead.

Massage helps break up blockages and trauma stored in our muscle's fascia allowing for better energy flow.

Meditation (see Chapter 15) quiets the mind, allows time for reflection, and is a place "to find ourselves." The mind-clearing techniques of meditation help raise our vibration and clear the path for ascension.

Mindfulness is being consciously aware of what we do, say, and think at that instant. Mindfulness raises vibrations by connecting ourselves with present moment-to-moment awareness, and "being in the Now." Paying attention to our thoughts, feelings, and negative emotions requires being mindful to what is happening around us. The key is to notice and catch ourselves when our thinking goes downhill so we can immediately shift it to a more positive direction.

Mindset is how we view the world. A growth mindset is being able to stretch ourselves and stick it out even when things aren't going well. Changing our mindset is like creating a new habit. It requires the mindfulness to know when our thoughts or actions aren't beneficial so we can replace them with better thoughts. We must create a mindset of what we want and who we want to be before we can manifest it.

Music (see Sound Therapy, Chapter 12) is an emotional outlet that raises our frequency, especially when the music is happy and upbeat. Music that we particularly enjoy helps induce the alpha brain state of relaxation and releases the happy hormone, dopamine.

"Music gives a soul to the universe, wings to the mind, flight to the imagination, and life to everything." — PLATO

Nature is a natural healing energy and vibration raiser. Being in nature grounds our Earth Star and Root Chakras, helping to balance our sense of security, energy, and emotions.

Play takes us back to having the curiosity of kids when we were full of wonder, adventure, and had imaginations as big as the Universe. The fun of playing "pretend," belly laughing, or making mud pies is a natural vibration raiser. When we engage in life in a less serious, more curious, and playful manner, it keeps our vibrations high and helps us experience life to its fullest. Having youthful fun helps us find the carefree spirit of our inner child and may spark a new-found hobby or interest.

Positive Thinking is a natural vibration raiser and shifts the aging process. Those with positive thinking and positive mindsets tend to live an extra ten years than those with pessimistic tendencies.

Prayer is a form of meditation and method of communicating with our higher self. When we use prayer as healing words and not as needing words, we raise our frequency by 15 Hz.

Qi /chee/ or chi, also called prana, is the intelligent, subtle, vital, life energy that flows through all things in the Universe. Qi flows within the body's prana and meridian channels and is the dynamic and fundamental force underlying all creation. Qi energy comes from three sources: sunlight, air (zero-point energy of the Universe), and the Earth.

Reclaiming Our Power boosts our vibrational levels once we decide that we're the ones in charge of our destiny and that our full power lies within us and not in educational, religious, or governmental constructs. Reclaiming our power from others opens doorways to new possibilities and inspires vision and creativity for future endeavors.

Release Techniques are stretching movements that remove old energy and blockages held in muscle fascia, cells, DNA, and chakras. Techniques to release stagnant energy are given in Chapters 8-14.

Rest, Relaxation, & Reflection are necessary when our bodies are signaling that it's tired. Resting without judgment and without guilt lets positive energies flow. When we don't allow our bodies the time it needs to relax, the body will take the time for itself in the form of sickness, a migraine, or another manifestation of pain. Resting gives the needed time to peek inside ourselves and makes space for creativity to occur.

Rituals intensify and magnify energy back to the Universe, increase life span, and give a sense of purpose.

Rituals are not routines, but more like sacred givers of energy. We can create personal rituals using intention, visualization, mudra gestures, mantras, and incorporating them into special activities or something we do daily, like taking a morning walk, preparing a cup of chamomile tea, or lighting a candle for dinner.

Sacred Geometry is the building blocks and driving force of everything around us including matter, nature, and energy. Sacred geometry is the divine, geometric coding of the Universe that shows itself through Fibonacci spirals (growth patterns of nature) and cymatics (visual pictures of sound). Each shape has a vibrational frequency that has a healing effect on us. Working with these patterns connect us to our inner Source, release tensions, and increase vibrations to bring transformation to our body, mind, and soul.

Self-Expression and Speaking Our Truth raise our vibe. Not holding things in allows energy to flow. When we are clear with our conversations with others, don't swallow our words, and speak truthfully and diplomatically when we have a grievance, it keeps the Throat Chakra open and vibrations high.

Self-Love is not a narcissistic love, it's a necessary component for healing, clearing blocked chakras, and achieving ascension. Self-love is allowing ourselves to heal from past trauma, past pain, and finally realizing our value by just being our true selves. When we make peace with who we are, even undesirable aspects of ourselves, we open the Heart Chakra, raise our vibration, and make room for things we desire.

Service to Others is important in freeing ourselves from our karma and in raising vibrations. When service to others is completed with a pure heart, it raises vibrations and makes ascension to 5D easier. Jobs on 5D Earth will have the underlying premise of selfless service to others.

Shadow Work raises our vibration by uncovering the parts of ourselves that we repress and hide from others and allows our authenticity to shine through.

Silence clears excess energy and puts us in a high vibrational state of expectation and possibility. When we settle into the quiet space of silence, creativity and healing flourish.

Simplify by clearing out the old and making space for the new. Space is the place where energy lies and manifestations occur.

Sleep rejuvenates the mind, body, and soul. The soul departs from the body during sleep via the silver cord to roam the Multiverse and free itself from the constraints of the physical body's dense energies.

Smiling can train our brain into believing that we're happy when we turn our frown upside down. The intent here is not to suggest that we have to smile or be happy all the time, but it works in times of need. Much like Botox® works, smiling relieves muscles from their ability to frown, making those who smile and those who use the product feel happier. However, Botox® injection sites tend to be a little too close to the Third-Eye Chakra for a neurotoxin hangout.

Instead of Botox®, try holding a fake smile for twenty seconds for seven days. This creates new neural networks in the brain. After 21 days, fake smiling becomes a new neurological habit operating on autopilot as a genuine smile! If we desire, we can turn smiling into a vibration-raising *ritual*.

Sound Therapy (see Chapter 12) shifts the low vibrating energies from an emotion such as grief and upgrades its frequency to a more harmonious emotional state such as acceptance. Sound therapy can transform emotions that turn guilt into acceptance and despair into hope. Sound frequencies keep our bodies in "sound resonance" by removing energy blockages in chakras and DNA that prevent us from vibrating at full speed.

Stones & Crystals (see Chapter 10) clear, absorb, and magnify energy. Stones and crystals clear energies around auras, absorb negative energies of our bodies and a room, and magnify their high vibrations to entrain with our own. Stones are often held in clothing pockets so that their vibrations can easily enter the body. Always consider acquiring ethically sourced stones or taking on our own rock-hunting adventure before buying.

Subtle Energy is the all-encompassing term for life force energy, the energy of all things, the energy of the Universe, divine energy, cosmic energy, vital energy, chi, qi, kundalini, and prana. Subtle energy enters through the Crown Chakra at the top of the head and flows to the rest of the chakras and all parts of the body through energy channels called nadis and meridians.

Meridian channels are our body's energy grid that connects to Earth's energy grid of ley lines. This connection of One gives Earth the ability to heal us through the grounding of the Root Chakra, and gives us the ability to heal Earth through ley lines and through the high-energy thoughts of the collective conscious.

Subtle energy constitutes the light of the aura and therefore, the soul. The subtle energy of the soul continues to exist even after the physical body dies and reincarnates to complete karmic obligations. Although subtle energy is faster than the speed of light, it can be measured in units called hertz (Hz) or megahertz (MHz) and can be accessed through conscious awareness. Western allopathic medicine is the only healing system that does not recognize subtle energy as a role in maintaining health.

Sunlight and rays from light codes raise frequency by bringing more light into the body to activate DNA.

Tithing is a form of giving. A tithe means tenth and the purpose is to give ten percent of our salary or selves for charitable purposes. Tithing's act of giving sparks energetic manifestation in the form of more abundance. The Law of Attraction says whatever we put out will be returned to us *ten*fold; what we give, we get back multiplied.

Vision Boards are a collage of images representing our dreams, desires, and aspirations. They are powerful reminders that help attract our desires. Cut-out magazine pictures on a posterboard, in a spiral notebook, or internet images for a desktop collage screen saver work great as vision boards. Adding personal affirmations is another great technique towards making vision boards our own and bringing our goals to fruition.

Visualization (see Chapter 14) is the process of creating powerful pictures in the mind—it's imagination with a purpose and thoughts with pictures. It's the creative force that allows us to "see" what we desire in our mind. Visualization inspires the mind to find a way to make our pictures a reality. Anything that's been created was once a picture in the mind and we can create whatever we desire by picturing it in the mind first.

Water (see Chapter 13) raises vibrations through the power of affirmations, intent, thoughts, words, prayer, and music.

Wisdom is the height of ascension and the cumulative effect of raising energy through the chakras. The Third Eye Chakra symbolizes wisdom and is a divine trait on the Tree of Life.

Yoga can be a gateway to understanding ourselves better, when used with intent. The mindful stretching of yoga activates chakras along the spine helping to increase energy and well-being.

Zen Living incorporates living simply and being in the moment into daily life by using rituals that bring meditative and restorative peace of mind.

Although this list is in no way meant to be exhaustive, it does give various ways to up our energy. The next section shows how thoughts turn into things that we either desire or don't, through the influence of thinking, beliefs, and emotions.

PART II

From Thought to Thing

"All that we are is the result of what we have thought."
— BUDDHA

Thoughts change physical matter.
Reality is created from our thoughts.
What we think, we experience.

Our thoughts are the beginning of everything we create. All possibilities of creation and reality exist from what we think. If thoughts have the power to create physical reality, then thoughts must have the power to shape our internal reality as well.

If thoughts affect the outcome of things and "what you think you become," then ideally, we should all be living perfect lives and have lots of money without a care in the world. For most of us, this doesn't seem to be the case. Somehow our thoughts have become stuck in nojoland, and we've created exactly what we didn't ask for.

Quantum physics tells us that just like a proton's behavior changes when it's being observed, we too can change our behavior when we observe ourselves. By looking within and observing what we're thinking, we can change and create our reality.

Like a sculptor, we can mold the quality of our thinking by consciously shaping the direction of our thoughts, words, and actions to match what we desire. Consciously shaping our thoughts requires nonstop monitoring, but this is the road to consciousness and being able to create the life of our dreams.

CHAPTER 4

What You Think Is What You Get

"What we believe ourselves to think and be, we are."
— BUDDHA

Like everything else in the Universe, thoughts are made of intelligent vibrational energy that make matter. Everything in our physical world was first a thought come to life. Thought gives birth to all things. In every moment of every day, our thoughts create things. Whether good or bad, consciously or unconsciously, we have created and manifested every*thing* we have in our lives. Our thoughts have created the person we are today—our life is a manifestation of our thoughts. Everything we have previously thought, said, or accomplished has created the experiences of our present life. If past thinking creates our present life experiences, then we can create a new and improved present life experience by improving our thoughts. So, if the person and life we have created is not what we desire, then we can create anew by consciously thinking better thoughts.

Nothing in our life can occur without our invitation through thought.

Thoughts mirror beliefs and take form through hopes, wishes, dreams, and fears. According to the Law of Attraction, thoughts are like magnets that bring the good or the bad to us. When our thoughts emit positive pure energy, we magnetize good health and fortune. When our thoughts are negative and lackluster, we attract bad health and misfortune.

<u>We have three choices when it comes to choosing our thoughts:</u>
1. We can unconsciously allow our thoughts to control our reality.
2. We can allow our thoughts to follow the crowd of the collective *un*conscious.
3. We can consciously choose our thoughts and create our reality.

Although thinking is easy, consciously changing the way we think is not something we do naturally. It takes mindful effort and practice, just like building any other skill. Instead of letting our thoughts come and go as they please, now our task is to be aware of them and change the ones that don't benefit us. How do we know which thoughts don't benefit us? Simply, if our life is not what we want, if we have more negative than positive emotions, or if we have sickness or a disease, then our thoughts have not benefitted us well. Places in the body where we *feel* is a sign that we are holding onto negative thoughts. Negative thoughts and emotions manifest in our body as pain and in places where we ache. Interestingly, when negative thoughts turn into physical disease, someone will literally ask, "What's the *matter*?" because thoughts make matter.

Negative Talk and Words are an extension of thoughts and carry positive or negative energy. Negative words are dull, dense, and have low-vibrating energy. Positive words and thoughts have light and high-vibrating energy. Even speech that *sounds* negative has detrimental effects on our energy and in our manifesting intentions.

If we could see and hear ourselves during a conversation, what would our words say about who we are? Do we use empowering language or do our words have a defeated tone? Do we have a friendly voice, or do we overreact with anger and frustration? Are we positive or complaining? Do we talk about what we don't like rather than what we do want or like? Are we confident or do we sound doubtful? Do we curse a lot? When we begin to notice our negative language, we can consciously change these words to more positive and empowering language and thoughts.

We often use unconsciously uttered phrases whose energy decreases our vibration. Although they seem harmless, we should try to eliminate them because the subconscious can't tell the difference between whether a thought is real or imagined, true or false, or intended as a joke; the mind still believes it as real and true.

- ☹ *That burns me up.*
- ☹ *Give me a break. You crack me up.*
- ☹ *I'm working feverishly. I worked until I was blue in the face.*
- ☹ *I got tripped up. That's so nerve-racking. I'm a mess. I choked.*
- ☹ *What a pain in the neck. My head is splitting. That hurts my heart.*
- ☹ *You're killing me. I'm dying to see you. That would be the death of me. Over my dead body. I would die if that happened.*
- ☹ *I feel so bad for you. I feel horrible that happened to you.*
- ☹ *I'm sick and tired of this.*

These phrases are mostly used for defusing a situation or for giving empathy, but the underlying message is literally asking the Universe to make us sick. Whenever we catch ourselves thinking a negative thought or saying something we didn't intend, we can immediately substitute it with a new thought that is opposite to the negative statement we just said. We can intentionally switch our words out for something that sounds better by simply stating, "I take it back!" "Cross that off," or whatever personally works to negate and upgrade the energy of the undesirable phrase and turn it into something better.

Say This Not That

That 🚫	This ✅
Sorry I'm late.	Thanks for waiting!
Sorry, I forgot.	Thanks for reminding me.
I hate this.	It's not my favorite.
I suck at this.	I'm learning.
It's such a drag.	It's an opportunity for growth.
I hate the way I look.	My looks give me character like no other.
I'm stressed out.	I'm under divine pressure.
I'm so stupid.	Every day I gain new knowledge.

To get past negative events, we must actively choose not to engage in emotional drama. If we happen to get involved, before reacting, we can first choose to mentally observe what's happening. Mental observation helps us notice our part in instigating emotional drama and helps us create and choose a more ideal response. Consciously choosing a better reaction ahead of time keeps us from saying things we'll later regret.

How to Stop ✋ Negative Thoughts
- Disengage from negative thinking.
- Choose an alternative positive thought.

- Use daily reflection, breathwork, and meditation.
- Talk back to our thoughts to take away their power.
- Visualize the image of the thought shrinking until it disappears.
- Take back bad thoughts and words by declaring, "I take that back!"
- Change the negative thought to a better thought using positive affirmations.

Changing negative-sounding phrases to more positive ones gets us one step closer to manifesting and creating the life of our desires and becoming the best version of ourselves. Consciously choosing to upgrade the vibration of our thoughts requires being mindful and being aware of the present moment. By choosing thoughts that make us *feel* good, we can think and feel our way into vibrational alignment.

> The secret to life is that you have ALL the power. If you can change your mind, you can change your life. You don't need any amount of money, education, or the right connections. You just need to be in control of your thoughts and your mind. Program your mind to believe in yourself and know that you have what it takes to achieve greatness and watch greatness manifest in your life. THE KEY to success is overcoming your limiting beliefs and aligning yourself with the energy you want in life.

CHAPTER 5

Blasphemous Beliefs

"Everything changes when you start to emit your own frequency rather than absorbing the frequencies around you, when you start imprinting your intent on the universe rather than receiving an imprint from existence." — BARBARA MARCINIAK, Author

Beliefs come from long-term thinking that something is either right or wrong and are often confused as truth. Beliefs are not truths and are merely opinions instilled upon us, thus, how we were raised and how we view ourselves are often based on the beliefs of others. Many beliefs that we have "downloaded" as truths come from our family, friends, and social media. To be happy and authentic, we must follow the beliefs of our heart and not what others believe is true.

Follow the heart instead of the crowd.

Beliefs of lack and limitation are stored in the subconscious whether they're true or not and this is where we gain access to change them. When false and limiting beliefs are accepted by our subconscious as true, this is how we perceive ourselves to be. False beliefs make us feel unworthy, incapable, and keep us from feeling our best and experiencing our full creative potential because they focus on lack, on not having, and on not being enough.

Family may have subconsciously given us the belief that having money is bad. A teacher who inferred that we weren't smart, kids who taunted us at school, or parents that humiliated us in public could have contributed to false beliefs of low self-esteem. When someone does or says something that hurts, we repress the feelings until they turn into the low-vibrating emotions of shame and blame. Negative beliefs that we have adopted as our own keep us from achieving our desires, so the goal is to identify, reprogram, and let go of those that don't serve us.

Identifying the root belief is necessary to let go and move on. Sometimes finding the root cause of false beliefs can be difficult, but we can start by paying attention to the excuses we replay in our mind and to those we tell others. When we hear ourselves use words such as *if, when, maybe, might, must, should, could, would, can't, always, never, and have to,* it's an indication that a false belief has control of our thoughts. Feelings like having a pit in our stomach, having a bad taste in our mouth, uneasiness, and the "freeze" response are signs that we're operating from a limited belief system. Past events that we replay over and over in our minds and haven't been able to get over often reveal hidden beliefs. A belief becomes a conviction when we allow our ego to run the show.

The following statements are indicative of a belief system that needs upgrading:

Nobody likes me.
I'm not smart enough.
I'm not good at anything.
I could never do something like that.
I'll be happy when I find the right job.
I don't have a creative bone in my body.
I'd like to help you, but I can't because of my illness.
My lack of education keeps me from making a lot of money.
I'm sure I'd be more successful if I were given opportunities like you.
I'd have more talent, but my parents couldn't afford to pay for my lessons.
I could have been successful, but I'm from the wrong side of the tracks.
I have to keep this job because there's nothing else available.
My messed-up childhood is why I can't keep a relationship.

I'd like to date someday, but all the good ones are taken.
My past is what keeps me from being happy.
I'm afraid to start a new business.
Money is the root of all evil.
I got dealt a bad deck.
I'll never find love.

Reprogramming limiting beliefs can be accomplished by replacing fear-based beliefs with love-based beliefs using *I am* affirmation statements. Occasionally the subconscious will try to sabotage our new belief system by bringing up doubt and unwanted emotions. If this happens, consciously and deliberately redirect our thoughts back to our "new me." Although we all have our own limiting belief system, these underlying beliefs often plague our thinking. Positive, love-based beliefs are written in italics as affirmations and are intended to reprogram any fear-based "poor me" limited thinking patterns that may resurface. Creating a new inner dialogue helps replace old beliefs with a new set of complementary self-beliefs.

"Poor Me" Fear-Based Beliefs	"New Me" Love-Based Beliefs
Victim Mentality	I create my life and am accountable for all my actions.
Scarcity Mindset	I have a millionaire mindset.
Says Yes to Everything	I create healthy boundaries for myself.
Survival/Stress Mode	I can create and achieve anything I desire.
Follows the Crowd	I trust my intuition and the knowledge it brings.
Happens by Chance/Fate	I have complete control of my choices and my destiny.
Logical, Rational Mind	I am grateful my mind is open to new beliefs about myself.
Coincidence	Synchronicities assure me that I'm on the right path.
Driven by Ego	I trust that my actions are in mine and everyone's higher good.
Living in the Emotional Past	I release all negative associations with people who may have hurt and hindered me in the past.
Making a Living	I am the architect of my life. I build its foundation and choose its contents.
Doubt	I believe in myself and all that I am capable of.
Complainer	I am grateful for the big, the small, the good, the bad, the All.
Competition	My heart is full of love and cooperation knowing that we are all One.
I'm always sick.	My body is healthy, and my mind is tranquil.
I don't have enough money.	Money flows to me from known and unknown sources.
Money is the root of all evil.	I release all negative associations with money.
I'll believe it when I see it.	I believe it, then I receive it.
I'm too fat/short/ugly.	I'm perfectly imperfect.
Life is nothing but problems	I am grateful for the lessons life brings.
Everything makes me mad.	I am full of love, peace, and acceptance.
I don't have enough.	I have everything I need.

My life sucks.	I consistently take advantage of opportunities that come my way.
It's too good to be true.	I have complete certainty in my ability to attract good fortune and know that anything is possible.

Combining affirmations with breathwork and visualizations, in which we act the way we wish to be, strengthens the conversion between old and new beliefs in the subconscious. Visualizing having already accomplished our goals combined with deep breathing and feeling high-vibrating emotions like excitement, optimism, and empowerment reprogram the subconscious to believe it as true. Looking in a mirror while repeating affirmations is also beneficial in integrating new beliefs.

Letting go of limiting beliefs can be done once we understand why we've been holding on to them for so long. During meditation or time alone, we can ask ourselves why we have perpetuated our limiting beliefs by questions such as: *What am I learning from this belief? How is this belief serving me? How is this belief keeping me safe? Why do I believe that I can't get what I want? Why would I want to stay the way I am? Why am I not able to let go of this limiting belief that's holding me back?* Answers will come when we're ready to give up our stories of being the victim, let go of our psychological baggage, and release the emotions of shame and blame we associate with our stories.

Once we understand why we've been holding on, then we can consciously reprogram old beliefs to new beliefs with affirmations, desire, intent, imagination, visualization, meditation, and sheer willpower.

"No matter how hard the past, one can always begin again today." — BUDDHA

<u>Clearing Limiting Beliefs Meditation</u>
1. *Sit comfortably with our arms and legs uncrossed; close our eyes and take three deep, relaxing breaths.*
2. *Place attention on the Root Chakra near the pelvic area. This is our creation space for change.*
3. *Place one hand 8-12 inches from our body and move in counterclockwise rotations. These rotations release birth energy from the Root Chakra.*
4. *Repeat the following to release negative and false beliefs:*

- I release that I am a bother, an interruption, or that others' needs are more important than mine.
- I release looking outside myself for validation or checking to see if I am still loved.
- I release DNA patterns that keep me stuck in my family's dysfunction.
- I release feelings of being stuck and feeling unable to move forward.

- I release all the times I have felt powerless and feeling that nobody was there for me.
- I release feelings of not being touched enough, of not being the right sex, or of not being wanted at all.
- I release feelings of anger, frustration, resentment, and of being exhausted from living in this energy struggle.
- I let it all go once and for all.

5. *Take a deep breath, exhale, and Let It Go while imagining pulling all the negative energy out of the chakras down the spine and sending it into the Earth.*
6. *Now, imagine a color filling our new inner empty space.*
7. *Now rotate our hand in a clockwise direction to open and activate our chakra energy while repeating:*

- I am wanted. I came at the right time. I deserve to have my needs met. My parents are grateful I am alive. I am a joy to others. I am loved and wanted. My needs are important. I am birthing new experiences that bring me joy. I easily receive that which brings me pleasure. I rejoice in my sexuality. I am a gift to the world.
- I am supported. I now choose to be born in the energy of love and joy. I am moving forward with ease. What I desire and need show up for me effortlessly. Everything supports me. I stand in my truth. I take pleasure in my life. I am creating my life and I like my results.

- I am creating success. I am creating wealth. I am creating a healthy body. I am creating joy-filled relationships. I take pleasure in my success. I pleasure in my wealth. I pleasure in my healthy body. I pleasure in sharing my affluence with others. It is my birthright to thrive.

Every thought can be an opportunity for growth when we're able to shape its energy and change what we think is a problem into a blessing. When we step out of old beliefs to create new beliefs based on what we desire, not by default, we consciously change the direction and outcome of our lives.

CHAPTER 6

The Emotions of Manifestation

"Love is what we are born with. Fear is what we have learned here. The spiritual journey is the unlearning of fear and the acceptance of love back into our hearts."
— MARIANNE WILLIAMSON

Most of our lives, we have been taught that showing and expressing our feelings is "acting like a sissy" and a sign of weakness. The truth is, feelings give validity to our intuition and immediate feedback to what we're really thinking. In this sense, feelings are never wrong because they speak our truth. If we want to know what's true and right for us, all we have to do is see how we feel about it. Feelings are energy, and energy doesn't lie.

Emotions are energy that carry different frequencies for each emotion. Love and fear are opposite sides of a coin, and these highly charged emotions make manifesting easy because strong emotions attract. If we feel strongly about it, we will attract it, whether good or bad.

The frequency of fear is a slow and low-vibrating energy that activates very few DNA antennae. It causes harm and manifests sickness, unhappiness, and misfortune. The frequency of love is a high-vibrating and fast energy that activates many more DNA antennae and manifests health, wealth, and happiness.

Like a navigation app, feelings are our inner guidance system that let us know what's right or wrong for us. If our feelings cause emotions like joy, happiness, and love, then we know that we're on the right path. Likewise, if we're feeling unsure, hesitant, and confused, then we know that our path is off, simply by feeling uncertain instead of confident.

There is no *wrong* way to feel about what's going on inside, negative feelings are merely a detour on the road to desires but will still get us to our destination. That's why we should trust our feelings and let them guide us. If it *feels* right to us, then we should trust that it is, as feelings are the wisdom of our intuition and heart speaking to us.

Emotions and Manifestations of Fear
"Thinking will not overcome fear, but action will."
— W. CLEMENT STONE

Negative emotions, like fear, have strong feelings attached to them and cause us to act in the fight, flight, freeze, or fawn mode. These emotions usually arise without warning because they are triggered by subconscious memories of the original event. When something triggers a fearful memory, vibrations from the initial encoding are activated, causing the same negative reaction to resurface as experienced by the original trauma.

Fear plagues us because of the high emotional attachment to it. Feelings of fear and shame are our go-to mode that remove us from our ability to create. Fear manifests as the insecure feelings of not being good enough, unworthiness, and of being undeserving.

Since we can choose to feel afraid or choose to feel love in our hearts, they're really intentions, and intentions are malleable. What we choose is what we will experience. When we choose fear, it expresses itself as hate, anger, control, worry, tension, doubt, nervousness, anxiety, competition, impatience, irritation, frustration, yelling, criticism, procrastination, resentment, aggression, distrust, judgment, rigidity, separation, envy, jealousy, greed, comparison, dissatisfaction, pessimism, bitterness, and a lack of integrity. When we engage in gossip and drama, act fake, worry about the future, avoid activities, have hidden motives, and take advantage of other people to get ahead, these are forms of fear that dramatically lower our vibrational frequency.

Physical effects of fear show as a weakened immune system, cardiovascular damage, ulcers, acid reflux, fatigue, depression, accelerated aging, and extra cortisol release, causing weight gain in the face and belly.

Fear of death may be the largest fear of all, mostly because many of us were raised to believe in hell ever after if we didn't live a life of salvation. Religion uses the ultimate scare tactics to keep us in acquiescence, but that era is over; in the Fifth Dimension, religion is replaced by "spirituology," which is fueled by love, not fear.

Death is not to be feared because it isn't real. All humans are matter, matter is energy, and energy cannot be destroyed. When we die, the physical body of this lifetime is put to rest, but the energy of our soul lives on. Souls are made from the light energy of the Universe—the energy that has always been and will always be, the Source. This energy surrounds the body and ascends to the Afterlife awaiting its next incarnation, and therefore, never dies. The soul energy of our loved ones is waiting to meet with us again.

Finding the root cause of fears, like finding the root cause of limiting beliefs, can be accomplished by simply asking ourselves, *"What am I afraid of? What is my fear telling me that I need? Do I have a fear of attachment because I need love? Do I have a fear of success because I need to prove myself? How is hanging onto this fear benefitting my life? Where and why do I need this fear in my life now? Can I trace this fear back to a painful memory?"* When fears show up, we should try and become consciously aware of what originally triggered the fear. Answers lie in the subconscious mind, cells, DNA, and in the second Sacral Chakra, where our fear was first energetically encoded.

We shouldn't try to bury emotions of fear. Instead, when shadows of fear creep in, our job is to consciously create and cultivate the emotions we desire by visualizing ourselves responding and reacting ahead of time with courage and confidence.

The change in thinking will cause our fears to dissipate, then eventually disappear. We don't have to get rid of every dark shadow to cultivate courage and confidence. When we let in love and light, we let darkness out. We let light and love in by letting go and thinking thoughts opposite of fear.

If we are feeling angry, we can let in more light by consciously creating and thinking opposite thoughts of peace and calm. If we are feeling frustration, we consciously imagine ourselves performing with mastery. If we are feeling worthless, we envision ourselves helping others. When we're sad, we imagine ourselves feeling happy and laughing with others. By being a master of our emotions, we move closer to raising our powers of consciousness and ability to create.

<u>To Release and Let Go of Fear</u>
1. Identify the root cause or triggers associated with our fear,
2. Acknowledge our feelings of fear and where we feel it in our bodies, and
3. Consciously change fearful feelings to opposite feelings using visualization.

Also, visualize ourselves achieving our desired goal for one minute. After that, take one action step to further overcome feelings of fear. By performing the action step, we form positive new neural patterns that reset the fear circuitry. Using affirmations also help support the new circuitry and reinforce new behavior patterns.

When we continually think about or avoid the cause of our fears, they will eventually manifest as disease; but fears go away when we look inside to see what shadows linger. The better we get to know ourselves through alone time and self-reflection, the less we will fear the unknown and the more we will come to know our true potential. When we change our thoughts from fear mode to love mode, insecurity becomes confidence, anger becomes understanding, sickness becomes health, and procrastination becomes action. Love gives us answers and a reason for being.

Emotions and Manifestations of Love
We overcome, advance, and progress when we act out of love and not fear.

Love, in the sense of manifesting or raising consciousness, is not a sentiment or relationship between two people. Love is a way of life with all living things. Love is an emotion that makes us experience feelings such as joy, gratitude, compassion, excitement, wonder, and awe. It's the highest vibrational frequency we can achieve while still being in a physical body. Feeling love in the heart is the *only* way to move forward on our path to knowledge and higher awareness. Love is a vibrational choice, and when we choose the frequency of love in our hearts, it gives us the power to create, manifest, and heal.

When we choose love, then we experience and align with high vibrational emotions such as gratitude, appreciation, openness, positivity, presence, acceptance, kindness, compassion, peace, trust, joy, forgiveness, happiness, encouragement, inspiration, creativity, contentment, harmony, and balance.

One way to intentionally create feel-good emotions and increase our vibrational output is to have a mental or physical list of thoughts, images, events, or things that make us feel good. These could include the birth of a child, a graduation, past successes, work accolades, our honeymoon, or even conjured visualizations that create positive emotions inside. Because the subconscious mind doesn't know the difference between intend and pretend, any emotions that cause the heart to flutter will work.

Whenever we need to change negative feelings into positive emotions, we can replay these images in our mind. *The degree to which we can feel and turn up the emotions of love to their highest, is the degree to which we're able to create and manifest.* To create a life we desire, we must become the master of our mind and the director of our emotions.

MIND BLOWN

We become a master director by cultivating our feelings and emotions before our experience occurs. We live, act, and feel the future as if it's happening *now*. We consciously choose to *feel and act* abundant before the money comes in. We consciously choose to *feel and act* empowered first, before we're successful. We consciously choose to feel and act healthy before we feel healthy. We consciously choose to feel love before we have love. If we desire it, we must first imagine what it feels like having it. This is why it's helpful to have ideas and images of what empowerment, success, health, and love feel like to us—so we can direct our emotions to feel the way we desire.

Self-love is not about narcissism but about respecting and feeling good about ourselves first so that we can share our love with others. It's about having self-esteem, self-worth, self-appreciation, and self-awareness. Without self-love, we manifest ailments doctors can't find a cure for, or medicine simply doesn't work. Self-love affirmations help retrain the subconscious towards having a more loving nature.

- ☺ I love myself in every way.
- ☺ I have a great sense of humor.
- ☺ I'm smart, kind, and generous.
- ☺ I'm witty and fun to be around.
- ☺ People like hanging around me.

The heart center of our body encompasses the Heart Chakra and the "Sacred Heart at the Thymus" area, a secondary Heart Chakra located in the center of the chest. Both encompass our sense of who we are and our intuition. Thus, to develop intuition and understand ourselves and others better, our Heart Chakra should be free and clear of blockages.

To Open the Heart Chakra
- ♥ Visualize happy memories.
- ♥ Think of love and loving thoughts for other people.
- ♥ Listen to 594 Hz music.
- ♥ Have a forgiving nature.
- ♥ Incorporate pink & green stones into our surroundings.
- ♥ Use rose essential oil.
- ♥ Get the heart pumping with coffee, offering a slight buzz of 223 Hz.

Intuition, sympathy, and empathy are precursors of compassion, the uniting energy that helps raise the vibrations of Earth and of the collective conscious.
- ♥ Sympathy gives us the ability to identify *with* others' anguish; it's the first step in developing intuition.
- ♥ Empathy is the ability to *feel* others' sorrows and is a component for developing intuition.
- ♥ Compassion is the uniting energy that brings us closer to the plights of humanity and helps in ascension to 5D.

The Emotional Guidance Scale Chart is an energy scale that correlates to levels of consciousness, dimensional planes, colors of the chakras and the visible light spectrum, and measures the vibrational output of our emotions. Every step up the chart implies increased awareness, understanding, and the ability to create and transform our lives. The higher we are on the chart, the closer we are to realizing our true potential and power.

The frequency of love at 500 Hz is the highest we can ascend on the chart while still being in a physical body, while 1000 Hz is the ultimate frequency encompassing full awareness and ascension, and zero is the frequency of death. Being neutral at 250 Hz is the state of unconditional acceptance—we accept how things come; we accept how things go. As soon as we form a judgment about someone or some thing, we move down the scale from being neutral to being biased and lower our vibration. We can move up the chart by letting go of judgments about ourselves and others, by feeling emotions associated with love, or by consciously creating the next highest vibrating emotion.

"The ability to observe without evaluating is the highest form of intelligence." — KRISHNAMURTI

To create the next highest-vibrating emotion, choose to mentally observe the situation. Through neutral self-observation, we may see our role in causing the situation to happen in the first place, or we may better understand the other person's point of view. Seeing our role in upsetting situations makes it easier to practice forgiveness and choose better emotions.

For instance, if we feel mad, registering at 150 Hz, we can consciously choose to feel an improved emotion, such as annoyed, which registers at 175 Hz and is better than being and feeling mad. Intentionally choosing a better emotion to feel helps us get through difficult situations and helps us ascend to higher vibrating levels and dimensions.

The Emotional Guidance Scale Chart

DIMENSIONAL LEVEL	VIBRATIONAL FREQUENCY	LEVEL OF CONSCIOUSNESS
12th Dimension	1000	Full Consciousness
	900	Freedom Empowerment
	850	Gratitude
	800	Compassion
	780	Appreciation
	700	Enlightenment
	600	Peace
5th Dimension	540	Oneness Joy
	500	**LOVE** Happiness Enthusiasm
	400	Hope Optimism Understanding
	310	Forgiveness Willingness
	250	Neutrality Trust Acceptance
4th Dimension	200	Courage
	175	Annoyed Pride Worry Doubt
	150	Hate Anger Rage
	125	Jealousy Disappointment Wanting
	100	**FEAR** Anxiety
3rd Dimension	75	Grief Regret
	50	Apathy Depression
	30	Guilt Blame
	20	Shame Worthlessness
	0	Death

T. S. Martin

We know we're on the right path when we're able to express our feelings without arguing or shouting; we can apologize when we need to; we know our boundaries and can communicate them clearly; we don't take things personally; we work on our vulnerabilities; we're reliable and we love ourselves as much as anyone else. Being in the neutral zone of not judging, not caring what others think about us, and loving and honoring our imperfections is a path to happiness and health.

With purpose, intent, and focus, we can consciously and deliberately change our thoughts, feelings, and emotions out of the negative and into the positive and become the master of our emotions. By converting the emotional energy of fear to the energy of love, we create and manifest desires, not disease.

CHAPTER 7

Conscious Creation

Manifesting Desires not Disease

"Life isn't about finding yourself. It's about creating yourself." — GEORGE BERNARD SHAW

Image Courtesy of @Snakes.N.Roses

When energies of thoughts, words, feelings, intentions, and beliefs align with our heart, they manifest as inspirational action, the energy of creation. So, manifestation isn't magic; it's an inside job of aligned energies.

To have things we desire, it's essential to vibrate at high frequency. Desires vibrate at 528 Hz, the frequency of love, and correspond to the solfeggio musical note *mi*, meaning miracle. To manifest our heart's desires, we must vibrate at the frequency of love. It's harder to manifest when we're operating below 500 Hz. This is why it's important to get rid of old, stagnant energy before we consciously manifest. The key is to match the frequency of our thoughts to the frequency of our desire.

"There is not enough action in the world to make up for energy that is not moving." — ESTHER HICKS, Author of *Ask and It is Given*

Conscious creation combines all the components of thinking and turns them into reality. Manifestation usually begins with having a need that leads to a desire. With unwavering focus on a desire, we match our intention, emotional energies, and energetic output to the vibrational level of our desire. When we have absolute belief that there are no limitations and accept that we deserve our desires as much as anyone, then we've come closer to consciously creating the life of our dreams.

Components of Conscious Creation

Action is the energetic, inspirational force needed for manifestation to occur; it's the baby step needed for follow-through. It's our part—the doing and effort required for manifesting. Only through action do we achieve ambitions. When we act as if we are what we desire, it will come. What we act as, we become.

I AM
Intention + Action = Manifestation

Affirmations are short, simple, and specific declarations that remind us of our goal and have the ability to transform brain pathways. Affirmations and visualizations work well in manifestation because the mind cannot distinguish between the vibrations of an imagined thought, a spoken word, or an outward action. These money affirmations are borrowed from abundance guru John Assaraf:

I can achieve anything I desire.
I now have an abundant mindset.
I consistently use my money wisely.
Money is everywhere, and I find it with ease.
I release all negative associations with money.
I love the choices making lots of money gives me.
I am now fulfilling my financial destiny to be rich.
I am consistently in the right vibration to earn money.
Money flows to me from known and unknown sources.
I give myself permission to earn as much money as I choose.

I have the confidence to make as much money as I choose.
I now live, feel, and expect an abundance of money.
Once I choose my financial goals, I achieve them.
The more people I help, the more money I earn.
Money is easy for me to earn and attract.
I think and act rich because I am.
I deserve all the money I want.
Making money is fun for me.

Asking is part of the manifesting process. If we don't ask, we'll never receive, so it's a necessary component. Although asking for what we desire suggests a statement of lack, asking with gratitude is acceptable for manifesting. We should be as specific as possible about what we desire, much like writing goals. We only need to ask once, but we can visualize our desires happening as much as possible.

Attention is where our predominant thoughts lie; it's our level of focus. The more laser focused our attention, the better our chances of consciously creating.

> WHAT YOU THINK ABOUT ALL DAY IS WHAT YOU END UP MANIFESTING

Belief is 100% faith, knowing, and trusting that our desired manifestation will come true. Positive belief is necessary to have the energies of the Law of Attraction work in our favor. We have to believe and feel it in our heart and soul that what we've asked for is already ours.

Desires are what we want to manifest, our wishes, wants, goals, needs, and our intentions. It's been a common belief that we should "resist our desires;" however, having and receiving desires is not selfish. It's part of our natural birthright to want to be happy and to achieve our full potential. Being abundant and having our desires met enables us to give and help others. We can't pour from an empty cup. Since the expansive forces of the Universe allow for unlimited creation, it's in our divine nature and the Universe's to constantly create and manifest new desires.

Expectations are how we think things should be and what we think we deserve and should receive. Having total acceptance of the outcome no matter how things turn out is receiving without expectation. *Let go and let be.*

Feelings are a crucial and indispensable component of creating and manifesting. We don't have to be abundant to attract abundance, but we do have to *feel* abundant to manifest it into being. Things that we have manifested in our lives, we have done so by having the same prolonged feelings for them. When we hold on to feelings of hate and fear over time, we unconsciously manifest disease. When we hold on to feelings of love, we manifest desires. Manifesting desires and manifesting disease use the same intensity of feeling and focus that has the power to create. When we consciously feel all the accompanying emotions of achieving our goals, it accentuates the manifestation process.

Focus is a combination of attention and awareness, and the more concentrated and unwavering our focus is on a desire, the better our manifestation outcome. Focusing on one desire at a time aligns thoughts with our ability to create. With consistent focus on what we desire, we can manifest anything.

Gratitude vibrates at a minimum frequency of 500 Hz and is necessary for ascension to higher dimensions. To cultivate gratitude in our hearts, think about the qualities that we love about people we're with, appreciate the beauty around us at that moment, or use gratitude journals to develop skills of appreciation. To manifest, ask for desires with gratitude in our hearts as if the desire has already been granted.

Before consuming food or drinks, try giving "Gratitude Energy Blessings" by being grateful, thankful, and imparting good health into our food.

Even "bad" things can receive gratitude when we reframe our outlook. We are meant to learn from the lessons the Universe sends us, and whether we understand the messages or not, we should always be grateful for the opportunity to learn and grow.

Imagination is meant to take us from the smallest beginning of a thought to the farthest limits and deepest realms of what we think is possible. With imagination, all things are possible.

Einstein said, "Imagination is everything. It's the preview of life's coming attractions." What we think and what we see in our minds is what we're going to experience, meaning, what we imagine, we achieve.

Inspiration is the intuitive, divine guidance component of manifestation that helps us follow through with our actions. Inspiration is an internal power that requires no outside force to motivate us.

Intentions are energy, like thoughts, so the more powerful our intention, the better the chance of vibrationally matching to our desire. Intentions have a twofold purpose: one is the motive behind a desire and two is the amount of energy that goes toward our intended manifestation. Like the type of gas we give to our car, the higher the grade of our intention, the more enhanced our performance. Intentions should be positive, in the now, and specific, without stating what we lack. We can increase our intention and what we want by writing it down and visualizing as if it's already happened. Our goal is to make life completely intentional by consciously and deliberately choosing everything that we manifest.

> *"Intention is desire to make manifest the decisions of the mind."* — ARISTOTLE

When we combine crystal-clear intentions with goal setting, it amplifies our manifesting abilities. To get crystal-clear intentions, begin with creating only one desire at a time and attach feelings of achieving the desire to the intention. In the 3rd Dimension, intentions are mirrored back to us through the Law of Attraction; in the 5th Dimension, intentions manifest instantly.

Intuition is listening to the voice of our heart and letting our feelings guide us in the right direction, as they always do. Intuition tells our thinking mind what the next step is.

Love is a must component to have in our hearts if we wish to manifest. No amount of hate will manifest a heart's desire. Love vibrates at 500 Hz, the necessary frequency to raise our thinking to manifesting levels. Once we learn to love ourselves, then it becomes easier to love All as One.

Receiving our desires is left to higher powers, intuition, or synchronicity; we don't have to figure out how our desires will manifest in the receiving process. We may receive our desires differently than we anticipate, so it's always best to keep an open mind.

Visualizing is seeing the experiences of our desires in our mind. Using all the senses, visualizing future manifestations as already given, and living the experience as Now, bring manifestation to realization. When visualizing, start by thinking of a happy moment—one that fills us with the elevated emotions of love, joy, and happiness. Once we have these feelings inside us, switch our thoughts to what we desire. This is a great way to supercharge our manifestation with positive emotions and feelings to bring them to reality. We can use visualization to assist in the manifestation process when we imagine that our desires have *already* come true, and we are simply living out the details of our desire.

Visualization helps design our day when we decide in advance how we'd like the day to unfold. Imagining scenes in our mind that haven't happened yet is a potent manifestation tool to make thoughts come true. The mind doesn't know the difference between real and imagined; therefore, we can visualize *anything,* and the mind finds a way to make it materialize.

Like affirmations, visualization is often used with meditation to change thoughts, habits, and beliefs to reprogram our mind to manifest our desires.

> **IF ENERGY IS NEITHER CREATED NOR DESTROYED**
>
> Everything you will ever want is already here. It is simply a matter of choosing the thoughts which will put you into harmonious vibration and alignment with what you deserve.

Although there are variations, here is a condensed method for manifesting:

Think It, Speak It, Act It, Have It.

Think It Into Being: We can think our desire into existence. As fast as we are thinking, we are creating. Thinking creates what happens to us, so we can create our reality by thinking about what we desire first.

Through willpower and intention, we have the power to change our thinking: we tell our thoughts, *I am going to think this way to create this*. We manifest our reality by consciously designing our thoughts of how we desire our life to be ahead of time. When we first deliberately decide what we want to think and be, our thoughts will create the experience.

Speak It Into Being: We can speak our desire into existence. Vibrations from our voice send powerful messages that activate the subconscious mind. Mantras, affirmations, and nada yoga stimulate vibrations that modify our cells and DNA; thus, we can change our reality at the quantum level through the vibrations in our voice while speaking.

Act It Into Being: We can act our desire into existence by being and doing. When we act and believe as if our desire has already happened, then our desire will manifest. What we act as, we become. Thinking, visualizing, and imagining are effective tools for acting like what we desire to be because the subconscious cannot distinguish between real or imagined. Using the senses to imagine how our desire looks, feels, sounds, smells, or tastes, encourages the mind to bring it into existence.

It's essential to pair elevated emotions with thoughts and visualizations, as strongly felt emotions are crucial to manifestation. Feeling emotions of love, joy, compassion, and excitement attract the high-vibrating frequency necessary to manifest. When we think, speak, act, and feel as if we have already received our desire in our minds, then it will show in our physical reality. Imagine watching ourselves playing out different scenes of our desire as if it's really happening, and then adding feelings, dialogue, and details to make our visualizations seem more real and come alive.

Sometimes we may wonder, "Why am I not getting what I want? I'm thinking about it all the time!" Although we think about things that we want all the time, we have an unconscious habit of negating our desires by thinking of the *absence* of what we want. For instance, we may think, "I want a new car, *but I don't want the payment,*" or "I need more money because *I can't pay my bills,*" or "I want new clothes, *but I don't have any money,*" or "I wish I didn't *feel so poor.*" Our own contradictory thoughts keep us from getting what we desire. We unconsciously manifest lack by focusing on, believing, and stating that we don't have enough, and that's what we get, not enough. We disaffirm our desires with negative thoughts and statements because they are focused on the *lack of having*, and that's what the Universe delivers.

Telling the Universe *why* we want something negates our desires as well: *"I need more money because my family will go without if I don't have it."* And when we say, "I *want*…," the Universe hears, "I *am wanting*…" Our words literally put us in a state of wanting and not having. This is why "I am" affirmations work and "I want" affirmations do not.

The Merriam-Webster Dictionary definition of "want" describes it as 'a state of lack, a deficiency, to be needy or destitute, and extreme poverty that deprives one of the necessities of life.' The mere act of asking for something is really a statement of lack as well, because it implies that we don't have what we are asking for. To correctly ask for something from the Universe, show appreciation in advance as if we already have it, and use affirmations as a statement for what is so. For example, "Thank you for the knowledge I have to start a new business," "I am so grateful that I am fulfilling my destiny to be rich," "Thank you Universe for supplying me with the tools I desire to access my subconscious," or "I am so grateful for the money I am receiving."

Can We Attract Money through Conscious Creation? Yes, says the Law of Attraction because money is energy.

NEVER FEEL BAD OR HAVE A NEGATIVE ATTITUDE ABOUT SPENDING MONEY. When we complain about having to pay for food, rent, bills, and gas, we send our negative and disempowered energy towards money. This programs our subconscious mind to attract less money. Instead, be happy when spending money, and know we can always make more of it. This will help manifest more money-making opportunities into our lives.

Thoughts of *already having* are thoughts of abundance, which in return, attract more abundance. To attract abundance using the Law of Attraction, visualize what it's like having unlimited money. Mentally see all the ways money could appear in our lives: a windfall, an inheritance, lottery winnings, a higher-paying job, finding a sugar daddy (or mama), or imagine being born wealthy. Remember, the mind doesn't know the difference between intend or pretend, and we're trying to train the brain to attract like energies. Continue imagining what it's like living a life with no money worries and all the things that having money can do for us. Envision paying the monthly bills and mortgage or rent on time, all the time. Imagine the feelings associated with being debt free, paying cash for expenses, and money worries become—poof! gone. Imagine taking family or friends on first-class luxurious trips, the taste of freshly-prepared meals by a gourmet chef, the touch of silky sheets or the smell of a Cuban cigar. Imagine driving our dream car, the sound of music softly playing on an Italian vineyard, or the ultimate in acquiring wealth: giving and helping others in need on a grander scale. The Law of Attraction says we can attract desires of abundance when we keep our thoughts and intent focused on the positive and match them to the frequency of love.

Remember that wanting and using the phrase *I want* signifies not having, a sign of lack, so we should think thoughts of already having, as if our wish has already been granted. Therefore, to manifest, we must eliminate thoughts of being without, and consciously change and replace them with thoughts of already having.

When the timing's right, desires manifest. We have to be at a place in our lives where we are capable and able to accept desires. The time lapse between wanting and getting creates the illusion that things are happening *to* us and not because of us. This is the illusion of time. Once we know that we have done everything we can to mentally prepare, we have to wait and anticipate. This keeps us from manifesting too quickly, from changing our minds, and allows us to exhaust all other possibilities of what else we might desire. When the timing is right, desires materialize and stick around. If every thought were instantly manifested, low-vibrating frequencies would manifest instantly as well.

When you've been working hard and have been manifesting abundance all year and now are just patiently waiting for the Universe to deliver the goods.

Summary of How to Manifest our Desires

♥Consciously change negative thoughts to better thoughts.

♥Choose one desire at a time and visualize daily.

♥Practice thoughts that make us feel the elevated emotions we want to create.

♥Believe and act as if our desire has already come true and we are living its life.

♥Use affirmations to train the brain to form new and improved neural pathways.

♥Visualize and imagine having our desire using all our senses.

♥Keep thoughts vibrating near the frequency of love, 500 Hz.
♥Have pure intentions and unwavering focus and belief.

> The only thing that stops healing and manifestation from happening is fear, doubt, disbelief, and lack of virtues.

When things are looking bleak for us, the process of choosing new desires brings consolation. Thinking about what manifestation we would like to choose next encourages our spirit to carry on. When things aren't going as planned, we can mentally change the words, rewrite our script, choose a new desire, and deliberately decide how we want things to go next. When we don't receive what we have been intently manifesting, the best we can do is pick up our pride, wish it well, blow it off with a kiss, and make a new wish.

PART III

A Vibrational Toolbox

"The secret of health for both mind and body is not to mourn for the past, nor to worry about the future, but to live the present moment wisely." — BUDDHA

Energy healing helps us at our deepest levels, whether it's a physical, mental, emotional, or spiritual challenge that we're facing. Since virtually all illness is created in the mind first, energy healing begins with addressing our emotional issues. If the emotional issues of our mind create illness in the body, then we can create wellness by releasing the negative emotional memories of the past.

If we have manifested sickness or disease, it's our subconscious' way of letting us know that there's something in our body that needs more love and attention. We may think of sickness as being bad, but instead of labeling it as *bad*, we can consider it more of a *blessing* since awareness gives us an opportunity to change our circumstances. If illness didn't show up on a physical level, we would easily keep our buried emotions where they are, never realizing that something might be wrong with us.

Fix it in the Field First.

Bad experiences can be *fixed* in our energy field before they turn into illness. Before signs of disease show up, when we tune into our body's feelings, listen to its subtle signals, and address our emotional imbalances, we can fix ourselves at the quantum level before negative emotions develop into disease.

Signs and symptoms of disease often take a metaphorical form of what we're feeling, much like dreams of the subconscious mind. We may have a sore throat when we "don't speak up for ourselves." Digestion problems could indicate that there's something in our life we're "unable to digest." Arthritis in the knees could suggest we're having "difficulty taking the necessary steps" to move forward. If our neck hurts, something is giving us a "pain in the neck." Ulcers could mean that something is "eating us up inside," or we have the flu because we are "sick and tired" of a situation in our life. When we listen to the subtle, or not-so-subtle signs of what our body is telling us, we get a glimpse of the language necessary to understand our mind.

The vibrational frequencies of health and disease are affected by whether we're sick or well. Being sick lowers our vibration and being well raises our vibration. Human bodies have a frequency of about 62-72 megahertz (MHz) and different sicknesses lower our frequency.
- The brain vibrates between 72-90 MHz
- Healthy humans vibrate between 62-70 MHz
- Cells mutate when their frequency drops below 62 MHz
- Colds and flus vibrate at 58 MHz
- Candida vibrates at 55 MHz
- Epstein-Barr virus vibrates at 52 MHz
- Cancer appears at 42 MHz
- Death appears at frequencies of 20-25 MHz

Sickness seldom results from a true imbalance in the body and more often is initiated by repeatedly thinking negative thoughts such as criticism, anger, resentment, and guilt. If we are sick, we need to ask ourselves what critical, angry, resentful, and/or guilty thoughts have we been ruminating over repeatedly to create this condition? Continually thinking negative thoughts releases the stress hormone cortisol, which causes inflammation—the substance of knots, kinks, blockages, and pain in the body.

We've all been known to overthink a situation. When we repeatedly think, "I don't want to get sick…I don't want to get sick…" we send out low energy vibes that attract sickness, due to the Law of Attraction. Also, the

Universe doesn't acknowledge the word *don't*, thus it hears, "I want to get sick." Another way we attract sickness through our thoughts is when we say, "I'm sick." Every time we think it, say it, and feel it, we attract more sickness. Repetitive thoughts of not wanting to get sick, yet saying and speaking that we're sick, attract low-vibration energies that manifest as illness and disease.

Finding the root cause for healing requires courage to bring out our buried feelings of the past to the surface and is necessary before healing can happen. Although pain and hurt are emotions we don't intentionally like to remember, it's empowering and at the essence of self-healing to understand the lessons they bring. To understand lessons of past pain, we need to know what's behind the stories we've told ourselves for so long. What story, emotion, or experience do we need to honor in order to heal?

During meditation or a time of solitude, we can ask our subconscious to identify and bring to awareness the original cause of our illness or pain. We can ask why we have been holding onto it for so long and what benefit we have received from keeping and having this disease. (Do I enjoy the attention I receive from being sick? Does having this sickness make me feel less lonely?)

One way to find the root cause is to think about what was happening in our lives at the time our sickness started. Ask ourselves how we added fuel to the fire to keep it growing; we obviously didn't *fuhgeddaboudit*. Ask ourselves what is it about *us* that needs to grow in order for this to go away. We should continue asking until our questions are intuitively answered to find the true motivation behind unintentionally manifesting and holding onto our illness. Once we understand the truth behind our pain, we are in a better position to release and overcome its hold on us.

After we have found what we believe to be the root cause of our problem, how do we heal ourselves? We start by taking personal accountability for our thoughts, beliefs, and actions. If we created it, then we can change it. When we accept our imperfections as our own creation, then we can accept and manifest healing as our creation. Being honest, self-aware, and realizing that we are the cause of our creations brings us one step closer to being able to heal ourselves.

The Placebo Effect proves that we are capable of healing ourselves from sickness and disease simply from the *belief* that we will get well or by taking a healing medicine. Sugar pills work just as effectively as real drugs when we believe the placebo is the real thing.

As a culture, we are overly critical of ourselves and others, and this is why pills cannot fix many ailments. When we catch ourselves being critical, we need to recognize it immediately and *take back and change our words*: "I take that back!" We can literally take back our negative words and replace them with opposite and kinder words. Choosing new thoughts releases resistance, helps us let go, and gives us a sense of empowerment.

We can release and let go of our illness by *not* focusing directly on our illness, but on thoughts of being well. If we're thinking about how to overcome our sickness or how to beat our condition, then we are using the Law of Attraction to hold on to it. The focus of our thoughts should be *"Every day I get better and better; all my cells are well; thank you, Universe for allowing me to feel healthy; or I am in perfect health."*

Getting past previous trauma, pain, hurt, negative thinking, and all the behaviors that lower vibrations can be accomplished by moving beyond previous patterns of thinking and creating anew. With each Now moment, we can change from before to create what we desire, whether it's past patterns of negative thinking or outgrown beliefs, we can make a conscious choice to change our thinking. We must release and let go of pain, beliefs, and expectations—trust and surrender are part of the process needed for self-healing.

Adopting our inner child initiates the healing power of play and is one way to release and create ourselves anew. Imagine asking a younger version of ourselves what would bring us joy. Even if our answers are wild and random, we should listen and use our intuitive advice as a guidepost to give ourselves what we missed out on as a child.

Inner Child Wounds

Guilt Wounds

- Feels "sorry" or "bad"
- Doesn't like to ask for things
- Uses guilt to manipulate
- Is afraid to set boundaries
- Attracts people who make them feel guilty

Neglect Wounds

- Struggles to let things go
- Has low self-worth
- Vulnerable and gets angry easily
- Represses emotions
- Attracts people who don't appreciate them

Abandonment Wounds

- Feels "left out"
- Dislikes being alone
- Co-dependent
- Threatens to leave
- Attracts emotionally unavailable people

Trust Wounds

- Is afraid to be hurt
- Doesn't trust themselves
- Finds ways to not trust people
- Insecure and needs lots of external validation
- Attracts others who don't feel safe

Thinking back to when we were a kid, what made us happy? What is it that made us feel happy, carefree, and completely safe? Maybe it was watching cartoons, Disney movies, or reruns of *I Love Lucy*. Maybe our fondest memories were eating sugary cereal for breakfast or fishing on the dock with our dad. What else could we do that would ease and release tensions and trauma from our youth? Over-zealous holiday decorating is a festive way to let our inner child shine. And so are the littler things: riding a bike, ice skating, or building a tent in the living room. Playing in the rain, fingerpainting, and blowing bubbles are expressive ways to be a kid again and make up for things we may have missed out on. Sometimes, it's the simple things that renew our spirit and give us a chance to heal.

What if we're not getting well? When we identify with and have emotional attachments to our sickness, those attachments prevent it from going away. We may be afraid to get well because our identity has been based on our illness, and this is how people know and identify with us. How grand it would be that instead of, "They're the one with cancer," we could say, "They're the one who healed themselves from cancer."

When we know and understand our motivation for holding onto sickness in the first place and accept and forgive our reasons without judgment, this helps us heal. Accepting, forgiving, and knowing that we are worthy on our own merits and that it's only our limiting thoughts and beliefs that keep us from having perfect health.

Just like manifesting desires, similar elements are needed for manifesting health. We must have desire, intention, focus, belief, and feelings of love. Additionally, healing requires forgiveness and letting go of the past. The vibrational energy needed to manifest healing and get past buried emotions is through love and understanding. The power of love and positive thoughts is the vibrational perk needed to change any diagnosis given us. We heal by opening our heart and letting in love. When love flows, healing happens.

Any traditional treatments during the self-healing process should continue, but the power of the mind and energy as medicine has been a focus of medicine for thousands of years and has helped many heal. The following chapter looks at the chakras, or the energy system of the body, and the remaining chapters of this section examine vibrational therapies, most of which are outside of the norm of conventional medicine.

Patient: Doctor, I don't feel well and I'm not sure why

Doctor: I want you to meditate for 20 minutes twice a day, exercise for at least 30 minutes a day, avoid processed foods, eat plenty of organic fruit and veg, spend more time in nature and less indoors, stop worrying about things you can't control and ditch your TV. Come back in 3 weeks.

CHAPTER 8

The Chakralatory System

"There is more wisdom in your body than in your deepest philosophy." — FRIEDRICH NIETZSCHE

What I affectionately refer to as the "Chakralatory System," is a portmanteau from *chakra* and *circulatory*. What blood is to the circulatory system, energy is to the chakra system. Like blood in veins, energy flows to all parts of the body through chakra channels called meridians. When blood in the circulatory system is blocked, it causes disease. When energy in the chakra system is blocked, it causes disease.

Emotional energy flows through the chakras, and when it is flowing freely, our bodies are healthy, happy, harmonious, and free of disease. When chakras are blocked, we may not feel well without knowing a reason why. Energy medicine and energy healing help us heal the underlying emotional issues at the root of dis-ease and dis-comfort.

Although there are many thousands of chakra locations, this chapter focuses on the seven physical/emotional chakras and five spiritual chakras located within and around the body. The chakra centers are made from swirling vortexes of subtle light energy known as *qi* (aka *chi*) or *prana*, the energy of life and the Universe.

Chakras affect energy throughout the body. Whether a chakra is open or closed, aligned or misaligned, underactive or overactive, can drastically alter our energetic, physical, and spiritual states of well-being. When our chakras are open, we feel healthy, balanced, and more enlightened. When chakras are closed, it shows up as body imbalances and emotional distress.

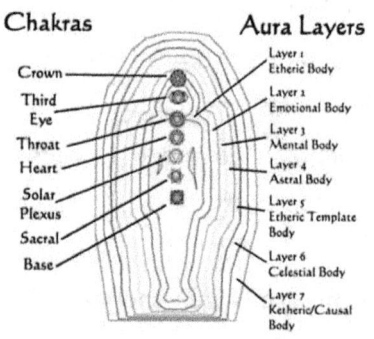

Our body's energy level is displayed through the aura via the chakras. Our physical health can be determined by looking at the first layer of the aura closest to the body, the etheric body layer. When energy is flowing freely in our bodies, it shows as a vibrant and colorful egg-shaped aura. When energy is sluggish or we are sick, the aura is less vibrant, smaller, and may appear as a haphazard shape surrounding the body.

Chakras provide the light energy for the holographic blueprint, as well as the aura, correspond to the light wave spectrum of the rainbow, DNA strands, levels of consciousness as shown on the Tree of Life, and dimensional planes anticipating interdimensional travel. Most of us have only evolved to the second Sacral Chakra level of consciousness, so there is still work to be done in opening our chakras and DNA strands.

The location of the chakras along the spine correlates to the location of the body's endocrine system, responsible for hormones in the body.

Chakra	Endocrine Gland	Emotional Purpose	Energetic Feeling
#1 Root	adrenals	survival and trust	adrenaline rush
#2 Sacral	gonads	sexuality & creativity	arousal
#3 Solar Plexus	pancreas	personal power	butterflies
#4 Heart	thymus	love & healing	broken heart, flutters
#5 Throat	thyroid	truth & communication	speechless
#6 Third Eye	pituitary gland	awareness & intuition	inner knowing
#7 Crown	pineal gland	dimensional spirituality	tingly scalp

Different Ways to Balance and Cleanse the Chakras

Affirmations help balance and cleanse the chakras through vibrations of the voice.

Root - I am safe.

Sacral - I am creative.

Solar Plexus - I am strong.

Heart - I am loved.

Throat - I am expressive.

Third Eye - I am connected.
Crown - I am divine.

🌀*Colors* of each chakra center are related to a color of the light spectrum. Activating color frequencies corresponding to a specific chakra, release energy blockages in that chakra. The frequency of the Root Chakra resonates with the color red, so using red-colored crystals, eating red foods, or wearing red clothing help restore energy in that chakra. To balance other chakras, use their associated ROY G. BIV rainbow colors to cleanse, restore, and unblock stuck energy.

Root - **R**ed
Sacral - **O**range
Solar Plexus - **Y**ellow
Heart - **G**reen
Throat - **B**lue
Third Eye - **I**ndigo
Crown - **V**iolet

🌀*Sound* has healing frequencies, just as color does. Chakras resonate to specific musical notes and frequencies and listening to music and sound therapy in these notes activate that chakra center.

Root	Note A - 432 Hz
Sacral	Note B - 480 Hz
Solar Plexus	Note C - 528 Hz
Heart	Note D - 594 Hz

Throat	Note E - 672 Hz
Third Eye	Note F - 720 Hz
Crown	Note G - 768 Hz

🌀 *Toning* is using vibrations from our voice to stimulate and balance the chakras. Place both hands on the chakra center to be balanced. Vibrate our voice using the deepest seed sound (in italics) or vowel tone possible, and then gradually increase the pitch. The chakra center should feel lighter afterwards, resonating with the higher pitches.

Root - *Lam* - Uh
Sacral - Vam - Ooh
Solar Plexus - *Ram* - Oh
Heart - *Yam* - Ah
Throat - *Ham* - Eye
Third Eye - *Om* - Aaa
Crown - *No sound* - Eee

🌀 *Essential oils* help to balance chakras due to their similar vibratory essences. For chakra balancing, oils can be applied directly to the skin with or without a carrier oil or through inhaling. These are some common oils used for the chakras:

Root - frankincense, sandalwood, vetiver
Sacral - clove, orange, ylang ylang
Solar Plexus - lemongrass, grapefruit, helichrysum
Heart - rose, jasmine, cardamom

Throat - peppermint, blue chamomile, bergamot
Third Eye - angelica, sage, blue lotus
Crown - angelica, frankincense, lavender

🌀 *Chakra Meditation* opens and activates the chakra centers. Use the corresponding chakra color in the meditation to unblock each chakra.

Begin by sitting in a quiet space. Imagine a glowing (color of chakra) ball of energy on the chakra energy centers, spinning smoothly in a clockwise motion, while slowly releasing pent-up energies. Silently repeat a chakra affirmation for each chakra. Start with the Root Chakra and work our way up the chakras, practicing for ten minutes at a time. This can be done with or without holding a corresponding crystal for each chakra.

🌀 *Crystals and Stones* help the chakras resonate at high frequencies through the principle of entrainment.

Root - Red Jasper, Black Tourmaline, Hematite
Sacral - Carnelian, Tiger's Eye, Sunstone
Solar Plexus - Citrine, Amber, Yellow Jasper
Heart - Green Aventurine, Rose Quartz, Emerald
Throat - Turquoise, Lapis Lazuli, Aquamarine
Third Eye - Amethyst, Labradorite, Sapphire
Crown - Clear Quartz, Diamond, Selenite

🌀 *Sacred Geometry* shapes connect us to the Universe and our higher self. Looking at sacred geometry figures during meditation clears the chakras and wearing the shapes as jewelry calms the mind. Placing crystals and stones in the shape of geometric figures on the body also help unblock chakras.

Root - *hexahedron* – grounding
Sacral - *icosahedron* - flowing
Solar Plexus - *tetrahedron* - balance
Heart - *star tetrahedron* - healing
Throat - *octahedron* - balance
Third Eye - *dodecahedron* - higher self
Crown - *sphere* - spirit

Tapping (EFT—Emotional Freedom Tapping) helps unblock chakras by releasing blocked energy while tapping on meridian channels and simultaneously repeating affirmations.

Start with the Crown Chakra at the top of the head and tap 10-15 times, more if needed. Next, tap the Third Eye Chakra in the middle of the forehead, then gently tap the middle of the throat for the Throat Chakra. Use a small fist to tap the Heart Chakra in the middle of the chest. Tap just below the sternum to unblock the Solar Plexus Chakra and just below the belly button for the Sacral Chakra. Using a gentle fist, tap the lower back near the bottom of the spine.

Earth Star Chakra Zero

Meaning "Daughter of the Earth"	Earth & ancestral wisdom
Colors Deep red, infrared	**Element** Earth
Musical Note All Notes / **Hertz** / **Sound** Om	**Planet** Pluto
Location	6-18 inches below the soles of our feet into the Earth
Physical Body	not directly related to any specific body parts
Emotional Body	grounded, connection to Earth, stability, security, sense of belonging, fight-or- flight-response, primal needs, survival instincts
Spiritual Body	the center from which we ground ourselves and connect with Mother Earth
Affirmations	"I am safe, steady, strong, and secure," "I trust and love myself," "I have everything I need," "I am kind to myself," "I am fearless."
Gemstones	black kyanite, brookite, petrified wood, red jasper, sardonyx, Tibetan quartz, ruby, bloodstone, obsidian
Essential Oils	black & pink peppercorn, ceremonial tobacco, frankincense & myrrh resin, all root oils and flower oils
Herbs	red clover, white sage, galangal root
Unbalanced Signs	addictions, difficulty handling money and maintaining a job, self-destructive tendencies, DNA, heredity, and bone marrow-related issues
Balanced Signs	equitable distribution of work/life balance, feeling centered and grounded
How to Heal	reconnect with nature by walking barefoot—"earthing"

Root Chakra 1 (DNA Strand 1)

Meaning Root + Support			Survival, trust, grounding	
Colors Red, brown			**Element** Earth	
Musical Note A	**Hertz** 432	**Sound** Lam	**Planet** Saturn	
Location			coccyx (first three vertebrae at base of spine), tailbone	
Physical Body			adrenals, kidneys, immune system, blood, base of spine, perineum, muscles, bone marrow, legs and feet, rectum, sense of smell, pheromones, male reproductive system, elimination, colon	
Emotional Body			grounded, connection to Earth, stability, security, sense of belonging, fight or flight response, primal needs, survival instincts: food, shelter, and safety	
Spiritual Body			the center from which we ground ourselves and connect with Mother Earth	
Affirmations			"I am safe, steady, strong, and secure," "I trust and love myself," "I have everything I need," "I am kind to myself," "I am fearless."	
Gemstones			red jasper, smoky quartz, black tourmaline, garnet, ruby, hematite, black onyx	
Essential Oils			sandalwood, myrrh, vetiver, frankincense, white sage	
Herbs			dandelion, rosemary, paprika, clove, cayenne, allspice, nutmeg	
Unbalanced Signs			being afraid, fearful, anxious, tired, stubborn, unwilling to accept change, mentally scattered, clumsy, frazzled, nausea, autoimmune disorders, financial instability, ungrounded, materialistic, cynical, and greedy	

Balanced Signs	financially secure, physically safe, emotionally stable, grounded, connected to Earth, sense of belonging, happy to be alive
How to Activate	listen to our body's signals, release ancestral limiting beliefs, prejudices, and toxic patterns, use mindful movement, journal our feelings, spend time in nature, practice traditions like cooking with a grandmother's recipe, or organizing kitchen cupboards

Sacral Chakra 2 (DNA Strand 2)

Meaning "The Place of Self"			Sex, creativity, abundance
Colors Orange			*Element* Water
Musical Note B	*Hertz* 480	*Sound* Vam	*Planet* Jupiter and Mercury
Location			a couple inches below the bellybutton, between the hips and lower stomach
Physical Body			gonads, female reproductive system, bladder, lymphatic system, kidneys, prostate, pancreas, bladder, large intestine, appendix, sense of taste
Emotional Body			sexual desires, passion, creativity
Spiritual Body			the center from which we create and give birth to new life and new ideas, ascension corridor
Affirmations			"I enjoy the pleasures life has to offer," "My life is full of adventure," "I attract healthy relationships," "I have lots of energy," "Creativity comes to me easily."
Gemstones			carnelian, orange sapphire, imperial topaz, red goldstone, yellow tiger's eye, orange calcite, citrine, unakite
Essential Oils			vetiver, ylang ylang, rosemary, clove, cedarwood, angelica
Herbs			calendula, coriander, fennel, licorice, cinnamon, vanilla, dandelion, nutmeg
Unbalanced Signs			feeling emotionally stuck or codependent, apathetic, no creativity, low libido or hypersexual, low energy, unmotivated, ashamed, jealous, territorial and isolated, lack of trust, feels victimized, money issues, possible addictions, unhealed trauma, manipulative

Balanced Signs	energized, motivated, healthy sex drive, adventurous, generous, creative, curious, passionate, optimistic, goes with the flow
How to Activate	follow our passions and curiosities, give to others, try tantric sex, explore new hobbies, connect with the water element by spending time in the ocean, a pool, or bathtub

Solar Plexus Chakra 3 (DNA Strand 3)

Meaning "Lustrous Gem"			Power, vitality, manifestation	
Colors Yellow, gold			**Element** Fire	
Musical Note C	**Hertz** 528	**Sound** Ram	**Planet** The Sun	
Location			a couple inches above the bellybutton below the ribs	
Physical Body			pancreas, small intestine, liver, gallbladder, spleen, upper spine, stomach, metabolism	
Emotional Body			self-confidence, self-esteem, self-control/willpower, identity, personal power, determination, inner strength	
Spiritual Body			the center from which our self-power and inner strength come from	
Affirmations			"I accept all parts of myself," "I am strong and I know my worth," "I am comfortable in my own skin," "I make great decisions," "I am capable in all I do."	
Gemstones			pyrite, citrine, yellow sapphire, peridot, amber, red creek jasper	
Essential Oils			sandalwood, lemongrass, helichrysum, juniper, grapefruit, neroli	
Herbs			anise, celery, cinnamon, lily of the valley, marshmallow, mint, melissa, turmeric, cumin	
Unbalanced Signs			personal power issues from powerless and timid to domineering and power hungry, perfectionism, critical, frustration, inferiority complex, low self-esteem and self-confidence, doubtful, feeling incapable, conformist or overly assertive, anxious, nervousness, people-pleaser, feelings of guilt and anger, nervousness, stomach tightness	

Balanced Signs	calm, decisive, confident, courageous, empowered, worthy, capable, in control, positive self-image
How to Activate	set clear and healthy boundaries, learn to say no, be assertive with personal decision making, try new things, high-intensity exercise

Heart Chakra 4 (DNA Strand 4)

Meaning "Unhurt"			Love, healing, relationships	
Colors Green, light pink			**Element** Air	
Musical Note D	**Hertz** 594	**Sound** Yam	**Planet** Venus	
Location			center of chest	
Physical Body			thymus, heart, lungs, ribs, cardiovascular system, pulmonary system	
Emotional Body			love, compassion, kindness, self-love, joy, forgiveness	
Spiritual Body			the center from which we integrate our earthly needs with our spiritual endeavors (connects lower three chakras to upper 3 chakras)	
Affirmations			"I am loved, and I am loving," "I love and forgive myself," "I send love to everyone and everything," "The past is over and I release it."	
Gemstones			rose quartz, jade, emerald, green aventurine	
Essential Oils			rose, jasmine, cacao, cardamom, palmarosa, bergamot, black spruce	
Herbs			cayenne, hawthorn berries, jasmine, lavender, marjoram, rose, thyme, cilantro, parsley	
Unbalanced Signs			hurt, grief, heartbreak, jealousy, loneliness, lack of compassion and empathy, bitterness, hatefulness, feeling closed off, cold, intolerant, lacking kindness towards us and others, self-sacrificing, smothering people with affection and gifts, resentful, judgmental, difficulty forgiving, chest pains, heartburn, heaviness, stooped posture	
Balanced Signs			compassionate, loving, accepting, peaceful, forgiving, joyful, tolerant, warm, open, understanding	

How to Activate	practice forgiveness, cuddling, intimacy, gift-giving, express love to oneself and others, keep a gratitude journal

The minor chakra Sacred Heart at the Thymus is located here.

Throat Chakra 5 (DNA Strand 5)

Meaning "Very Pure"			Expression, communication
Colors Azure blue			**Element** Sound, music
Musical Note E	**Hertz** 672	**Sound** Ham	**Planet** Mercury
Location			middle of throat
Physical Body			thyroid, throat, tongue, teeth, mouth, tonsils, salivary glands, voice, esophagus, ears, bronchial tubes, neck, shoulders, jaw
Emotional Body			self-expression, honest communication, speaking one's truth, authenticity, self-expression, feeling heard, verbal and non-verbal communication, intuition, personal power, clairaudience, claircognizance
Spiritual Body			the bridge between thinking with the heart and thinking with the brain
Affirmations			"I speak the truth and openly express myself," "It's okay to say what I feel," "I speak my truth with ease," "My opinions have value."
Gemstones			turquoise, blue topaz, aquamarine, sodalite
Essential Oils			peppermint, bergamot, basil, geranium, blue chamomile, bay laurel, blue yarrow, fir balsam
Herbs			coltsfoot, blackberry, elderberry, sage, salt, lemongrass, bay laurel, chamomile, eucalyptus, geranium

Unbalanced Signs	fear of speaking up and sharing opinions, telling lies, lack of self-expression, gossiper, shyness, tendency towards oral fixations, feeling withdrawn, speaking too freely and openly, poor listener, dictatorial, inability to take a stand, stress eating, sore and strep throat, dental issues, halitosis, TMJ, thyroid disorders, ear infections, stiff neck, writer's block
Balanced Signs	having confident expression, and clear and honest communication
How to Activate	offer our perspective in conversations, sing in the car or shower, speak at a volume loud enough to be heard, say hello to strangers, practice honesty, chant affirmations

Third Eye Chakra 6 (DNA Strand 6)

Spiritual Body	"the mind's eye," "the seat of consciousness," where our ability to see within ourselves and others is combined with a greater universal understanding, allowing us to see the truth and the meaning behind it
Meaning "Beyond Wisdom"	Awareness, intuition, thought
Colors Indigo	**Element** Light/dark

Musical Note F	Hertz 720	Sound Om	Planet The Moon

Location	on the forehead, between the eyebrows extending to the brain's pineal gland
Physical Body	pituitary gland, hormones, eyes, brain, nose, sinuses, face, pineal gland
Emotional Body	intuitive guidance and insight, clarity, psychic phenomena, telepathy, extrasensory perception, clairvoyance, psychic vision, ability to examine our thoughts, balance between the creative mind and analytical mind
Affirmations	"I am open to exploring what cannot be seen," "I trust myself and my gut feelings," "I trust my inner wisdom," "I recognize and take inspired action on my intuition."
Gemstones	lapis lazuli, amethyst, fluorite, Iolite, sapphire, tanzanite
Essential Oils	angelica, sage, blue lotus, juniper, cypress, yarrow
Herbs	eyebright, juniper, mugwort, poppy, mandrake root, blue lotus, cypress

Unbalanced Signs	poor judgment, lacking focus, intuition, and imagination, stuck in a 3D world, headaches, migraines, clogged sinuses, nightmares, poor sleep, stubbornness, narrow-mindedness, denial of spiritual world, materialistic, repeating same mistakes, obsessiveness, always needing a logical explanation, unable to see the big picture, unaware of others' energies, doubtful of one's success, hallucinations
Balanced Signs	in touch with one's feelings, a good judge of character, open-minded, a healthy balance between logic and emotion, trusts gut feelings, able to process unwanted emotions, imaginative and intuitive, sees beyond the physical, ability to interpret dreams
How to Activate	incorporate frequent meditation, visualization, manifestation, and mindfulness practices, listen to our inner voice, trust intuition and messages from our dreams

Crown Chakra 7 (DNA Strand 7)

Meaning "Thousand Petaled"			Spirituality, enlightenment
Colors Violet, white			**Element** Water
Musical Note G	**Hertz** 768	**Sound** Consciousness	**Planet** Jupiter
Location			top of head, the crown
Physical Body			central nervous system, head, brain, pituitary and pineal glands, spinal cord, skin, biological cycles including sleep
Emotional Body			life purpose, sense of self, connection to a higher power or spiritual realm, source of dream activity, wisdom, attunement with the Universe
Spiritual Body			wisdom, pure consciousness energy, transcendence, connection center of our energy to the Universe
Affirmations			"I am a vessel for love and light." "I am connected to all of life and the Universe." "I am in complete alignment with my soul and divine purpose." "My life is beautiful."
Gemstones			amethyst, selenite, quartz, rutilated quartz, moonstone, howlite, diamond
Essential Oils			frankincense, jasmine, sandalwood, angelica, rose, lavender, pink lotus
Herbs			lavender, gotu kola, pink lotus, St. John's wort

Unbalanced Signs	learning difficulties, making foolish decisions, brain fog, isolation, depression, self-sabotage, apathy, headaches, migraines, dogmatic, judgmental, overly analytical, nerve pain, hormonal imbalances, poor sleep, mental illness, inability to quiet the mind, no conception of a greater existence, spiritually disconnected, feeling purposeless
Balanced Signs	awareness of the Oneness with all of life, aware, wise, understanding, connected with everything, spiritual practices, empathetic, blissful, joyful, drama-free, doesn't care what others think, enjoys time alone, and listens to their intuition
How to Activate	ground the lower chakras, stargaze, travel, lucid dream, meditate, use mindfulness, stare at a candle flame, try aromatherapy, read spiritual books

Soul Star Chakra 8 (DNA Strand 8)

Meaning "Holy Star," halo to the crown	Connection to the stars
Colors Foam green, magenta, ultraviolet	**Element** --

Musical Note	Hertz	Sound	Planet North and South Lunar Nodes
Golden C	--	All Notes, Om	

Location	6-12 inches above the top of the head above the Crown Chakra
Physical Body	connection to all internal chakras, encourages spiritual development and ascension, a toroidal portal for Merkabah activation and access to other dimensions, past life Akashic records access, communication with spirit guides, aka "Seat of the Soul" or "Halo Chakra"
Gemstones	any clear quartz, diamond, moldavite, rainbow moonstone, optical calcite, scolecite, Lemurian crystal, silver, opal
Essential Oils	anise, basil, elemi, jasmine, gardenia, red myrtle, tuberose, white lotus
Herbs	lavender, gotu kola, pink lotus, St. John's wort
Balanced Signs	embodies peace, capable of channeling and manifesting energy, ability to access Akashic records easily, consciousness time travel
How to Activate	incorporate spiritual practices like meditation, visualization, and yoga

Stellar Spirit Star Chakra 9 (DNA Strand 9)

This chakra's color is aqua. It's located about two feet above our head, and it's our connection to our soul's destiny and communication with angels, light beings, and spirit guides. Activation connects us with our true purpose and opens us to the expanse of our soul's powers.

Universal Chakra 10 (DNA Strand 10)

Chakra #10 is pearly white with the merging of physical and spiritual, and masculine and feminine energies. When activated, our light being is completely aligned with our physical being resulting in harmony with the Universe.

Galactic Cosmic Chakra 11 (DNA Strand 11)

Cosmic Chakra #11 is pinkish orange and is related to teleportation, instant manifestation, travel beyond space and time, and communication with higher ascended masters and spiritual beings. This chakra is activated with light language, light code symbols, and vocal meditations.

Divine/Stellar Gateway Chakra 12 (DNA Strand 12)

Chakra #12 is gold and represents full ascension, universal consciousness, and complete Oneness with Source. It's the portal to the Cosmoverse, and its activation opens spiritual knowledge to help others on their journeys.

Auras are the energy source known as our "vibe"—the energy we put out to the Universe. It's also known as the lightbody or biofield surrounding the body that's made from geometrical shapes, electromagnetic light, and sound waves. The seven layers of the aura correspond and are powered by the light energy of the chakra system.

When chakras are out of balance, it is reflected in the aura. The aura reflects the spiritual, mental, and emotional part of us that determines our physical health. Observing an aura's color and size over time indicates health issues and level of spiritual development.

The aura is home to the Akashic records, the mind, memory, soul, and survives what we know as death. Immediately before death, the aura/soul leaves the body; it doesn't die or dissipate but moves into the Afterlife until its next incarnation. Via the aura, the soul leaves the body nightly to astral travel to higher dimensional planes. The aura is the connection to our higher self, the Creator Source, or that which is "above."

YOUR AURA IS WEAKENED BY:	YOUR AURA IS STRENGTHENED BY:
• a poor diet & lack of exercise	• eating fresh, organic, & colorful foods
• a lack of fresh air and sunshine	
• being near crowds, noise, & toxic people	• daily sunshine & being in nature
	• avoiding toxic & negative people
• saying yes to everyone & everything	• setting healthy boundaries
	• using energy healing techniques
• a lack of rest & sleeping near electrical devices	• listening to music & dancing
• fears, traumas, & negativity	• limiting alcohol & drinking F7 water
• too much TV, alcohol, drugs, & other bad habits	• being nice, enjoying life and having fun!

Energizing and cleansing auras can be accomplished using light, color, and energy healing therapies as described in this book. Cleansing the aura balances the chakras, as both are interconnected through light energy.

To see our own aura, begin by gazing at the third eye area in the middle of our forehead against a white background. Relax our eyes' gaze and focus on the forehead and the area surrounding the head. The outline of a white-colored glow around our head and shoulders may appear. With practice, colors will begin to show in our aura. The color of the aura changes frequently depending on the state of our physical and mental health.

Aura Layer 1—*The Etheric Body* is anchored to the physical body and has the slowest vibrational frequency of the aura layers. The etheric layer links qi energy to the physical body through meridian pathways and connects to the Root Chakra. Injury or illness to the physical body shows in this layer.

Aura Layer 2—*The Emotional Body* is associated with feelings, moods, and emotional well-being. This aura level changes color according to our mood and is what we see as the "aura." The emotional body extends about three inches from the body and connects to the Sacral Chakra.

Aura Layer 3—*The Mental Body* contains vibrational thoughts, ideas, and thinking processes of the mind and ego. It connects to the color yellow and the Solar Plexus Chakra. Overactive minds tend to radiate strong mental body auras.

Aura Layer 4—*The Astral Body* level connects the first three aura layers with the lighter vibrations of the higher spiritual levels. The astral body is the first of three levels that comprise the soul. The astral body connects to the Heart Chakra and is made from energy patterns of organized symbols.

Aura Layer 5—*The Etheric Template* represents the body's blueprint/template for personality, identity, and overall energy. This layer controls communication and connects to the Throat Chakra. Sound vibrations from this template create matter on reality's holographic template. Healing is accomplished through this aura level, which extends up to two feet around the body. The etheric template represents the second level of the soul, its archetype, and is home to the Akashic records.

Aura Layer 6—*The Celestial Body* unites the physical to the spiritual through awareness, enlightenment, intuition, and manifestations. The celestial layer emits a white light color and connects to the Third Eye Chakra. Layers four, five, and six of the aura comprise the three levels of the soul.

Aura Layer 7—*The Ketheric Layer* (or Causal Body) is the highest frequency field uniting kundalini energy to One Universal energy. The ketheric layer connects to the Crown Chakra and reflects a golden color.

The Akashic Records is an energetic database of soul knowledge and memories kept in the etheric body level of the aura and in the consciousness of the Earth. It is where all past life experiences are recorded. Information about any future or past choice our soul has ever made is stored here—as well as knowledge of our galactic origin. Accessing the records helps us understand recurring patterns that need to be cleared, as well as information about the lessons we're meant to learn right now. Sometimes information may be disturbing, as we realize how we have contributed to the cause of our problems and ignored challenges meant to move us forward. Missed opportunities constitute the basis for karma and are revealed in the records.

To access Akashic energy, begin in a deep meditative state with a clear intention or purpose for accessing the records. We might say something like, *"Hello Spirit Guides, please help me access my Akashic records to gain wisdom with this problem."* Or, we could say, *"Please allow me access to my Akashic records so I can understand my past faults to improve my current situation."* If we want to elaborate, we could say something like, *"Hello, soul records. I have a matter in my life that I am unable to solve. I have been working on trying to fix* [describe problem] *to no avail. Is there a past life issue that I should be made aware of that will help me solve this problem?"* Like all intuitive information, answers may come in the form of synchronicities, visions, symbols, or we may hear, smell, or taste it, according to which of our "clairs" (see Chapter 18) we most closely resonate with. Akashic records that reveal the most uncomfortable truths have the highest potential for karmic redemption and self-transformation.

The energy flow of the chakra system dictates our level of health, happiness, and harmony in our life, and opens the doors to our spiritual and psychic powers. It's through opening and activating these portals of energy that we can begin to truly know and understand ourselves better. When the chakras are out of alignment, we don't function at full capacity.

We can loosen stagnant energy and get qi flowing freely again through meditation, visualization, sacred geometry, and various energy healing methods given throughout the next chapters of the book.

CHAPTER 9

Matters of Light and Color

"There are many levels of Life which we cannot see and know, yet which certainly exist. There is a larger world, vast enough to include immortality...Our spiritual natures belong to this larger world...If death is apparently an outward fact, immortality is an inner certainty." — MANLY P. HALL

The colors of light either turn us on or turn us off. The red of a rose, the blue of the sky, the green of grass, the orange of a summer sunset…when we see colors, they stir and persuade our emotions, stimulate our senses, and make us *feel* certain ways.

The colors we see come from light photons of the Sun. Within its streams of light rays are organized geometric patterns of sacred shapes that have the ability to awaken our energy. Light is consciousness and makes matter on the holographic template. Therefore, all things, including us, exist as a form of light energy emanating from the life-giving Source of the Sun, and where the term humans as *light beings* originates.

Since our body is made of light energy, using color for healing makes sense. As humans, our bodies are encased in the light energy of auras, whose innermost layer touches the physical body, so treating the aura with colored light helps treat conditions of the skin.

Color and light therapies use colored light frequencies of the light spectrum to support and heal the body, aura, and DNA. The healing frequencies of light and color are absorbed through the eyes, skin, acupuncture points, meridians, reflexology zones, and the chakras. Most of our bodies are light deficient, so bringing more light into our bodies heals and makes us happier.

When colored light enters through the eyes, it produces a psychological effect in the body that affects our mood. Every color has a different effect, so different colors are used for treating different moods and emotional conditions.

Every frequency of energy has a unique color combination and corresponding rainbow color that resonates with similar frequencies in the body. Since every disease state is associated with a color, an undesired condition can be treated at a vibrational level by applying the opposite color. For example, if we're feeling angry, we would apply a calming color of green, opposite of red on the color wheel.

To treat a chronic problem, identify the problem and treat according to the chakra color to which it relates.

Colors have an inverse relationship with their energy, meaning the most energetic colors like blue, indigo, and violet are calming and relaxing, while lower-vibrating colors such as red, orange, and yellow generate feelings of energy. The general principal is that warm colors (red, orange, and yellow) are stimulating; cool colors (blue, green, and violet) are sedating, and green is balancing and toning. Color therapy is highly individualized, so it's important to associate a color's intrinsic meaning to our own interpretation. What may be a relaxing color to one person, could be agitating to another.

How Color Therapy Affects the Chakras and Us

Color therapy, or chromotherapy, helps to rebalance the chakras through the energy inherent in its vibrational frequency. The color red has the longest wavelength and carries the least energy while violet has a shorter wavelength that carries a higher frequency. The higher the frequency, the more powerful the energy of the color.

Color	Hz (approximate)
Infrared	62 – 91 Hz
Red	91 – 105 Hz
Orange	106 – 116 Hz
Yellow	117 – 124 Hz
Green	128 – 139 Hz

Blue	142 – 148 Hz
Violet	159 – 175 Hz
Ultraviolet	180 – 244 Hz

Red relates to the Root Chakra and is considered the color of energy itself. Red represents courage, strength, survival, passion, love, primal emotions, and materialism. It signifies our connection to the life "blood" of Earth, the physicality of matter, and the grounding of our energies. Red helps with circulation, as it energizes the heart and blood. The kidneys, spine, gonads, and sense of smell are associated with the color red. Red should be avoided if we feel anxious or have emotional drama.

Orange associates with the Sacral Chakra and is the color of warmth, joy, happiness, creativity, generosity, success, sensuality, enthusiasm, and pleasure. Orange helps depression, cramping, heart disease, raises blood pressure, helps circulation, is antibacterial, and purifies the adrenals and kidneys. Orange clears fear when combined with blue. Orange is associated with belly laughing, playfulness, and gut feelings.

Yellow links to the Solar Plexus Chakra and symbolizes intellect, alertness, empowerment, self-esteem, mental clarity, creation, confidence, cheerfulness, and creativity. Yellow assists the digestive and lymphatic systems and the pancreas, liver, and stomach. It also helps as a decongestant. As a stimulant, yellow helps with depression.

Green connects to the Heart Chakra and is known for being sedating, cooling, detoxifying, soothing, and balancing. Green calms the spirit and helps us let go. It signifies new beginnings, nature, healing, money, luck, compassion, and fertility. Green is helpful with matters pertaining to the nervous system, heart, lungs, and thymus, and assists with insomnia, irritability, and ulcers.

Blue associates with the Throat Chakra. This calming color signifies forgiveness, peace, nurturing, expression, and communication. It's the color of transition and the "door to the other side" as it links the warm colors of the lower chakras with the cool colors of the upper chakras, providing the first level of access of communication with our higher self. Blue corresponds with the thyroid, ears, throat, hands, and mouth. It helps alleviate pain, stops bleeding, reduces fever, treats liver disorders, jaundice, and eliminates toxins. Blue helps calm strong emotions like anger and aggression.

Indigo correlates with the Third Eye Chakra, abstract concepts, inner power, the Akashic records, consciousness, and "the other side." Indigo stimulates beyond the five senses to the wisdom of inner vision and intuition. Indigo helps control bleeding, brings relief to abscesses, and is a sedative, calming color for nerves.

Violet is the communion of the color red of matter and the color blue of spirit connecting at the Crown Chakra. Violet conveys the expression "keeping our feet on the ground with our head in the air." Violet is known for wisdom, tranquility, inspiration, transformation, spiritual awakening, and its association with the pituitary and pineal glands. It helps with meditation, opening inner doors, and letting go of old beliefs. Violet is antiviral, helps build white blood cells, neutralizes mercury from fillings, assists with menopause symptoms, and helps with sleep and dream cycles.

Color Therapies

 Color Ball Healing helps release trauma in the aura formed from low-vibration emotions and replaces it with the higher vibrations of love and light.

> *Imagine and feel the location of the emotion we're feeling in our body. Give the emotion a color. How does the ball of color feel? Is it heavy or light? Does it trigger pain? Does it spin? Using the right hand, send our color ball energizing love and white light until the color we gave to the ball turns completely white.*

> *How do our emotions change when we add love to them? Now that the ball is filled with light and love, make it spin faster and faster. When we feel love radiating from the ball, pull the white ball back into the original spot where we felt our trapped emotions. Replace the old density with the new frequency of the white color ball. Continue*

doing this until we feel that our trapped emotions have been completely changed into love and light.

Color Cloud Visualization is a meditation that uses imagination, creativity, and intuition to impart a color's healing effect on us based on the color's meaning.

Begin by choosing a color based on its effects and that we would like to impart its influence on us. Take a few grounding breaths. Once our breath is slow and controlled, visualize a small cloud of our chosen color floating above our head. Every time we exhale, imagine the cloud coming down and filling our body with the energy of that color.

Colorpuncture™, or light acupuncture, uses therapeutic colored lights on meridians, chakras, and acupuncture and reflexology points in combination with crystals and oils. Hand-held pens emitting infrared light are available for personal use.

- *Samassati Color Therapy* is similar to Colorpuncture in that it uses light color, crystals, and essential oils to positively affect energy pathways. This color therapy additionally uses intuition and feelings to guide and direct energy.

🌈 *Color Silks Therapy* uses colored silk fabrics draped over the chakra areas. Silk has the highest vibration of any natural cloth, next to cotton and wool; because of this, its frequency radiates into the body and aura to aid healing.

🌈 *Color Viewing* is another method to take advantage of the therapeutic effects of color. Simply look at a chosen color for a few minutes and allow the colored light to enter through our eyes. Visualize the healing we would like to accomplish while viewing our color.

🌈 *Color Wearing* affects our mood and how we like to be perceived. Red makes us feel bold and powerful, and orange makes us feel the enthusiasm and energy of a social butterfly. Wearing yellow is an attention-getter and the color to choose when we feel joyful or need a pick-me-up. Green is an approachable color, good for meeting new people. Blue connotes confidence and calmness, good when we're feeling anxious or stressed. Purple is the color to wear when we want to feel unique among others. Brown is grounding and good for taking it easy, whereas black is slimming, and asserts intimidation and authority. Wearing white conveys a feeling of renewed spirit and fresh beginnings.

🌈 *Hydro Color Therapy* uses water and frequency-colored light to heal the body and energy fields. Nontoxic colored glass bottles are filled with filtered water and placed in the sun for at least one day. Drinking blue-charged water before bed relaxes nerves. Red-charged water restores energy and vitality. Orange-charged water stimulates sexual desire. Yellow-charged water detoxifies. Green-charged water is an overall harmonizer and balancer. Turquoise water brings tranquility while violet water calms the mind.

> *How much does a rainbow weigh?*
> *Not much, it's pretty light.*

Color is visible light. Since we can only see 1% of the visible light spectrum, 99% of our world is completely imperceptible to us, leaving us very little to believe in when we say, "I'll believe it when I see it." We assume reality to be what our fingers can touch and what our eyes can see, but even the atoms that make matter are made from mostly undetectable empty space. So, the reality is, there's much more out there than the sliver our eyes can detect.

We can't see infrared and ultraviolet rays on the light spectrum, but they exist. The rays of light that are visible on the spectrum constitute the acronym ROY G. BIV, standing for red, orange, yellow, green, blue, indigo, and violet, the colors of the rainbow and the ascending colors of the chakras; these are the colors of light that we see—the 1% that fall in between infrared and ultraviolet rays.

Infrared rays lie just below visible red light on the light spectrum and correspond with powerful low frequencies while ultraviolet light lies just above visible violet light on the spectrum and corresponds to more subtle, high-vibrational frequencies. Light therapy allows us to use colors outside of the visible light spectrum, those in the infrared and ultraviolet range of perception, to help certain skin conditions and cancers.

Light Wave Spectrum
ROYGBIV: Red, Orange, Yellow, Green, Blue, Indigo, Violet

91 Hz --- Visible Light --- 175 Hz

Infra*Red* Rays

- activate Earth Star Chakra
- relieve pain, stiffness, & spasms
- help arthritis and carpal tunnel
- help wrinkles, acne, psoriasis, warts, cellulite, and alopecia
- treat certain skin cancers
- help with postpartum depression

Ultra*Violet* Rays

- activate Soul Star Chakra
- treat sun damage and rosacea
- fight viruses and bacteria
- help Seasonal Affective Disorder and depression
- help actinic keratosis
- help burns and wounds

> Sunglasses and sunscreens are cellular suicide. On sunny days, specific wavelengths of light from the Sun filter into the eyes. This feeds the pineal and pituitary glands, and lets the brain know that it's sunny outside. The skin then prepares for direct sunlight and gets ready to make vitamin D. Wearing sunglasses starves the pineal gland and tricks the brain into thinking it's cloudy outside, which stops the skin from preparing for sun exposure. This is one of the main reasons people get skin cancer—not because of the Sun, but because of sunglasses and sunscreens.

Light Therapies

💡 *Blue Light Therapy* is a type of phototherapy treatment that helps damaged and diseased skin. Specific wavelengths of blue light destroy abnormal cells to treat skin cancers, acne, varicose veins, fatigue, and Parkinson's disease. Blue light's therapeutic and anti-inflammatory effects promote blood circulation and detoxification and kill bacteria. Hand-held devices are available for personal use.

💡 *LED Lights* infuse color healing into the body. The lights' colored energy is beamed through water, allowing the body to completely saturate the benefits through the skin. These lights are usually found in bathtubs, showers, pools, and jacuzzies.

💡 *Light Language,* or Light Linguistics, is channeled healing through an attuned practitioner, higher vibrational beings, or it comes from the sun's rays. Light Language is not a system of words but is perceived more

Image Courtesy of @starseed.lightcodes

as sound vibrations from light codes. Light Language can be psychically seen as colors, symbols, and sacred geometry and has a healing effect on energy fields. Any physical manifestation is a form of light language since matter is condensed light energy. To absorb the effects of light language, follow the pattern's shape with our eyes.

Light Language's healing can be expressed through speech as a type of glossolalia (unknown language), or through tapping, drumming, toning, art, or hand and body movements. With intention, this linguistic light programming removes blockages, synchronizes the brain's hemispheres, heals chakras, and increases DNA's frequency. Using light language during meditation helps access the Akashic records to reveal and heal past life issues.

♀ *Optogenetics* is a form of light therapy that targets nerve cells. The light-influenced nerve cells send messages around the body that treat many neurological and psychological disorders. Currently, the therapy involves using a brain implantation device.

♀ *Photodynamic Therapy* (PDT) uses LED laser lights to target cancer cells. Cancerous cells absorb photosensitizing drugs that die when LED lights are applied. This therapy is useful for localized skin conditions and cancers that light is capable of reaching.

♀ *Red Light Therapy* isolates red LED lights to target skin conditions such as cold and canker sores, blemishes, and genital herpes. Personal devices are available as well as doctor-prescribed therapy for larger areas.

💡 *Terahertz Lights* are hand-held wands that blow light frequencies at one trillion hertz; visible light is around 150 Hz. Terahertz lights may treat cancers and other diseases of the skin.

💡 *Toning* beams colored lights to larger areas using lamps or pens to promote healing of the chakras.

Color and light complement each other as therapeutic tools for transforming and healing our minds and bodies. They have the unique capacity to enter the subconscious mind to bring suppressed feelings into awareness to promote healing. Both help release past traumas to bring health and harmony into our lives. Color is also a useful identifi cation tool when choosing healing crystals as the next chapter will illuminate.

CHAPTER 10

 Rock Steady: Geodes, Gems, and Jewels

"Let us carve gems out of our stony hearts and let them light our path to love." — RUMI

The abundance of the Earth comes forth in her gift of energetic crystals. Crystals amplify and help us become *crystal clear* about our intentions and what we desire. Crystal healing restores balance to the chakras that heal our body, emotions, and soul. Crystal therapy is based on the principal that every crystal has a unique vibrational frequency that can stabilize our emotions and clear blockages based upon its mineral content, crystalline geometry, and color.

Why do crystal colors matter? Crystals' colors are a vibrational match to chakras' colors. Because of the vibrational match between like colors, we can choose a crystal color that matches the chakra color we want to heal.

Using both crystals and sacred geometry together maximizes the energetic benefits of both. Through their geometric light patterns, crystals open energy channels, and when they are placed in sacred geometric patterns, their healing effect is amplified. To use crystals and sacred geometry together, create a grid or geometric formation on our body or on a sheet of paper and place it under our bed or meditate upon it to allow the energy to download.

Because some crystals magnify and channel energy with their energy and light vibrations, and some crystals absorb and dissolve negative energy and emotions, we can "program" crystals with what we wish to create, and the crystal will magnify that intention and energy back to us. Occasionally, stones should be cleared of absorbed energies; this can be accomplished by using salt baths or placing them in the sun or moonlight.

Crystals can be worn as jewelry, placed on our bodies, in clothes, used in meditation, placed under pillows, or around the home. When we hold a crystal in our hand that has high vibrations, it causes our body's vibrations to activate and align (or entrain with the crystal. When crystals are placed on the body or in clothes' pockets, their higher energy promotes healing by breaking up internal energy blocks.

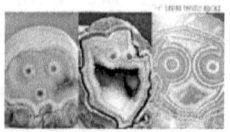
Me, every time I walk into a crystal shop:

The following are healthful and helpful crystals and stones and are listed according to the chakra that they help support.

Connective Earth Star Chakra Stones (Brown, Black, and Red)

Black Kyanite clears all energies from people, places, and things.

Black Tourmaline shields and repels negative energies. It purifies and transforms dense energy into lighter vibrations and provides an emotional and spiritual detox.

Petrified Wood conveys messages from the past.

Red Jasper strengthens personal energy and stamina.

Tibetan Quartz supports, soothes, and hydrates the body.

Protective Root Chakra Stones (Brown, Black, and Red)

Black Tourmaline protects and guards against negative energies.

Jet removes curses, hexes, and protects from diseases.

Obsidian shields negative energies.

Onyx absorbs low vibrations, negative energies, and attracts good luck.

Red Aventurine detoxes and clears stored trauma.

Red Jasper provides strength and fortitude to fight personal battles.

Shungite protects against EMF radiation.

Terahertz is a man-made crystal with super powerful frequencies, making it one of the strongest healing stones available. It provides protection from pollution and clears toxins and negative energies from the body. The high vibrations of terahertz make it useful as a gua sha tool for blood circulation and strengthens the bones and teeth.

Creative Sacral Chakra Stones (Orange)

Carnelian stimulates energy, creativity, and confidence.

Goldstone improves blood flow and increases energy to bring balance and alignment.

Imperial Topaz brings strength and power and is considered an aphrodisiac.

Orange Calcite brings stamina and endurance associated with sexual performance and helps counter the effects of menopause.

Peach Moonstone harnesses the creative powers of manifestation.

Tangerine Quartz is a male aphrodisiac that boosts sex drive.

Attracting Solar Plexus Chakra Stones (Yellow)

Amber channels ancient wisdom.

Citrine opens us to abundance, success and prosperity. It boosts confidence, self-esteem, and promotes joy and enthusiasm.

Pyrite brings confidence and inner strength.

Tiger's Eye enhances intuition and activates a protective shield around us.

Yellow Jade improves digestion, burns calories, reduces appetite, and increases metabolism.

Yellow Fluorite brings prosperity, manifestation, and wealth.

Healing Heart Chakra Stones (Green and Pink)

Mangano Calcite nurses a broken heart and heals trauma.

Pink Tourmaline opens energy to unconditional love and reminds us that it's safe to love.

Rose Quartz is known as the "heart stone;" it activates, magnifies, and helps us be more open to unconditional love.

Ruby brings passion to physical love and honors the legacy of a passed loved one.

Clarifying Throat Chakra Stones (Blue)

Aqua Aura Quartz purifies the aura and promotes strength, tenacity, and prosperity.

Amazonite promotes truth and boosts confidence while speaking.

Celestite connects us to our personal guides of the angelic realms.

Turquoise strengthens, purifies, heals, protects and is known as a source of good fortune.

Transformative Third Eye Chakra Stones (Indigo)

Amethyst helps in opening our Third Eye and Crown Chakras. It promotes mental clarity, intuition, and spiritual wisdom. Amethyst purifies, detoxifies, and brings balance and peace. It clears negative thoughts and energies, improves sleep quality, and guards against psychic attacks.

Azurite facilitates mastery with psychic visions.

Blue Aventurine heightens intuition.

Labradorite deflects energies and ignites the imagination to new desires and new beginnings.

Lapis Lazuli enhances confidence, self-esteem, and intuitive power.

Sodalite or the "dreamcatcher," prevents nightmares, releases fears, and keeps us focused on the present.

Tanzanite is a healing and foretelling stone that guides us towards our personal best.

Restorative Crown Chakra Stones (Violet)

Auralite promotes self-healing from emotional and physical trauma and reduces inflammation.

Lepidolite brings peace and relaxation that allows energy to flow freely through all the chakras.

Purple Fluorite cleanses the soul and attracts new opportunities to manifest our purpose.

Selenite is a ceremonial stone that removes blockages, clears others' energies, and carries vibrations of peace.

Quartz is a powerful all-purpose stone good for any condition. It is a natural life force attractor that uplifts vibrations, channels positive energies, clears negative energies, and brings awareness to our higher self. Quartz can be used for amplifying intentions during manifestation and helps trigger the piezoelectric effect during kundalini ascension.

Spiritual Soul Star Chakra Stones (Clear)

Diamond reminds us of our inner strength and imparts the energy of unconditional love.

Herkimer Diamond is the highest vibrating crystal and a source of wisdom and clarity to help identify our soul's highest calling.

Moldavite transfers energy from other universal dimensions.

Optical Calcite brings clarity, enhanced perspectives, and optimizes interdimensional travel.

Rainbow Moonstone creates energies of joy and gratitude and possesses manifestation potential.

Scolecite is the stone of ascension that accelerates spiritual development, manifestation, and higher awareness.

CHAPTER 11

The Shapes and Spirals of Sacred Geometry

"The spiral is the age-old intuitive symbol of spiritual development and our identity with the Universe."
— GEOFF WARD

Everything created has a repeating spiral pattern inherent within its shape. The repeating patterns are mathematical and scientific proof that the Universe and everything in it are created and connected by the same energy; all that we see, or don't, comes from the same unified energy Source. The spiral patterns of sacred geometry show how vibrational patterns of energy organize using the path of least resistance to create virtually all matter in the Universe.

Sacred geometry is found in virtually every pattern of biological growth such as DNA, snowflakes, crystals, flower petals, shells, the cornea of our eyes, coiled snakes, air, stars, and galaxies.

The spiral is found in all of creation from the swirl of the galaxy to the spirals of DNA.

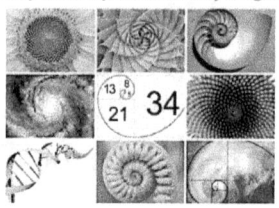

Image Courtesy of Medium.com

⌑ *The Fibonacci Sequence* is an aspect of sacred geometry whose numerical spiraling sequence begins with 0, followed by 1, 1, 2, 3, 5, 8, 13, 21, 34, 55, 89, 144…and keeps unfolding in a never-ending pattern. The Fibonacci spiral-forming sequence is found everywhere in nature, suggesting its importance as a basic characteristic of the Universe.

The Fibonacci sequence and its geometric spirals show patterns of growth, the infinite expansion of the Universe, and the nature of consciousness. The numbers of Fibonacci sequencing are also found in computer algorithms, piano keys, pyramids, hieroglyphics, pinecones, tree branching, sunflowers, hurricanes, human faces, fingers, lungs, chakra energy, the Vitruvian Man, DNA's double helix, the brain, and many other biological systems. The Fibonacci sequence symbolizes beauty, creation, harmony, perfection, proportion, and Oneness of All.

T. S. Martin

The Golden Ratio, Golden Mean, or Divine Proportion of 1.618 is the principle of energy flow that occurs when a number in the Fibonacci sequence is divided by the previous number. The Golden Ratio is often called the code of creation, a built-in numbering system for everything, as all shapes come back to the Fibonacci sequence and the Golden Ratio. The Golden Ratio is the energy-efficient path of least resistance for the flow of energy.

Shapes of Sacred Geometry

The Seed of Life symbolizes the creation of life. The seven overlapping circles connect with the seven chakras to form the shape of DNA. When the Seed of Life is transformed among dimensions, the Flower of Life forms.

The Flower of Life pattern symbolizes the mitosis of cell division and the origin and creation of the Universe. Each intersecting point in the flower represents an atom of consciousness. The interlocking triangles form a matrix of light and sound making up the 3D blueprint of consciousness that radiates unlimited zero-point energy.

The petals in the Flower of Life symbolize the spiritual awakening associated with the Crown Chakra and the interconnectedness of life on Earth. Placing images of the Flower of Life under our bed can help us get a restful night's sleep or help release buried emotional trauma during dreaming. Meditating on the Flower of Life reorganizes and reconnects the body and mind to promote healing and increase the flow of energy.

Metatron's Cube is a mystical cube that contains every geometric shape that exists in the Universe. These shapes are the building blocks 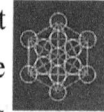 of all physical matter and appear throughout creation, in everything from crystals to DNA. They are known as Platonic solids because Plato linked them to the spirit elements of heaven and to the physical elements of Earth. The cube represents the 3D reality of our physical body while the sphere represents the consciousness of our soul. Metatron's Cube is useful in healing by pushing away unwanted energies.

The Platonic Solids represent the life force and building blocks of reality and of the shapes we see around us. They are called Platonic because Plato was the first to relate the shapes to the five elements of air, water, earth, fire, and ether (akasha, the medium of space, or zero-point energy). The Platonic solids hold the geometric codes of creation and are considered to be the most stable, balanced shapes in the Universe. Like other forms of sacred geometry, Platonic-shaped objects balance the energies in our body and our environment. The Platonic solids correspond to the chakra and light spectrum systems, to musical scale notes, to dimensions of Earth's radius, and references which dimension we're in. Currently, we're in a Third Dimension, that of the Octahedron, but are moving into the Star-Tetrahedron Dimension, or the Merkabah (the Source of interplanetary travel).

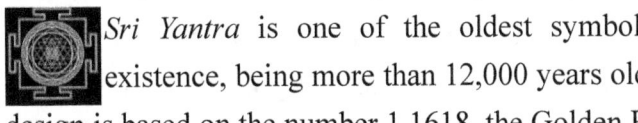*Sri Yantra* is one of the oldest symbols in existence, being more than 12,000 years old. Its design is based on the number 1.1618, the Golden Ratio or Divine Proportion. The symbol protects against negative energies and is used as a meditative tool to bring Universal Oneness.

Torus Yantra symbolizes the constant state of energy flow in and out of a torus vortex and that all things are naturally made from balanced energy flow. Meditating with the torus yantra brings happiness and harmony.

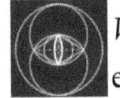*Vesica Piscis* represents a union of opposite energies symbolizing the power of three. The overlapping circles create a center portal signifying the threefold nature of existence: body, mind, and spirit. The portal signifies the convergence of light into matter through the birth canal. The portal acts to unify the past, present, and future in our minds and bridges the ego with higher consciousness.

All Images Courtesy of 7chakrastore.com

Sacred geometry opens our minds to using the symbolical shapes of creation as a healing tool. The shapes inspire our minds to rise to new levels of consciousness. Because all energy is information and light, sacred geometry works because it contains high frequencies of light that activate, heal, awaken, and transform.

Sacred geometry shapes connect us with Source energy in a natural and visual way to heal and purify at the transforming root level. Healing occurs on a physical level as sacred geometry realigns us with the creation of nature and the Universe. Sacred geometry also heals on a spiritual level by raising our vibration, increasing our intuition, and by developing inner trust with ourselves.

Like the effortless flow of Fibonacci sequencing and the rising spirals of DNA and kundalini energy, our life is meant to flow. When our energy flows with little effort, we are more open to having the most ultimate life experiences.

CHAPTER 12

The Healing Vibrations of Sound

"The medicine of the future will be music and sound."
— EDGAR CAYCE, "Father of Holistic Medicine"

Like other forms of vibrational therapy, sound therapy works on the same principal that everything in the Universe is energy that carries its own unique vibrating frequency. All sounds produce vibrations that synchronize brainwaves; therefore, using vibrations from sound is a natural way to treat pain and illness. Most sound therapies use the principle of brainwave entrainment, aligning brainwaves to sound frequencies to get into alpha, delta, and theta states of consciousness more easily. Sound therapy uses music, instruments, or our voice to activate chakras and DNA to release energetic blockages, restore cells' frequencies to normal, and bring health. The healing frequencies of sound lower stress, bring relaxation, and have the power to hypnotize, heal, and induce higher states of consciousness.

When we're feeling heartbroken, sounds from music heal the space inside when we have no words to express how we feel. When emotions are too confusing to express verbally, music opens the door to feeling again. Music helps us reflect on what we're unwilling to feel, which allows healing to occur. Healing happens in the space between the notes of music where there is no sound. This "sacred pause," the empty space, is found in meditation and breathwork, and is where we find answers to questions we seek. This emptiness makes space for healing and for new things to come.

Our soul is composed of harmony and disease is a form of disharmony. The healing sounds of music balance our chakras to bring us into harmony, holistic resonance, or "sound health." When we are in a state of "sound" health, our body is vibrating in resonance with itself. This is why it is said our heart "beats" and our insides are called "organs." If our body is out of harmony, sound vibrations bring it back to sound resonance.

Types of Sound Therapies

♪ *Binaural Beats* frequencies induce a theta meditative state by syncing our brain's hemispheres with tones below the range of hearing.

♫ *Chanting* is a voice meditation that harmonizes the chakras through vibrations from our voice. When the mouth forms shapes to make sounds, it stimulates eighty-four reflexology meridian energy points. Here are the related mantra chants (bija seed sounds) to activate DNA and the chakras:

Root Chakra: Chant *Lam*
Sacral Chakra: Chant *Vam*
Solar Plexus Chakra: Chant *Ram*
Heart Chakra: Chant *Yam*
Throat Chakra: Chant *Ham*
Third-Eye Chakra: Chant *O*
Crown Chakra: Instead of chanting, we just listen

To chant, either sit in a chair with our feet flat on the floor and our hands in an upward cupped position, or lie down, supporting the head and neck. Place our hands lightly on the body to direct sound to the appropriate chakra. For the throat, cup the hands just below the jaw. For the third eye, gently put our palms over the eyes, etc.

- *Gregorian Chanting* is famous for its use of the solfeggio frequencies in its chants. Singing these chants relieves fatigue, alleviates depression, and activates DNA.

♫ *Cymatics* is the science that makes sound vibrations visible as geometric patterns. When a membrane (such as a drum) is activated by sound, unique patterns emerge forming shapes reminiscent of sacred geometry. Although cymatics is not a sound therapy, its relevance comes from its ability to affect sound vibrations needed for healing.

Alphabet letters from the first alphabet were formed from cymatic sound patterns. Sound patterns are also the basis for letter formation in other languages, as all languages are sound vibrations formed within the Flower of Life pattern, adhering to the laws of nature and sacred geometry. Just as images are formed from sound vibrations on a cymatic membrane, sound vibrations form images on the 3D holographic blueprint to make matter.

♪ *Drumming* has long been used in shamanic traditions to transport shamans out of their body and into other states of reality. Striking a drum four and a half times per second produces a constant, rhythmic drumming vibration, granting access to the subconscious by inducing a trance-like theta state (4-7 Hz) on the brainwave chart.

♪ *Gong Bathing* is the only instrument with sound waves more powerful than our own voice. (That's why affirmations and mantras work so well!) Water is not used, and clothes are not removed for gong bathing. Gong vibrations quickly put us in a deeply relaxed and meditative theta state. Their strong vibrations clear fears and emotional blocks, realign cells, and improve mental clarity. Ancient people believed that listening to gong sounds for ten days would cure one of anything. 🔔

♪ *Humming* (as well as chanting, singing, and laughing) has been shown to heal because of its low frequency vibrations. Humming lowers blood pressure, calms nerves, and produces the "love hormone," oxytocin. Humming activates a multitude of mouth meridians, stimulates the vagus nerve, and helps reduce stress and other chronic diseases. Humming the sound *mmm* draws us toward inner peace and away from our ego.

♪ *Isochronic* music balances the brain using intermittent single tone sound patterns. This stimulates the vagus nerve to reduce disease-forming inflammation. Wearing headphones and listening at low volume levels enhances isochronic music's effects of relaxation and enhanced sleep.

♪ *Music for the People* (MfP) is a type of sound therapy that utilizes singing between the client and the therapist. Based on the principle that our voice is how we express our deepest truths and feelings, opening this avenue of expression brings intuitive healing to our heart center.

♪ *Popular Music's* deep bass sounds take us back to our ancestral roots of drum rituals that thumped our heart to the core. The Grateful Dead uses low frequencies in their music to induce a state of euphoria, and any music that we personally love can have great health benefits by its ability to release the "happy hormone," dopamine.

♪ *Singing Bowls* create vibrations that carry a sense of calmness and slow the rhythms of the heart, breath, and brain. Each bowl produces a unique vibration that helps reduce stress, anger, depression, and fatigue and promotes healing. The bowls elicit a light dream state and activate the pineal gland to trigger the piezoelectric effect.

To use a singing bowl or tuning fork on ourselves, strike the bowl with the puja wand to create vibrations. Guide the puja from the Root Chakra at the bottom of the spine to the Crown Chakra at the top of the head. Wait until the vibration has completely stopped before moving to the next chakra. Healing happens as vibrations diminish and release into our body.

♪ *Solfeggio Frequencies* are based on a range of frequencies that open a divine channel of communication with our higher self. Interestingly, the solfeggio frequencies have a set of sacred numbers with a repeating sequence of 3, 6 and 9. Using the Pythagorean method of numeral reduction, adding the numbers in each solfeggio frequency until it becomes a single digit, results in a number that will always be a 3, 6, or 9. The solfeggio frequencies correlate with the musical scale we know from *The Sound of Music:* do, re, mi, fa, sol, and la and the frequencies of the chakras.

Do	Root	396 Hz	3 + 9 + 6 = 18	1 + 8 = **9**
Re	Sacral	417 Hz	4 + 1 + 7 = 12	1 + 2 = **3**
Mi	Solar Plexus	528 Hz	5 + 2 + 8 = 15	1 + 5 = **6**
Fa	Heart	639 Hz	6 + 3 + 9 = 18	1 + 8 = **9**
Sol	Throat	741 Hz	7 + 4 + 1 = 12	1 + 2 = **3**
La	Third Eye	852 Hz	8 + 5 + 2 = 15	1 + 5 = **6**

"If you only knew the magnificence of the 3, 6, and 9, then you would hold a key to the Universe."
— NIKOLA TESLA, Scientific Visionary

Tesla believed that the numbers 3, 6, and 9 held the key to the pathway to the divine and higher dimensions, symbolized by the Holy Trinity of mind, body, and spirit. Thus, the numerology of solfeggio frequencies suggests that they open our connection to Source and is the pattern that holds the fabric of life together, the ley line pattern of the matrix Although not indicated, zero represents the Tree of Life and zero-point energy. Three signifies the triangle of creation and our progression through life. Six is the unification of heaven and earth, and nine represents the completion of creation.

As well as opening a connection to the divine, solfeggio frequencies open blocked energy channels, helping to harmonize and balancing qi energy. The healing solfeggio scales connect to consciousness levels of the chakras and to the natural harmonic vibrations of the Universe:

- 174 Hz is the lowest frequency of the solfeggio scales and acts like an energetic anesthesia. It reduces pain and helps us feel safe, grounded, and secure.
- 285 Hz is beneficial in targeting blockages in the chakras and aura and is the frequency of choice for many energy healers.
- 396 Hz – Root Chakra (Mars) – is a low and smooth frequency that helps cleanse and release feelings of

guilt, trauma, and fear, and turns grief to joy.

- 417 Hz – Sacral Chakra (Mercury) is a frequency that relieves stress and tension, loosens tight muscles, and increases mobility.
- 528 Hz – Solar Plexus Chakra (Jupiter) – is a frequency of transformation and miracles. It helps with anxiety, pain, weight loss, repairs DNA, and helps rewire brain pathways.
- 639 Hz – Heart Chakra (Venus) – is the frequency of love, healing, and intimacy, and connects us to healthy relationships and the spiritual realms.
- 741 Hz – Throat Chakra (Saturn) – is a frequency that awakens expression and empowers us to speak our truth. It helps us generate ideas, find solutions, and increases our self-confidence.
- 852 Hz – Third Eye (Sun) – is a frequency that ignites intuition, improves clarity, and cuts through illusions. It connects us with dreams and astral projection.
- 963 Hz – Crown Chakra (Moon) – is a frequency that activates the pineal gland and is our connection to Universal Oneness, our higher self, spiritual channeling, and other dimensions.

The preferred frequency for sound healing is 432 Hz, not 440 Hz, the current musical standard, which some consider to be an abomination against nature. (Cross, 2018). The frequency of 432 Hz is mathematically consistent with the vibration of the Universe which vibrates with the Golden Ratio to unify light, time, space, DNA, and consciousness. Ratios of the Sun's, Earth's and Moon's diameters, the equinoxes, Stonehenge, pyramid measurements, the chakra system and visible light spectrum, and the sacred geometry of the Sri Yantra with its 43 interlocking triangles all show that the Universe's mathematically precise creation system is established on the Golden Mean of Fibonacci sequencing and a musical scale based on A = 432 Hz.

♪ *Toning* is repeating a single vowel sound or syllable on an exhale breath and directing the sound vibrations to body parts or chakras that need healing. As we vocalize the tones, our chakra centers become activated, helping to charge those areas with increased circulation, energy, and vitality. To activate the chakras with toning, start with the lower Root Chakra and work our way up, harmonizing our voice to balance their energy.

Root Chakra – *Uh* as in cup
Sacral Chakra – *Oo* as in you
Solar Plexus Chakra – *Oh* as in go
Heart Chakra – *Ah* as in saw
Throat Chakra – *Eye* as in my
Third Eye Chakra – *Aa* as in may
Crown Chakra – *Ee* as in me

After taking a slow, deep breath in, slowly vocalize the toning sound while breathing out. This can be done up to five minutes per chakra. To enhance healing, pair toning with gongs or singing bowls.

♪ *Tingsha Bells* are purifying bells used in meditation, yoga, and Feng Shui. Two cymbals are struck together to form a high-pitched tone. Vibrations from the toning sounds clear auras and fill the empty space of air with free-flowing qi energy.

♪ *Tuning Forks* are calibrated forks that can be held to specific parts of the body to send vibrations that release tension and open blocked energy channels. Although tuning forks are typically used to tune other instruments, they have healing powers of their own. Tuning forks induce relaxation quicker than meditation.

Music has healed where other therapies have failed. Sound shifts the low-vibrating energies of grief and depression and upgrades them to the higher vibrations of acceptance and happiness. YouTube has sound healing frequencies and music with differing healing intentions to choose from, and experimenting with all kinds of frequencies will help us decide which ones resonate best with us. Just as the shapes of sound show cymatic patterns inherent of the shapes of sacred geometry, the next chapter shows that within the memory of water, geometric crystals form when we infuse water with intention.

CHAPTER 13

The Fourth Phase of Water

"Water has a memory and carries within it our thoughts and prayers. As you yourself are water, no matter where you are, your prayers will be carried to the rest of the world. — DR. MASARU EMOTO

Virtually all of us were taught in elementary school that there are three phases of water: liquid, gas, and solid. However, a fourth phase of water has been discovered, known as Exclusion Zone, or EZ water. EZ water is found abundantly in auras, body cells, and tissues, and has an atomic structure different from regular water, changing from H_2O to H_3O_2. This more structured water has a hexagonal shape with a gel-like viscosity that naturally makes this biological water more crystalline than liquid with the unique property of being able to record and store information.

As a calming energy, water can be used for clearing, programming, and healing. Water molecules have memory that act as a catalyst for physical change. After water has been programmed through intentions of thoughts, words, desires, music, or light, its molecules form amazing, or not so much so, crystalline structures.

When water is infused with positive intentions and then frozen, the crystals form perfect shapes reminiscent of sacred geometry. However, when negative intentions are infused into water, the shapes become unpleasant, unsymmetrical, and haphazard. (See insert of Dr. Emoto's work.) This implies that because thoughts and emotions are held as memories within the molecular structure of water, and humans are mostly water, that whatever we're thinking or feeling will be stored within the cells of our body. Then, most literally, we are what we think. Our bodies are made from cells that store our thoughts in its biological water. Thus, water (and food) enables us to change our body physically and emotionally by its ability to hold the intention of our thoughts in cells' biological EZ water.

Healing Water Therapies

● *Cold Water Showers* relieve stress and depression and decrease the stress hormone cortisol. Cold water increases blood flow to the organs helping with circulation and overall health. To get cold water benefits, try blasting cold water for a couple minutes in the shower and finish with warm water to help dissolve and clear negative energy.

⬥ *Epsom Salt Baths* have properties that relieve stress, calm the mind, and relax the body. The salts are easily absorbed by the skin to help from discomfort from ailments such as pain, inflammation, stress, gout, muscle cramps, migraines, and bad moods. Soaking in the salts makes insulin more effective, relieves constipation, flushes toxins, and helps with nerve functioning, blood clots, and hardening of the arteries.

⬥ *Exclusion Zone or EZ Water* is the fourth phase of water found within the body's cells and tissues. Like a charged battery, it produces and stores energy. When we are at optimal health, cells' EZ water has a negative charge of 70. Diseased cells lack EZ water and have a -10 charge. We can intentionally lower the pH and change the structure of our cell's biological water to improve our health. Here are some ways to incorporate EZ water in to the body:
- get more sunlight
- try red light (infrared) therapy
- take saunas and ice baths
- drink more water (it converts in the body)
- drink EZ water (possibly sold in markets, spring water is the next closest thing)
- incorporate turmeric, holy basil, and ghee (clarified butter) into our diets

- connect by grounding to similarly charged Earth electrons
- use intention to turn regular water into EZ water
- use structured water devices
- drink vortexed water
- try plant juicing

💧 *Alkaline/Ionized/Oxygenated Water* uses electrolysis to create higher pH antioxidant water. Alkalinized water has anti-aging properties, helps with weight loss and detoxification, increases hydration, restores normal cell functions, and neutralizes acids from a poor diet. Alkaline water is also known as micro water, light water, miracle water, and micro-clustered water. Water ionizer machines are available to ionize tap water.

💧 *Cooking with Healing Water* cleanses and heals those who consume it. Expressing gratitude and prayer while cooking transmits the positive energies and intentions into the food. This can also be done before consuming any meal.

💧 *Gold-Treated Water* is an Ayurvedic practice for building a healthy immune system. Gold releases positive ions, purifies, and makes water lighter, helping to aid memory and fight disease. Boil a 24-carat gold chain in water before drinking this life-protection therapy.

💧 *Healing Showers* help take the weight of the world off our shoulders. While showering, wash away negativity by stating aloud, "This shower will wash away anything not serving me," or sing a jingle "I'm going to wash my pain straight down the drain." Then imagine pure, white light cleansing our body with healing intentions.

● *Hydrotherapy* uses water to heal through various means such as saunas, hot tubs, spas, showers, steam baths, ice baths, soaking in water, or water recreation activities like surfing. Listening to flowing water also has a calming and healing effect on the body. Hydrotherapy improves acne, arthritis, asthma, back problems, colds, constipation, coughs, cramps, digestive problems, the flu, food poisoning, headaches, infections, insomnia, nervousness, poison oak, sinuses, sore throats, as well as chronic fatigue, diabetes, heart problems, and high blood pressure.

THE POWER OF WATER.
Photo Credit @ tsapatakis_a

● *Intentional Water* is regular water that has been molecularly changed through the energy of conscious intention. Because water holds memory, healing occurs after drinking water with good thoughts directed towards it.

● *Music's Effects on Water* demonstrate that certain types of music, like classical, generate beautiful crystal patterns, and other

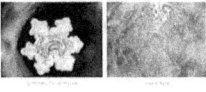

Image Courtesy of www. thewellnessenterprise.com

music, like heavy metal, makes ugly, blurry, and distorted images. Just like thoughts, words, and intentions affect and change our DNA, music also has the ability to upgrade or downgrade consciousness through the medium of water. Listening to water sounds is also a great way to ground and reconnect.

> Always say "I love you" and "Thank you" to your water and food before drinking or eating. The vibrational frequency generated from your voice box interacts with the molecular structure of the water, resulting in stronger hydration and a subtle raise in consciousness.

💧 *Programming Water, Food, & Objects* require focusing specific thoughts and energy into the water. (This can also be done with crystals.) Begin by touching, holding, or thinking about the object. Think about our intention for the water or object. Visualize and experience how it would feel when this object serves its purpose. For example:

Pour a cup of water and hold it between our hands. Visualize the intention of what we would like to happen in our life. Imagine or simply feel our intention being transferred into each atom of water. When it feels like the intention has taken hold, take a deep breath and a sip of the water. Allow ourselves to feel the message of the intention being carried into every cell in our body. Then, when we're ready, take a second sip and repeat the process until the water is gone.

Since water is programmable, infuse this homemade "Elation Spray" with good intentions like faith, hope, compassion, love, and laughter. This spray is great when our aura feels heavy, sluggish, or when the energy of a place seems depressing. It can be liberally sprayed to lighten the mood and clear negative energies and makes a nice gift.

Elation Spray ☺

1 glass spray bottle
¼ cup water
1½ tablespoons witch hazel
13 drops rose oil
13 drops hyssop or geranium oil
1 piece of rose quartz or seashell
Optional: a few rose petals or flower blossom
Recipe Courtesy of Eliza Swann, author of Auras.

We can also program water with words or an affirmation before bed and allow the intention to sit overnight.

Write an affirmation on a piece of paper and wrap it around a glass water bottle before going to sleep. When setting the intention, envision a healing light in the water. When we wake up, repeat the affirmation written on the paper out loud, and as we drink the water, feel the vibration of our affirmation penetrate every cell in our body.

UMH Structured Water Devices

- *The Aqua Energizer*™ is made from quartz crystals that reshape water to a biological state. When regular H_2O water flows through its specialized system of geometric patterns, it reenergizes and transforms the water into a healing state of H_3O_2.

- *Reverse Osmosis or Activated Alumina (AAL)* are useful water purification devices for removing toxins like fluoride from water.
- *The VitaJuwel* is a handcrafted drinking bottle that uses crystals for different healing and wellness intentions.

UMH water structuring devices resonate at high frequencies to raise the vibration of water. (See insert of crystalline changes in tap water using UMH).

Just like people are activated by the energy of light and sound, water functions in the same manner. It transforms our cells and DNA through the energy of our intentions; thus, water creates us and changes us. As we begin to understand water and its healing properties, we understand that its sacred creation brings life, love, and consciousness to our being.

"Learning about water is like an exploration to discover how the cosmos works, and the crystals revealed through water are like the portal into another dimension." — DR. MASARU EMOTO

Lastly, it is worth mentioning that because we haven't been able to create water on Earth, its existence may have come from the terraforming of Earth by outer space intelligence. It is well established that there can be no life without water, and that water is a necessary source for life. Water's conscious intelligence suggests that it was not created on Earth since it's never been able to be chemically created. If water came from outer space, then logic suggests that humans could have been created from outer space also.

CHAPTER 14

Other Energy Healing Techniques

"Time does not heal all wounds; it just gives them space to sink into the subconscious, where they will continue to impact your emotions and behavior. What heals is going inward, loving yourself, accepting yourself, listening to your needs, addressing your attachments and emotional history, learning how to let go, and following your intuition." — YUNG PUEBLO

The following are, again, alphabetical, and meant to be alternative energy healing therapies that, ideally, we can do on ourselves, but some do require a licensed practitioner.

Acupressure is a less invasive form of acupuncture that we can do ourselves. Firm but gentle pressure helps fatigue, insomnia, headaches, menstrual cramps, motion sickness, muscle tension, nausea, and vomiting.

☞ Massaging the tips of the shoulders in a circular motion with the thumbs releases tension and anger.

☞ To activate the leg area, sit in a chair with feet firmly on the ground. Lightly bang with our fist on both legs for 30 seconds; repeat 3-4 times. This strengthens immunity, increases energy, and provides grounding.

☞ Stimulating the center of the chest helps relieve anxiety and stress and gives a burst of energy. Activating this region with gentle pounding is known as the "Thymus Thump."

☞ Pressing about 1½ inches below the center of the wrist reduces stress, nausea, and regulates energy. Press this area for 10-15 seconds with the thumb and then slowly release; repeat 4-5 times.

Pressing between the webbing of the first and second toes relieves stress and improves circulation, as it controls qi throughout the entire body. Massage this point in a downward motion for 30 seconds, repeating 3-4 times.

The webbing between our thumb and index finger strengthens immunity, releases toxins, and improves circulation. Massage this area in a circular motion for 30 seconds; repeat 3-4 times.

The third eye area connects with the pineal gland to calm the body and reduce stress. Rapidly tap this area with a fingertip for 60 seconds to activate.

☞ The top of the ear relieves pain, relaxes the body, and calms the mind. Gently squeeze the front and back of both ears in a circular motion for 30 seconds; repeat 2-3 times.

☞ **Acupuncture** removes blockages and increases the flow of qi using thin needles inserted at various meridian points on the skin.

Auriculotherapy aka "Ear Acupuncture" inserts needles in the acupuncture points of the ear. To accurately insert needles in the ear requires a specialist, however relief can still be achieved by placing firm but gentle pressure on tender regions of the ear to relieve discomfort. Magnetic balls and ears seeds can be purchased and are used as self-ear acupuncture. Ear acupuncture helps with pain, insomnia, depression, anxiety, stress, and migraines.

Autophagy occurs about eighteen hours to four days after food fasting; the process of autophagy removes damaged cells and regenerates healthier cells. Autophagy has many health benefits such as protection from cancers, Alzheimer's, and it may reverse the effects of aging. Besides fasting, autophagy can also be induced through a 10-40% calorie restriction, exercise, and consuming foods that contain polyphenols such as red wine, green tea, nuts, berries, soybeans, apples, and turmeric.

Ayurvedic Medicine focuses on nutrition, lifestyle changes, and herbal medicine for whole-body healing. Ayurvedic philosophy maintains that people are made up of five elements: air, earth, ether (space), fire, and water, and that a combination of these elements manifest as energy in the body known as doshas. The doshas manage our physical, mental, and emotional health. Many believe Ayurveda to be the optimal method for maintaining health because it addresses the root cause of illness.

- *Vata* dosha is a combination of air and ether. People with vata dosha are slim, energetic, creative, and are easily affected by people, food, and weather. According to Ayurveda, vata dosha traits should meditate, eat warm foods, and avoid cold weather. Autumn is the season for vata dosha people.
- *Kapha* dosha is a combination of earth and water. People with kapha dosha are strong, thick-boned, slow and deliberate in their actions, and prone to weight gain. They are caring, trusting, and supportive. Those with kapha characteristics should focus on regular exercise, eating a healthy diet, and keeping a regular sleep routine. Spring is kapha's season.
- *Pitta* dosha is a combination of fire and water. Those with pitta dosha are muscular, athletic, and competitive. They are highly motivated, goal-oriented, and make great leaders, but tend to be aggressive. Those who are pitta dominant should focus on work-life balance and avoid spicy foods and hot weather.

Biodynamic Craniosacral Therapy (BCT) is a type of touch therapy that manipulates cerebrospinal fluid (CSF) beneath the skull to restore and correct balance. The stronger the CSF pulse, or "breath of life," the healthier we are. The pulse occurs about 6-12 cycles per minute. If we are doing BCT to ourselves, try to "sense" the presence of blockages and pain

Image Courtesy of www.healing-journeys-energy.com

in the skull. Using the fingertips, direct CSF energy to a numbered chakra area as shown in the picture insert. The numbered areas in the picture correspond to chakras: 1) Root, 2) Sacral, 3) Solar Plexus, 4) Heart, 5) Throat, 6) Third Eye, and 7) Crown.

Bioenergetic Frequency Devices are smartphone-controlled wearable personal healing instruments that tune into the body's frequencies to boost and heal in the quantum field. The Healy instrument and Qi Gong Infrasonic Massager are two types of bioenergetic frequency devices; they realign the chakra centers and alleviate severe pain using low-frequency healing vibrations. The devices also work on plants, animals, and the environment.

Black Cumin Seed (also called kalonji and nigella sativa) is an antioxidant used as a preventative stroke supplement that also kills cancer cells, improves rheumatoid arthritis, high blood pressure, asthma, diabetes, cholesterol, indigestion, obesity, leukemia, and other chronic pain and inflammation disorders.

Body Scanning is a form of meditation that brings attention to the breath. This process teaches us to observe, not react, and be in the present moment. Through breath and meditation, body scanning helps us recognize areas of stagnant energy and helps us locate energetic cords of attachment that need to be cut.

To do a Body Scanning Meditation, begin by focusing our attention on our breath as it comes in and out of the nostrils. Once we begin to feel sensations in our nose, then move our attention to our head. Silently scan our whole body from the head to the toes and back again. Feel all the different sensations, whether they're little pains or pins and needles. The more we are able to focus, the more we're able to notice areas of density.

Bone Marrow Breathing is similar to body scanning, but bone marrow breathing focuses attention on different skeleton and bone parts. Vibrations in our bones hold memories from generations ago, and bone breathing takes us to the parts of our body where we store old pain.

When bones are cleared of heavy energy and qi energy is able to flow up through the spinal cord, it will literally straighten the spine. This technique can also draw energy into specific organs for healing.

To do a Bone Breathing Meditation, sit or lie down. Keep the fingers open, stretched, and relaxed. Take several deep breaths through the nose. Start with the intention to clear the bones of stagnant energy, heaviness, pain, or trauma. Imagine and feel subtle energy around us. Bring attention to the fingertips on the left hand. Feel the energy around us move through our skin and into our bones while continuing deep, rhythmic breathing. Visualize our bones as sponges, soaking up energy from all around, into the bones of our hands, our wrists, forearms, upper arms, and shoulders. Repeat this process with our right hand. Next, continue drawing in energy into all the bones in the chest region (scapulae, collarbone, sternum, and ribs). Then bring attention to our toes, moving energy upward through the feet, to the ankles, calves, knees, thighbones, pelvis, sacrum, spinal column vertebrae, and then our teeth and skull. Breathe energy into the body for at least nine full breaths. Finish by bringing all the energy into the navel center and visualize "closing" this area.

Image permission granted by SpiritualResearch Foundation.org

The Box Spiritual Healing Treatment has been created and developed by Paratpar Guru Dr. Athavale and published by the Spiritual Science Research Foundation. The Box Treatment is an effective healing remedy for clearing the aura and removing negative energies using empty cardboard boxes. The emptiness of the boxes creates a powerful void effect relating to the principle of absolute ether and zero-point energy. The void energy essentially creates a black hole that sucks negative energy and vibrations out of the aura to bring healing.

Brainwave Entrainment uses frequencies embedded in audio tracts to synchronize both hemispheres of the brain. The subliminal frequencies positively influence emotions, feelings, and energy levels. John Assaraf's

NeuroGym® program is an example of brainwave entrainment.

Breathwork is one of our body's strongest tools for self-healing. Deep breathing lowers blood pressure, reduces heart rate, decreases stress hormones, alkalinizes the blood, improves immunity, and increases physical and mental energy. Breathwork helps dissolve wounds and reveals and heals past traumas. Breathwork helps us let go of thought patterns that don't serve us anymore and brings us back to the present. Breathwork dissolves the ego and can get us to state of euphoria without drugs. Different breathwork techniques are given in Chapter 15. Using sound and breath together bring in more oxygen in the body, which is the key to healing. This is why meditation, breathwork, and healing go hand-in-hand.

Low Frequency Sounds + Breathwork = Healing Effect

Celestial Vedic Healing is a multi-dimensional and self-transformational energetic healing therapy that clears karma, entities, curses, blocks, and ancestral spirits using Vedic methods and formations of the planets. Prayers, ceremonies, divine assistance, and meditation are some modalities used to assist healing.

Chakra Emotional Blockage Release (CEBR) accesses the subconscious mind to clear blocked energy and trapped emotions in the chakra energy system.

Cognitive Behavioral Therapy (CBT) is changing our thinking and actions to help with anxiety and depression.

Self-therapy includes:
- Paying attention to what we're thinking.
- Realizing that our thoughts determine the way we feel and act.
- Determining if our thoughts and long-held beliefs are accurate.
- Replacing old beliefs and with more constructive ones.

Common CBT approaches include:
- Planning activities that bring joy and a sense of accomplishment.
- Understanding how positive actions positively impact our thoughts and emotions.
- Making the best use of our time.
- Breaking down large tasks into more manageable ones.
- Gradually facing our fears so they diminish.

Cord Cutting is a method for cutting energetic cords of attachments from others. Here's a cord-cutting technique to release others' co-dependent and toxic energies. While visualizing and mimicking the hand and arm gestures of cutting an actual cord, use a similar phrasing:

"I (insert name) release (insert their name) from my life. They no longer have access to me in any realm or form. I remove myself from them physically, emotionally, mentally, spiritually, and energetically. I forgive myself and them for past actions and free myself from this attachment. I am free from any toxicity; I am free."

Other Methods to Cut Cords
- *Archangel Michael*—relax and take a few deep breaths. Connect with Archangel Michael using symbols or simply calling him forth. Ask to cut off any etheric cords that drain our energy and no longer serve us.
- *Reiki*—do a body scan and locate any cords of attachment. Imagine the cords in front of us and the person who has hurt us. Ask for forgiveness, bless them, and imagine cutting the cords with imaginary scissors, or imagine pulling the cords out.
- *Crystal Wand*—use a wand cleansed with Reiki energy. Beginning with the Crown Chakra, imagine slowly sweeping the crystal wand towards each chakra and cutting the cord wherever it is attached. Do this three times. Then, with another or cleansed wand programmed with healing light, sweep the wand slowly down each chakra, filling each chakra with light.

- *Pendulum*—invoke angels, spirit guides, and universal energy to cut etheric cords draining our energy. The pendulum will spin in two different directions, one for cutting, and one for healing.
- *Higher-Self*—meditate to connect to our higher self and those with whom we wish to cut cords with. Ask for forgiveness for whether we have knowingly or unknowingly hurt them. Cut or pull the cords from our aura and imagine them pulling out their cords. Send violet light to heal them and ourselves.

Digital CBD is a vibrational technology that extracts energetically encoded files from the quantum field of CBD (cannabidiol) products. The information is encoded into a smart phone that amplifies its vibrations. Unlike other CBD products, digital CBD only needs to be purchased once. Like other CBD products, it helps with pain, anxiety, cancer, diabetes, nausea, seizures, neurological disorders, cardiovascular health, and other inflammatory diseases.

EESystem (Energy Enhancement System) treatment generates bioelectric and scalar wave energy fields. The enhanced energy fields improve immunity, stimulate cell regeneration, provide pain relief, improve mood, increase energy, release toxins, repair DNA, and balance the brain's hemispheres.

EFT (see Tapping)

Electroceuticals are tiny electrodes attached to nerve bundles that block the sensation of pain. Electroceuticals include pacemakers, cochlear or retinal implants, and spinal cord stimulators. Newer devices work by sending electric signals directly to the vagus nerve to treat a wide range of chronic diseases.

Energetic Repatterning Technique (ERT), aka Spinal Release Technique, reharmonizes our emotional reaction to things that trigger us, i.e., helps us get a new mindset. ERT coordinates breath and eye movements to restore energy and release trauma. Here's a self-ERT technique:

While focusing on our "issue," wrap both arms around ourselves and thump on our sides from the armpits to the hips, or have someone thump both sides of the spine while repeating a sequence of breath and eye movements:

1. *Take a deep breath and hold it in. Exhale and hold it out. Hyperventilate or "huff and puff" breathe. Then slowly breathe in; slowly breathe out.*
2. *Roll opened eyes around in one direction in a big circle. Then roll them around in the other direction. Roll closed eyes around in one direction, then in the other direction.*
3. *For each eye and breath movement, thump, or have the thumper move up or down the spine once.*

4. When the trauma has been released, replace, and install a new, preferred response to our trigger/issue. Ex. If we were abused, we can say that we feel safe now.

Eye Movement Desensitization and Reprocessing (EMDR) requires performing eye movements that distract, relax, and synchronize the brain's hemispheres to realign traumatic layers of energy while simultaneously recalling traumatic memories. EMDR simulates REM eye movements that help treat anxiety, grief, childhood trauma, depression, PTSD, anger, addiction, and stress. Although a skilled therapist is best to administer EMDR, there are devices we can use to do it to ourselves.

- Light Bars are visual EMDR devices that have horizontal LED lights that help guide side-to-side or up and down eye movements.

  Image Courtesy of www.emdrhealing.com
- Audio stimulation devices require headphones and software that play alternating sounds in each ear.
- Tactile stimulation uses small handheld devices called tappers that vibrate in alternating patterns to mimic tapping.

Faith is the strength and power of belief. The result of our intentions matches the amount of faith we give it. The healing of the Placebo Effect could be due to the strength of our faith and power of belief.

Group Therapy is several people sharing similar experiences of trauma, anxiety, or mental health issues. Sharing like issues in a group imparts a sense of camaraderie and comfort knowing that others suffer from the same thing. Listening to others' perspectives and to the therapist's coping techniques gives new ways to handle difficult situations.

"Heal Your Life" by Louise Hay is a therapeutic healing method that involves learning to love ourselves more by releasing negative emotions. Nutritional cleansing and psychotherapy are part of the process of bringing the body, mind, and spirit into harmony. The therapy also uses positive affirmations, visualization, chanting, inner child healing, and mirror work to achieve its healing effects.

Herbalism has a 5,000-year-old history of using therapeutic tinctures and compounds from botanical plants and herbs to energize qi and treat conditions within the body. A naturopathic doctor is the best administrator of herbal medicine, although herbalism as a hobby could be a fun endeavor.

Holographic Kinetics (HK) Therapy uses muscle testing to access previous past life timelines to remove limiting beliefs, anxiety, addictions, and ancestral trauma stored in the body. HK Therapy takes us on own inner journey by accessing cellular memory to clear and change events from the past.

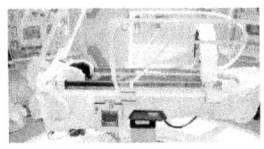
Image Courtesy of http://www.blissfulvisions.com/articles/med-beds.html

Holographic Medical Pod, aka the Med Bed, is a 3D anatomical life-saving scanning machine that works on the principles of energy medicine. The Med Bed uses tachyon (faster than light) particles and plasma energies to recalibrate DNA and RNA to increase the carbon to crystalline ratio in the body. Med Beds use a reatomization process that can grow back missing limbs, replace dying cells to slow the aging process, cure Stage 4 cancers, and make other diseases obsolete. This is currently alien technology that may be available to the public through certain outlets.

Homeopathy uses the philosophy of "like cures like" and the belief that a person can be cured by the substance that produces the symptoms of the disease. Homeopathic remedies use natural derivatives from plants, minerals, and animals for their therapeutic effect. Common homeopathic medicines include arnica, aloe, antimonium, borax, cadmium, calendula, comfrey, mercurius, belladonna, capsicum, goldenseal, mistletoe, St. John's wort, saw palmetto, pertussin, selenium, sulfur, thuja, tuberculinum, and witch hazel.

Ho'oponopono /ho-oh-pono-pono/ is a prayer and mantra known as the Hawaiian Code of Forgiveness that uses four simple phrases: I am sorry, please forgive me, thank you, and I love you. This phrase has healing power to forgive and release past pains.

Integrated Energy Healing is a wholistic approach to energy healing using principles from neuro-linguistic programming, cognitive behavioral therapy, acupuncture, and a combination of other complementary modalities to achieve healing.

Internal Family Systems (IFS) is a subset of psychotherapy that believes we are all made up of sub-personalities that protect our shadows. IFS is a type of talk-therapy that uses a 6F system of *Find, Focus, Flesh it Out, Feel, beFriend, and Fear* to integrate our mini personalities with our whole self. IFS treats depression, anxiety, panic, phobias, trauma, substance abuse, health conditions, and general well-being.

Kriyas is a yogic healing technique that combines six cleansing principles: 1) brain cell purification through intense breathing techniques; 2) Neti® nasal cleansing; 3) tear gland secretion; 4) abdominal toning; 5) intestinal cleaning; and 6) rectal cleaning.

LifeLine Healing uses symptoms of stress as a gateway to the subconscious. It releases emotional imbalances at the cellular level without bringing up past traumatic issues like shadow work requires. LifeLine rebalances energy fields to help addictions, anxiety, phobias, limiting beliefs, low self-esteem, insomnia, weight issues, and other physical ailments.

Light Codes are templates of light and sound from energy fields of the Sun's rays that promote healing in the body. The cosmic, light-encoded rays contain information that activate and reform dormant DNA strands and grant access to higher dimensions. Light codes are activated through sacred geometry, mudras, fire letters, sounds, tones, and frequencies.

Light Therapy (see Chapter 9) uses colored lights near infrared and ultraviolet frequencies to activate and heal the chakras and aura.

Listening is a powerful form of healing. When we feel ourselves being heard, we begin to heal. When we listen to others, they begin to heal. Listening is stepping outside of our ego to understand another's perspective without offering advice or passing judgment. Listening requires no words, just open ears and an open heart.

Magnets work to unblock trapped emotions. Because the aura is made of electromagnetic energy, running a magnet from the chin, over the head, and down the spine ten times helps rebalance the chakras.

Mantras are words, phrases, or vowel sounds chanted during meditation that help regulate the heart and release negative energy. Like an advertising jingle, chanting's rhythmic vibrations calm the mind, even if the meaning of the words is unknown. To unblock chakras, use the one-syllable 'seed' sound associated with each chakra starting with the Root: lam, vam, ram, yam, ham, om, and silence for the Crown Chakra. Practice each seed sound for about ten minutes each. We can create our own mantras depending on our needs, such as "I am worthy."

Marma Massage is an Ayurvedic massage that activates 108 energetic body points on the body. Stimulation of these points activates pathways to the mind, body, and soul.

Massage increases circulation, eliminates toxins, gets energy flowing, reduces anxiety, and improves sleep. Deep massage (myofascial) accesses meridian points that clear energy blocks and release past traumas. Massage can be done at home simply by pressing directly on tight areas or trigger points using small circular or kneading pushes and holding for about ten seconds.

Meditation is the number one tool for reaching the depths of the subconscious and improving our emotional health. Meditating helps remove fears by having us focus on the present. Meditation improves intuition, insight, self-awareness, and helps us become more empathetic. It improves our remote viewing skills (seeing beyond time and space) and helps us tune our 3D reality into a 5D reality. Meditation with breathwork is an effective tool for healing our body, chakras, aura, and DNA.

Meridian Stretching, or resistance stretching, is accomplished by squeezing muscles while simultaneously stretching them. It's a push-and-pull effect at the same time: stretching and holding a muscle in one direction while providing counter resistance at the same time in the opposite direction. Resistance bands are often used for meridian stretching which helps remove kinks (trauma) from dense fascia, the fibers of light channels connecting qi energy from meridians to chakras to organs.

Meridian Therapy is a form of acupuncture that doesn't use needles; it redirects qi energy to areas that need it through one of twelve meridians using low doses of electricity or lasers.

◯◉**Mirror Work** is a self-love practice developed by Louise Hay that uses mirrors to reflect affirmations back to ourselves helping us become less critical and develop self-confidence and self-esteem.

Mudras are hand positions or gestures used during meditation that channel our body's energy flow to areas that need healing. The hands have 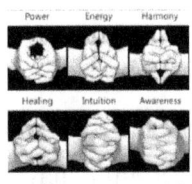 thousands of nerve endings and chakra points; mudra positions stimulate receptors to support healing. Mudras are the physical representation of spoken mantras. In many parts of the world, mudras are used to cure sickness in place of pharmaceutical drugs.

Myofascial Release uses foam rollers to apply pressure along meridians and muscle groups to remove tension, tightness, knots, trauma, and blocked energy stored in muscle fascia.

Neoshamanism is a doctor-led program that uses Shamanic approaches (fasting, plant medicine, and meditation), combined with energy medicine (light and oxygen therapy) to release trauma and attachments held in the energetic body of the aura where emotions are remembered and stored.

Neurolinguistic Programming (NLP) is a method for reframing our language to manifest new and better behaviors. This therapy often uses hypnosis to achieve change. We can try NLP on ourselves by being consciously aware of what we say. If we say something negative, we can immediately rephrase the words into something better.

Neuroscience uses behavior modification techniques and tools such as biofeedback, cognitive priming, reprogramming, brainwave entrainment, success meditation, subliminal programming, and positive and negative reinforcement to help induce or extinguish certain behaviors and belief programs.

> Your brain constantly rewires itself to suit the information that you feed it. If you constantly complain, gossip, find excuses, etc., it will make it much easier to find things to be upset about, regardless of what is happening around you. Likewise, if you constantly search for opportunities, abundance, love, and things to be grateful for, it will make it much easier to find a reflection of those things around you. With practice, this is a powerful way to reshape your reality.

Nootropics, aka as "smart drugs" and "cognitive enhancers," encompass a wide range of supplemental drugs that improve brain function, promote relaxation, increase concentration and creativity, and boost mood, memory, and motivation. Common nootropics include creatine, Panax ginseng, ginkgo biloba, nicotine patches, lion's mane, l-tyrosine, piracetam, caffeine, phenotropil, and Noopept.

Nyas is a self-healing technique that combines chanting while focusing energy through our fingertips. Through directed thought and mudra hand movements, energy is dispersed to a chakra center and to the organs associated with that chakra center.

Pet Therapy lowers stress, blood pressure, and heart rate, besides providing emotional and social support when pets become our best friend. Pets activate the "love hormone" oxytocin and the "happy hormone" dopamine. Caring for pets encourages a daily ritual which improves mental health and longevity.

Plants induce feelings of calmness, relaxation, and help reduce anxiety through their use of color and connection with being close to nature.

🌱 *Flower Essence Therapy* uses the energetic imprints of a plant's flowering essence to evoke specific qualities within us. Just as inspirational music carries its meaning through sound, flower essences work through the medium of water.

🌱 *Green Plants* clean the air, boost our home's aesthetics, and help create a sense of well-being.

> ❀ *Aloe vera* helps burns, scars, and cuts, and serves as a reminder to break toxic ties.

- ❀ *Dracaena* absorbs toxins from household cleaners.
- ❀ *Ficus* cleanses odors and provides extra oxygen.
- ❀ *Jade* absorbs toxins from paints.
- ❀ *Lavender* is an antiseptic, anti-inflammatory, and an aromatic bug deterrent, and helps us relax and stay calm.
- ❀ *Peace lilies* neutralize electromagnetic radiation and symbolize a harmonious work-life balance.
- ❀ *Snake plants* sanitize and cleanse air. Its strong durability reminds us of our own resilience.

🌱 *Plant Medicine* uses herbs and botanicals for mind/spirit healing and to clear energy. They can be grown around the home, burned, added to cooking, baths, and cleaning solutions, or used for creating sacred geometry images to meditate upon.

- ❀ *Anise* aids in divination and psychic powers, and is used for ceremonial rituals.
- ❀ *Basil* attracts prosperity.
- ❀ *Cayenne* is used for cleansing and purification rituals.
- ❀ *Cinnamon* brings prosperity, purifies, and boosts metabolism.
- ❀ *Clove* brings protection and helps with manifestation.
- ❀ *Cumin* is protective, healing, and connects us with creative energies.
- ❀ *Dandelion* facilitates communication with souls in the Afterlife.

- *Gotu Kola* expands awareness and perception of the third eye.
- *Eyebright* brings mental clarity and enhances both eye and psychic vision.
- *Galangal Root* facilitates astral projection and spirit guide connections.
- *Frankincense* purifies and is a ceremonial botanical.
- *Lavender* brings peace, calmness, and a sense of well-being.
- *Marshmallow* enhances clairvoyance.
- *Mint* is for luck, wealth, and mojitos.
- *Myrrh* invites angelic energies.
- *Palo Santo* clears and cleanses energies.
- *Paprika* is grounding and helps remove clients' negative energies from healers.
- *Peppercorns* bring protection, grounding, and courage.
- *Rosemary* clears stuck energy and entities.
- *Turmeric* is a powerful antioxidant and useful for decalcifying the pineal gland and increasing cellular EZ water.

Smudging is burning sage, incense, or other herbs to clear energy, auras, and the environment. Smudging helps kill airborne viruses, grounds vibrations, and generates negative ions that reduce stress and tension.

> Meditate with plants. Every species of plant has a certain resonant frequency. Roses have one of the highest, measuring at 320 MHz. When we meditate in proximity with plants with high frequencies, it can increase our thought patterns and frequency to entrain with the higher frequencies of plants.

Polarity Therapy is a type of touch therapy that transmits and manipulates energy using opposing locations with the hands. It combines diet, exercise, counseling, and self-awareness to help with fatigue, stress, anxiety, depression, osteoarthritis, pain, fibromyalgia, and other conditions.

Pranic Healing is a no-touch healing that directs qi/prana (pranic) energy from the therapist to cleanse, restore, energize, and balance the aura and chakras. Pranic Psychotherapy helps with psychological issues by using the technique of Prana Color Healing and Pranic Crystal Healing to focus prana energy.

Prayer is a form of meditation that accesses the inner self for guidance and wisdom. Prayer can induce a mild trance state through its repetition of sounds and words, which is the key to its healing effect. Prayer comes from the heart, so within its healing words are feelings of love and compassion. Mechanisms for prayer's healing effects include the placebo response, divine intervention, faith, its ritualistic nature, and quantum entanglement.

Psi Energy Balls are used for sending and giving unconditional love and healing energy to ourselves and others. Psi balls also remove energy blocks, dark energy, and negative energy.

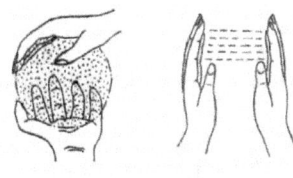

Image Courtesy of "Miracles through Pranic Healing" by Grand Master Choa Kok Sui

To make an energy ball: rub the hands together until they feel warm. Separate the hands 6-12 inches and move them like a ball is in the middle of them. Using positive words and feeling heartfelt emotions, state aloud the intent and send the energy to its destination.

Psychedelic Therapy (Entheogens) uses plant medicines, considered to be mind-expanding, drug-inducing ways to reach higher consciousness. Entheogens help reveal the root cause of limiting beliefs, bad habits, and negative programming. Long-term effects include increased clarity and intelligence, better memory, psychic, manifestation, and visualization abilities, and more youthful energy. Many entheogens treat and *reverse* anxiety, Alzheimer's, depression, ADHD, PTSD, and drug addictions with no withdrawal symptoms. Iboga has been described as "ten years of psychotherapy in one night," with the ability to completely rebalance the chakras for profound healing. Those who have used ayahuasca often make life-altering changes afterwards such as ditching bad relationships, starting new careers, and following the instincts of their heart.

Different Types of Entheogens

- *Ayahuasca/DMT* restructures repressed memories to relieve trauma.
- *Cannabis* is anti-inflammatory, anti-anxiety, and mood enhancing.
- *Hapé* is an herbal snuff causing increased awareness and psychological and spiritual healing.
- *Ibogaine/Iboga* is a Shamanic plant with psychological and physical healing properties; it opens the third eye.
- *Ketamine* or "Special K" causes detachment and separation from the body.
- *LSD* is a psychedelic that helps anxiety, depression, and dependency.
- *MDMA* or "ecstasy" reduces anxiety associated with trauma.
- *Peyote/Mescaline* or "cactus tea" causes hallucinations and spiritual insight.
- *Psilocybin* or "magic mushrooms" relieves depression, OCD, anxiety, and other mental issues.
- *Sananga* eye drops enhance spiritual awareness.

Psychorientology is also known as the Jose Silva Method, a combination of meditation and mind control that uses alpha brainwave frequencies to access the subconscious consciously.

Pulsed Electromagnetic Therapy (PEMF) is a type of magnetotherapy that sends magnetic energy waves from 6-75 Hz helping with pain, circulation, bone healing, and muscle functioning, inflammation, and stress.

Quantum Apometry uses mental projection of the therapist, mandalas, and symbols to access different dimensions of the body to find root causes of pain, trauma, and release ancestral memories.

Quantum Healing Hypnosis Technique (QHHT)®, or past-life regression, is a method developed by Dolores Cannon to access past lives using somnambulistic (deepest stage) hypnosis. QHHT® explores lives of our past to release pain and trauma of this lifetime. QHHT® connects with the higher self and aspects of the soul for transformative healing.

Quantum Neuro Reset Therapy (QNRT™) resets the brain's emotional response to trauma and stress by identifying triggers and changing the neurological response. QNRT™ uses chiropractic adjustments and cold laser therapy to readjust nerve signaling of the spine to reduce pain in joints and improve range of movement.

Radiant Circuits is an energy system along the central meridian pathway that helps trigger intuition by moving energy ourselves. Here are three DIY's:

1. *"The Belt Flow"* grounds and balances hormones. Rub the hands together, then shake them off, move hands from the center and across the stomach and down the legs. Another version for low back pain is to rub hands together, shake them off, put thumbs in

the center of the back, and then move hands forward to the front of the body in a swooping motion.
2. *"The Zip Up"* helps to strengthen the aura/biofield and personal power. Starting near the knees, do a "zip-up" motion with the hands while looking up the central meridian channel with the eyes and then release negative energy out from the head while stating an affirmation.
3. *"The Triple Warmer Smoothie"* reprograms and balances energy in the immune system and helps us snap out of bad moods. To begin, rub the hands together, and then shake them off. While breathing in, put the hands over the eyes and move them outward to the temples while breathing out. Then, move the hands around the ears, squeeze the shoulders, move toward the vagus nerve in the neck and finish by covering the Heart Chakra with the hands.

Radical Healing teaches those healing from racism and ethnic trauma how to change their emotional response to the trauma. It involves addressing root causes and becoming whole by practicing resilience and wellbeing. Healing happens when those oppressed gain consciousness by acknowledging their pain while fostering actions of justice.

Here are ways to cultivate Radical Healing:
- Develop pride in your ethnic group and culture.
- Share your story and listen to storytelling traditions.

- Join a collective action group to create change.
- Believe that your ancestors' contributions are a testament that things will be better in the future.

Practice self-care to benefit you, your community, and your cause.

Radionic Therapy uses electromagnetic devices to detect abnormal vibrations of the aura and the application of a counter, harmonizing frequency to bring health benefits. Some radionics healing is practiced through distance healing using intuitive capacities. Rife machines, pendulum dowsing, and accessing Akashic records are also forms of radionic therapy.

Rapid Transformational Therapy® (RTT) uses a combination of modalities from hypnosis, hypnotherapy, cognitive behavioral therapy, psychotherapy, and neurolinguistic programming (NLP) to access the subconscious mind to find disease-causing roots and remove energetic blocks.

RASHA is a scalar-plasma-energy system that reprograms DNA, detoxes and cleanses blood cells, and completely harmonizes the body. RASHA uses scalar waves, brain hemisphere synchronization, chakra realignment, and base-12 Fibonacci frequency matching to positively affect health. The RASHA energy device increases energy, reduces pain and stress, clears negative patterns, relieves anxiety, helps with PTSD, stroke, opioid addiction, depression, suicidal thoughts, Lyme

Disease, emotional traumas, cardiovascular disease, autism, and other body conditions.

Reconnective Healing™ defines itself as a comprehensive spectrum of healing composed of energy, light, and information. It works similar to reiki in that no touch with the hands is involved while interacting with the biofield (aura). Therapists' healings are usually immediate and permanent.

Reflexology, aka Zone Therapy, is a self-massage therapy done by applying pressure to the feet, hands, ears, face, or head using hand techniques such as pressing, kneading, twisting, pinching, pushing, rubbing, and jabbing. Cotton swabs can be used to apply pressure to smaller areas. Painful areas indicate stagnant energy that needs to be released.

Reiki /ray kee/ is no-touch energy healing with the palms. The hands have minor chakras that act as portals for energy and healing. The Source of reiki energy comes the empty vacuum in Space known as the zero-point field.

To Activate Our Hands' Chakras
1. Visualize white light healing energy entering though our head.
2. Channel that light down our arms and into our hands.
3. Bring our attention to our hands—they may feel warm or tingly.

4. Visualize healing balls of energy forming between our hands.
5. Cover the area to be healed with our hands.
6. Gently push the white light energy out of our hands and over the area to be healed.

Self-Hypnosis helps induce a trance state using self-talk and visual imagery to access the subconscious to "think away our sickness." Through relaxation and focused concentration, we can get to an unconscious state to reprogram our minds to adopt new and overcome unwanted beliefs, fears, habits, and illnesses. While counting, visualize "seeing" ourselves going deeper and deeper into trance.

Here's an example relaxation script used to induce a state of self-hypnosis:

❀ *Sit comfortably in a chair and fix our eyes on a point on the ceiling.*

❀ *Repeat a mantra such as "As I visualize, I sleep deeper" while visualizing ourselves performing our intended purpose.*

❀ *Breathe slowly and deeply. Mentally repeat "sleep" on each inhale until we feel drowsy.*

❀ *Suggest to ourselves to close our eyes.*

❀ *Deepen the hypnotic state by repeating a few times, "I will be more relaxed on the count of three."*

❀ *"One, getting more relaxed...two, deeper relaxation... three, total relaxation and in a hypnotic state."*

Like learning any other skill, it takes time to self-hypnotize. With practice, the counting method can program ourselves to do other things, such as:

- ❀ *"On the count of ten, I will be more loving to my family and friends."*
- ❀ *"On the count of ten, I will forgive my colleague completely."*
- ❀ *"On the count of ten, I will no longer have a headache."*

Following the same script helps with focus and quicker ability to fall into trance. With practice, the trance state can occur within seconds. If we find it difficult to get into the trance state, we can lengthen the "sleep deeper" phase and increase the counts for each suggestion.

Seraphim Blueprint Energy Work once existed in the days of Atlantis and is now channeled through intuitive angelic connections. Different modalities are used to create healing, including kundalini reiki, angel and integrated energies, and crystal and essential oil therapies.

Shadow Work is working with our subconscious mind to release past trauma or karma. Inner shadows are the dark, emotional parts of us that are often from negative and buried childhood experiences but can also be inherited from ancestors. The core of shadow work is recognizing and uncovering the parts of ourselves that we keep hidden because of shame or embarrassment. Once we acknowledge our shadows, we can learn to live with them or set them free. Remember, it's our light that casts the shadow, and it's our light can free the shadow. Just like a proton, shadows disappear when we look at them.

> *"I am not what happened to me.
> I am what I choose to become."* — CARL JUNG

Here is a mantra to be used during meditation or EFT (tapping) to help release inner shadows and trauma: *As I dig deep into my own darkness, I shine light on all the parts of myself that have been wounded, traumatized, neglected, shamed, and shunned. With all the pain, sadness, anger, and grief that I have endured, I now release it.*

Ignoring our shadows can cause poor self-esteem, anxiety, depression, self-sabotage, or bad relationships with others. Embracing, loving, and accepting our shadows brings self-acceptance and self-understanding. When we understand the wisdom that knowing our shadow imparts, it gives us a reason to look inside. Shadows no longer have power over us when we know the underlying cause.

> *"Don't cover the cracks."* — RUMI

Although trained therapists are available to help with shadow work, here are some guidelines for uncovering shadows:

- Start by paying attention to how we think, feel, and react when we interact with others. • Notice any repeating habits, triggers, and patterns that cause us to yell, retreat, act like a child, or retaliate. • Emotions that we were punished for having as a child often get repressed and turn into shadows. • Use self-observation, meditation, or have a conversation with our shadow to learn about what triggers us.

When another's actions cause us to get upset, it's a part of our shadow, projecting a part of ourselves that we haven't made peace with yet. Triggers are a shout-out from our shadow that it wants to be heard and are an invitation for us to listen, accept, and allow any emotions to come up without being judgmental. When negative feelings come up about the way another person acts, ask ourselves what part of *us* displays or hides the same emotions?

Understanding our shadows is the only way to live authentically and accept ourselves for who we truly are. Here are introspective questions we can ask ourselves if we feel our shadows are getting in the way of our happiness:

How would someone describe me to someone else? What are the worst traits someone could have? When did I start to demonstrate these traits? What makes me judgmental towards others? What memories am I ashamed of? Who do I envy? What frightens me the most? What emotions bring out the worst in me?

Why do I think this happens? When was the last time I engaged in self-sabotaging behavior? How was I feeling at that time? What are some things I wished people knew about me? What are some lies I've told myself? What is my worst memory from childhood? What are my parents' best character traits? Their worst? What makes me insecure? What makes me feel unsafe? Who do I have a grudge against and why am I not letting it go? Who has let me down? What makes me feel the most valued? What is another trait I see in others that I wish I had? Why don't I have this trait? When in my life have I been the hardest on myself? Why? What do I consider failure? How does failure make me feel? Am I afraid of failure? What am I afraid of? What do I enjoy doing? What do I do when I'm bored? What negative emotions do I try to avoid? Why?

To truly answer these questions may bring up a lot of painful emotions and memories. However, shadows long to be expressed so our inner light can shine free. We can express and let go of some of these emotions by keeping a journal, or through any type of creative art, like painting, sculpting, singing, etc. Mirror work and practicing affirmations such as "I trust and believe in me," "I am worthy of love," or "I have a lot to offer and deserve to be happy" are also helpful.

Our light casts the shadow that can free the shadow.

Shamanism is the practice of altering consciousness through channeled energy, combined with psychedelic drugs, fasting, and music or rituals, to induce trance and enter spiritual dimensions, often with healing intent.

> "In many shamanic societies, if you came to a medicine person complaining of being disheartened, dispirited, or depressed, they would ask one of four questions: When did you stop dancing? When did you stop singing? When did you stop being enchanted by stories? When did you stop finding comfort in the sweet territory of silence?"
> —Gabrielle Roth

Superconscious Recoding uses the brain's capacity for neuroplasticity to reconsolidate and rewire long-term memories stored in cells and DNA. Superconscious recoding accesses the deeper subconscious mind to neutralize and dissolve limiting beliefs, fears, and self-sabotaging behaviors without having to recall and share traumatic memories.

Tapping (EFT-Emotional Freedom Technique) rewires and releases trauma from the subconscious by deliberately having us think of traumatic memories while tapping on certain meridian points. Tapping helps us recognize our mind's stories and false beliefs, decreases the stress hormone cortisol, and increases our immunity to disease. It's being our own personal acupuncturist—

we can instantly change and restore our body's energy by finger tapping on different pressure points. Tapping helps pain, allergies, colds, anxiety, depression, phobias, cravings, and increases happiness levels.

To do tapping on ourselves, first identify the issue we would like to address. Using the fingertips, or small fist, tap firmly 5-7 times per point while repeating a phrase such as, "Although I have felt neglected and abandoned in the past, I now feel complete love and acceptance," or "Even though I am scared, I deeply and completely accept myself." Tap in a rotating sequence on the tapping points for about two minutes, increasing the number of times per day for more chronic conditions.

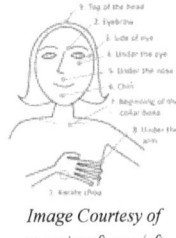

Image Courtesy of www.joyeft.com/eft

Therapeutic Touch (TT) is administered by a practitioner in a manner similar to reiki, but in TT, the hands are gently placed on the body or moved gently in the aura's energy field to deliver healing intent.

The Thymus Thump aka "The Happiness Point" and the "Fountain of Youth," energizes and boosts the immune system and white blood cells, decreases allergies, calms the mind, lowers stress and anxiety, supports healing and health, and neutralizes negative energy. To do the Thymus Thump, like a gorilla, gently

Image Courtesy of selfhealingonline.com

thump or tap with the fist or fingers on the thymus area 15-30 times. While tapping, breathe slowly in through the nose and out through the mouth.

Ultrasound Therapy is a noninvasive treatment in which sound wave vibrations are used to penetrate damaged tissues to decrease inflammation and pain and promote healing. Mini ultrasound devices are available for personal use.

Vagus Nerve Stimulation helps relax the body, keeps us healthy, and counterbalances the fight or flight system. The vagus nerve is longest neural network that begins in the brain and leads to the stomach with offshoots routing to every organ. When the vagus nerve is overworked, we put ourselves at risk for high blood pressure, stroke, heart disease, Type 2 diabetes, depression, anxiety, and other mental and physical health issues. Stimulating the vagus nerve helps combat these effects and promotes cells to regenerate, repair, and rebuild.

Breathwork increases vagal strength by slowing the heart rate during the "out" breath while suppressing its activity on the "in" breath. The larger the difference is in heart rate between in and out breaths indicate a healthy vagus nerve.

Different Ways to Stimulate the Vagus Nerve
- Alternate nostril, belly breathing, and box breathing
- Cold water face immersion (or cold compresses)
- Deep belly breathing with meditation
- Ear acupuncture
- Eating paleo (eliminating grains and dairy)
- Foot and neck massages
- Hand-held electrical impulse devices
- Intermittent fasting
- Interval training exercises, brisk walking, weightlifting, swimming, Pilates
- Listening to isochronic or binaural sounds through headphones
- Loud chanting, gargling, humming, laughter, or singing
- Om meditation
- Polyphenol foods (dark chocolate, red wine, leafy greens)
- Probiotics (kombucha, kimchi, sauerkraut, kefir, and yogurt)
- Sky yoga and tai chi
- Yoga asanas combined with deep breathing
- Zinc

Vibrational Plates involve standing on a platform (the plate) that vibrates up and down or side-to-side. The vibrational frequencies have a "tuning" effect on our bodies that support metabolism, circulation, muscle toning, bone density, lymphatic drainage, and help calm the nervous system.

Visualization helps with healing when we imagine our health as ideal. Visualization is powerful because the mind cannot distinguish between what is real and what we are visualizing. The same muscle pathways are activated when we imagine and when we're actually doing it. Using daily affirmations and visualizing ourselves walking, working, exercising, and doing all the things our physical bodies have been limited by, help reprogram the subconscious to accelerate healing.

Four Basic Steps for Visualization
1. Set a goal (intention).
2. Get a clear idea or picture in the mind.
3. Focus on it in the mind using all the senses.
4. Give it positive emotional energy.

Visualizations become multisensory and receive a mental upgrade when we add feelings, emotions, and incorporate all the senses. Words help create better mental pictures. If we think about what something looks like and can describe it by smell, touch, sound, taste, and by sight, then we are visualizing correctly. Try describing a scene to ourselves to help us recall it or visualize it.

Visualization Tips: Keep thoughts positive; be specific; imagine as if it's already happened; add elevated emotions and senses to make it more vivid; and, remotely view ourselves living in the picture.

★ Visualization DIY: *Look all the details of a scene or photograph for one minute. Then close our eyes and try to reproduce the image in our mind using as many details as we can remember. How accurate were we with our description?*

Here is a basic visualization and money manifestation; we can combine varied elements of each or add in our own variations to make them uniquely our own. As with all meditations and visualizations, first get in a quiet, comfortable space and relax our body through deep breathing.

Basic Creative Visualization
1. *Get in a comfortable, relaxed position with a goal of relaxation and mind clearing.*
2. *Close the eyes and visualize scenes of peace and beauty such as the ocean, a calm lake, the stars, or a beautiful garden. Get a clear picture of a tranquil scene.*
3. *Visualize taking in the splendor, beauty, and peacefulness of the scene using all the senses of touch, sight, sound, smell, and taste for at least five minutes.*
4. *Add emotions of love, joy, and gratitude until we feel calmness and tranquility.*

Money Manifestation Visualization

1. Start with the intention of manifesting money.
2. Imagine having the money we desire by seeing ourselves physically holding the money and walking into our bank to deposit the money in our account, or visualize having it show up as unexpected winnings, or perhaps we visualize money in the form of a high-paying job. How do we envision ourselves when money is unlimited?

    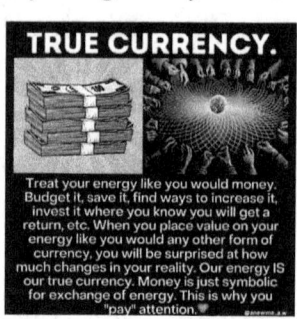

3. Create detailed images using all the senses. Clearly bring these pictures to our mind.
    - How do we look having all this money? Are we wearing stylish classic clothes sitting in first class? Imagine ourselves spending money on ourselves, family, and friends with dinner and nice gifts.
    - What does money feel like? Imagine stroking money with our fingers. Does having money bring a sense of serenity and calmness to us? Does it make us feel philanthropic, wanting to share with everyone?
    - What would money smell like if it had a smell? Imagine holding a handful of money next to our nose and taking in a few deep breaths. Does money smell like a gourmet meal or a bottle of French wine?

- *If money had a taste, what would it taste like? Imagine putting that taste on our tongue. Maybe it's a fancy dinner; what does it taste like?*
- *What does money sound like? Imagine we can hear the sound of money as we listen inside ourselves. Maybe it sounds like the purring engine of a luxury car. Visualize and incorporate taking the sights, sounds, smells, feelings, and taste of money until it feels good for us to imagine and enjoy our visualization.*

4. *Finish by pairing our visualization with heart-felt emotions of love and gratitude to manifest abundance into our lives. Add affirmations welcoming limitless abundance such as: "I am a money magnet," or "Money flows to me effortlessly." Feel deserving and grateful for our new-found fortune.*

Meditation and visualization often go together, both helping to complement each other. Like meditation, there is no one way that's "right" to visualize. We can change words and images in any way we need to suit our specific situation and needs. Remember that our subconscious doesn't distinguish between what's real and what's not, so visualizing encourages us to dream BIG. When we add heart-felt emotions and always imagine good things happening to us, our subconscious makes it happen.

Yoga postures relax the body and help release tension through stretching and breathing techniques. Yoga stretching helps activate the chakras and muscle fascia to release buried emotions where trauma is stored. All types of yoga and meditation help to reduce stress, increase self-awareness and self-compassion, induce a sense of calmness, and help create a more positive outlook on life.

Asanas are different yoga postures. Asana positions cultivate awareness, relaxation, concentration, and stimulate the chakras for better energy flow throughout the body.

Images Courtesy of voltlin.com

🧘 *Kundalini Yoga* incorporates asanas, breathing, meditation, chanting, and singing.

🧘 *Mantra Yoga* chants syllables, words, or phrases to focus vibrational energy inward. Mala beads are often used to keep track of the number of chants.

🧘 *Nada Yoga* uses music and the sound of our voice's vibrations to induce calmness.

🧘 *Nidra Yoga* uses guided meditation to enter a state of consciousness between wakefulness and sleep.

🧘 *Raja Yoga* is a classical yoga designed to create inner peace through asanas and meditation.

🕉 *Sahaja Yoga* is a combination of meditation and yoga intended to spontaneously awaken kundalini energy.

🕉 *Siddha Yoga* uses various practices including meditation, chanting, retreats, and service to others.

🕉 *Vinyasa Yoga* is the smooth flow of standard yoga asanas connected by breath.

Yunani (Unani) Medicine is based on the Four Humor theory of Hippocrates which states that imbalances in one of the body's humors (body fluids) of blood, yellow bile, black bile, or phlegm cause sickness. Unani detox methods include cupping, organ cauterization, sweating, urine excretion, Turkish baths, vomiting using emetics, blood drawing, massage, counter irritation using camphor and capsaicin, exercise, leeching, proper foods, and herbal medicine. Unani is the basic method of healing in many parts of the world.

Energy healing comes in many forms and experimenting with several methods may be necessary before we find the one that best fits our needs. We all carry our own unique blueprint and vibration, so one healing method may resonate better with us than others. We can incorporate one, or many therapies into our lives. If it feels good and resonates within us, it can be used as a doorway to the subconscious. As a reminder, these therapies are not meant to replace conventional healing we may be receiving, but more as an additive complement. The hope is that by incorporating high frequency therapies into our lives, we may no longer need to take medicine.

∽

PART IV
🚪 Doors to the Subconscious 🚪

"A man who as a physical being is always turned toward the outside, thinking that his happiness lies outside him, finally turns inward and discovers that the source is within him." — SOREN KIERKEGAARD

Accessing the elusive subconscious mind is opening the door to our full potential, including developing our psychic potential. The subconscious is where the imagination is stored, where answers lie, and can take us to the Fifth Dimension and beyond. Being able to act on our vibes, intuition, and feelings coming from the subconscious mind gives us a sense of power and control of our lives.

CHAPTER 15

Access and Answers of the Subconscious

"If the whole universe can be found in our body and mind, this is where we need to make our inquiries. We all have answers within ourselves, we just have not got in touch with them yet. The potential of finding the truth within requires faith in ourselves." — AYYA KHEMA

If we're one of those people who are always on the phone, always wondering what to do next, constantly running late, have emotions as unpredictable as the weather, are reliant upon something outside of us to make us feel better, or are anxious and unable to sleep, these are indications that that we need to reconnect with our inner self, the subconscious mind.

Access and answers from the mind come in many ways. This is why it's important to clear and quiet our mind so we're able to hear and receive the messages it gives. The techniques listed below help us reprogram, access, and receive intuitive info from the subconscious mind to help us expand upon all that is possible.

Affirmations can access and reprogram the subconscious mind and DNA through vibrations in our voice. Writing affirmations down as well as voicing them aloud amplifies the vibrations. Affirmations undo old programming when we replace them with new, more empowering beliefs. If there's something in our life we want to attract or change, we can use affirmations to change our reality. Combining affirmations with heart-felt feelings intensifies their effect. We can design affirmations to meet our own needs by keeping them specific, positive, and in the present tense by using the words *I am* and focusing on the result we desire, such as:

→ *I am a loving person and I attract love in my life.*
→ *I am financially secure and have an abundance of money.*
→ *I am healthy, wealthy, happy, and kind.*
→ *I am calm, confident, and in control at work meetings.*
→ *I am at my ideal physical weight, and I become healthier every day.*

A good time to practice affirmations is immediately after waking or right before falling asleep. The brain is in theta frequency, the state associated with hypnosis, so this is the best time to repeat or listen to affirmations with the intent of reprogramming the subconscious.

Alpha Brainwaves is the desired brainwave state to access the subconscious for meditation, self-reflection, and intuitive answers. Alpha state is where we can deprogram thoughts of doubt and fear without the judgment and criticism of our conscious mind interfering. Beta and gamma brain states are for thinking and problem solving and, therefore, too energetic for the needed state of mental relaxation. While beneficial, both theta and delta states are mostly sleeping modes, so it's difficult to consciously access, stay awake, and remember during these states.

The brain is a "bio-computer" and operates on small amounts of electricity, just like a personal computer. But unlike computers, the brain's electric frequency changes. Sometimes the brain's frequency will vibrate rapidly, and at other times it vibrates slowly. The rate at which brainwaves vibrate is divided into categories based on the number of cycles per second. The number of vibrations per second is called hertz (Hz). The higher the hertz, the more the brain is thinking.

> What happens when you get slapped with high frequency?
>
> It hertz.

Brain Wave Frequencies and Associated Cognitive States

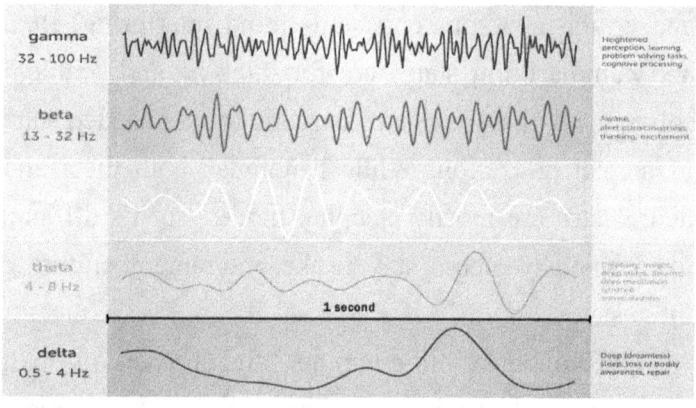

⎯⋀⎯ Gamma (32-100 Hz)	• Learning and problem solving.
⎯⋀⎯ Beta (13-32 Hz)	• Daily thinking uses eyesight and other senses for processing.
⎯⋀⎯ Alpha (8-13 Hz)	• Meditation, deep relaxation, light sleep, daydreaming, visualization, kids' brain state, common sense, intuition, self-reflection.
⎯⋀⎯ Theta (4-8 Hz)	• Deep sleep, dreaming, meditation, prayer, affirmations, hypnosis, frequency of the Schumann Resonance.
⎯⋀⎯ Delta (0.5-4 Hz)	• Detached awareness, healing, deepest sleep, communication with higher intelligence, doorway to the "other side."

Automatic Writing is a popular way to receive intuitive messages from the higher self or the spirit world. This method requires allowing messages to flow through us via pencil and paper without conscious thought or effort. As with other forms of psychic access, practice makes understanding the message easier.

Breathwork is a type of active meditation or breathing with intention. Many of us don't know proper breathing techniques, as we tend to breathe from the upper chest, without allowing ourselves the benefit of deep belly breathing. The ideal breathing technique is six breaths per minute— three in through the nose and three out through the mouth, with a longer out breath than in breath. The relaxation response is triggered when the exhale breath is longer than the inhale breath. We find answers to our questions in the "sacred pause" between breaths, the time when the ego is silent.

To properly "belly breathe," think of the stomach like a balloon: a balloon expands when it becomes filled with air, as does the stomach. When a balloon releases air, it contracts, just like the stomach. When we breathe in, the stomach goes out; when we breathe out, the stomach goes in.

While doing breathwork, we need let go and release any fears, anticipations, logical thoughts, expectations, or doubts, and let the power of the breath completely relax the body. Be still and silent enough to feel the beat of our heart. Breathe in love and exhale gratitude. Breathe in peace and exhale pain. Breathe in new and exhale old.

Respiration is Inspiration.

Focusing our attention on the ins and outs of the breath can bring about a light trance state because the lungs produce the most DMT (natural psychedelic) in our body. Conscious 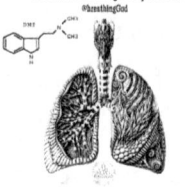 breathing releases DMT from the lungs and pineal gland, responsible for mystical experiences and spiritual insight.

Breathing Exercises Used with Meditation

🫁 *Alternate Nostril Breathing* through the left nostril while holding the right nostril closed with the right thumb. Then, alternate with right nostril and left hand.

🫁 *Ashtanga Yoga Breathing* uses equal length breaths through the nose while making gentle noises from the back of the throat.

🫁 *Attitude Breathing* (condensed and reworded from the HeartMath Institute).
1. *Identify an unwanted attitude we want to change (sadness, depression, judgment, guilt, anger, etc.)*
2. *Breathe in the feelings of a better attitude to replace the unwanted attitude. Do this slowly from the heart area to anchor the new feelings.*
3. *Turn our feelings into "no big deal" by taking the drama out, changing significant to insignificant, and taking a "so what" attitude.*

🫁 *Box Breathing* involves breathing in for four seconds and holding the breath for four seconds, then breathing out for four seconds, and holding the breath again for four seconds. Repeat this sequence for four minutes.

🫁 *DMT Breathwork* is usually done with tribal music and a practitioner with the intention of creating mind-altering experiences without drugs.

🫁 *Holotropic and Neurodynamic Breathwork* use deep, fast, rhythmical breathing combined with evocative music to lead to altered states of consciousness.

🫁 *Pranayama* is breathwork that directs the flow of prana and accompanies yoga asana positions.

Channeling is accessing information from the higher self or from extraterrestrials. Channeling accesses the subconscious and puts us on the receiving end of pure thought.

💭 **Daydreaming** is not necessarily a tool for accessing the subconscious, but it can still be beneficial because it puts us in a semi-trance state available to receive answers.

Déjà Vu is the feeling that we're currently experiencing is one we have already experienced before—the present feels like the past. It's the Universe's way of shouting out loud, "This is a sign!" Having a déjà vu moment is a signal to look inside and see if we can figure out what we're feeling. It could mean that a situation of our history is repeating itself, it could be a momentary crossover to a parallel universe, or it could be when two dimensional planes intersect.

MIND BLOWN

Dowsing uses a pendulum to connect to hidden information in the subconscious. Pendulums swing in certain directions based on vibrations from our intuition to answer yes-or-no questions. Pendulum charts are also used as reference for getting answers. Pendulums can be purchased at New Age stores, but can also be made from a weighted object, such as a ring and about 8" of string. To establish a pendulum's direction, hold the pendulum by the string and let it dangle. Close our eyes and ask the pendulum what our "yes" direction is. The pendulum may move left to right, counterclockwise, clockwise, or front to back. Whatever direction the pendulum moves is our "yes" response. Try the same process for a "no" direction. Directions other than yes or no may indicate an "unsure" answer.

Dreams are the "language of the unconscious mind." They are the language of symbols, signs, and imagery that connect us with the subconscious mind. Dreams may provide visions or premonitions to help us understand messages and come up with solutions to problems. Lucid dreams, especially in which we are aware we are dreaming and can manipulate the dream character's actions, give us best insight and access to our subconscious.

> Going to bed on an empty stomach induces more vivid and lucid dreams. This is because hunger stimulates the production of DMT in the brain. When we eat right before bed, our body works all night on digestion, which takes away energy from the brain. By producing more DMT naturally, we can achieve deeper states of meditation, stronger connection with our Higher Self, and easily tap into Infinite Intelligence.

Answers to questions we are wondering about often come in dreams. We can "create" dreams that will answer a question we have. Before going to sleep, ask ourselves what problem it is that we wish to solve. Write the question down, place it under our pillow, and focus on it a bit before falling asleep. This primes the subconscious to find an answer during our dreams. Then tell ourselves that we will have a dream that provides the information we need to answer our query.

> *"I dream my painting, and then I paint my dream."*
> — VINCENT VAN GOGH

Dreams speak in symbols and literal interpretations don't work. Paying attention to emotions experienced during dreams is one way to determine their meaning. Conscious intention and keeping a smartphone or journal near our bed can help with remembering dreams.

Recalling & Analyzing Dreams

We can program ourselves to dream about a particular problem, to recall that dream that solves that problem, and to be able to understand the message it conveys. Every morning, we can write our dreams down with the date and give our dream a title to help us remember its details.

- Try to relate our dream to something that happened during the day.
- Look for advice, guidance, or lessons in dreams.
- Decode a dream's symbols according to what it means to us.
- Look for the emotional impact and feelings within dreams to get an overall impression of its meaning.
- Focus on dreams that are recurring or evoke strong feelings during the dream, as emotions in dreams may reveal insight to situations that provoke similar emotions in waking life.

Dream Symbols

The best understanding of dream symbols doesn't come from a book; they are best understood by the connection of what the symbol means exclusively to us. However, there are common themes among dream symbol meanings that can help in our interpretations:

 Houses represent different areas of life: a basement could be the subconscious and an attic could be our spiritual side. A house crowded with junk or ill-fitting clothes could indicate outgrown attitudes or that work is needed in personal areas.

🚗 *Cars* symbolize movement through life. Who's driving the car? What's the condition of our car? Is the road we're on safe or perilous? Are we in the fast or slow lane? Can we see the direction the car is headed?

🌊 *Water* signifies emotions. Are we struggling to keep our head above water or is it smooth sailing? Is the water clear or murky, smooth or turbulent, deep or shallow?

📚 *Taking tests and school* dreams represent feelings about abilities. Being late or unprepared indicates feelings of inadequacy whereas acing a test could indicate good fortune.

💀 *Death dreams* indicate a transition from a previous stage, that something in our life is moving on.

👹 *Monsters* symbolize a part of our selves that scare us. Do we run and hide from them or face up and find out what happens?

👶 *Babies* signify the birth or beginning of a new phase in our life, creativity, and fertile ventures.

Eye Gazing establishes an energetic circuit that induces euphoria, visions, past life experiences, and remote viewing when we stare into another's eyes or a candle flame for an extended period. Eye gazing helps us reach higher states of consciousness, giving true meaning to the saying "the eyes are the window to the soul."

Inspiration comes from the subconscious mind; it's the feeling of fresh, unbridled enthusiasm, creative energy, and possibilities. Inspiration guides and leads us in the right direction.

> *"No man was ever great without divine inspiration."*
> — Cicero

Intention gives direction to our thoughts. Intention is necessary to access the subconscious mind, heal, act with compassion, and it gives a purpose to our creations.

Intuition is linked to our sixth chakra, the Third Eye. Therefore, the sixth chakra is our sixth sense, the sense of intuition. It's an inner knowing (aha moments and epiphanies) that something is true without understanding the reason behind the feeling. Intuition shows up as gut feelings, flashes of insight, hunches, vibes, or a sense of just knowing.

Serendipity, inspiration, mediumship, precognitive dreams, intention, channeling, the "clairs" (See Chapter 18), and ESP are subsets of intuition. Our intuition is always communicating with us and always guides us in in the right direction. Our ego, on the other hand, steers us off course from our well-being and true destination.

To use the wisdom of our intuition, it's essential we listen and pay attention to our body's signals and take the first hit of "knowing" before our brain starts using logic to decipher. Improving our other senses can help develop our intuitive capacities. Knowing the difference between butterflies in our stomach that mean we have a crush on someone, or butterflies that mean uneasiness makes it easier to understand intuition's message. Feelings come from the heart; thus, intuition is the voice and language of the heart.

Listening provides the silence we need to hear our higher self speaking to us. When we listen, our inner voice answers our questions through our intuition telling us which path to choose from or which action we should take.

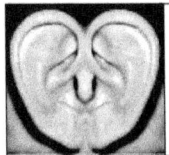
When two ears are put side by side, it forms the shape of a heart. Interestingly, the word "ear" sits right in the middle of the word "h-ear-t." The ear is the easiest way to the heart, so if you want someone's heart, learn to listen to them.

Meditation is the most popular access to the subconscious. If we want to bring energy to the chakra system, reach alpha brain states and higher levels of consciousness, access intuition, realign DNA, activate crystals in the pineal gland, or achieve kundalini, meditation is the ideal conduit to do so.

The goal of meditation is not to stop thinking; this would be unnatural. The intent is to calm the body, mind, heart, and thinking until we stop identifying with our thoughts and all we are left with is pure consciousness, pure awareness, the true essence of who we are. Just closing the eyes is enough to relax the mind and find silence between our thoughts.

Although many methods of proper meditation practices exist, the true beauty is that there is no right or wrong way. Many of us may not meditate because we don't understand its true purpose. We may believe that just sitting is a waste of time or it's something that keeps us from getting more important work done. However, if we have a goal of healing or discovering our psychic abilities, then meditation becomes essential. Meditation then becomes more than a mental timeout; it becomes a portal to inner transformation.

How To Meditate

- Find a comfortable spot and posture to meditate for at least ten minutes. • If desired, use a mudra hand position, or join the index fingers with the thumb and rest them on the knees. • Relax the shoulders, close the eyes, and take three deep breaths. • Set an intention for what we aim to improve or accomplish for the meditation. • Next, focus attention on our breath.
- Observe the ins and outs of the breath by mentally counting to three as our lungs fill with air. • Mentally count to six while exhaling. • Pause for a moment at the bottom and top of each breath. • Repeat this sequence about ten times. • The underlying goal is to reduce brain activity, so when the mind goes astray and begins to drift, bring the focus back to the breath and counting, without being judgmental.
- Over time, we will only be conscious of our breath.
- Each time a thought interrupts awareness, bring our attention back to the breath. • Finish with slowly opening our eyes and giving gratitude.

T. S. Martin

The only way out is in.

Playing meditation music in the background or repeating a mantra like *om* can help clear the mind of creeping thoughts. Sitting in a comfortable position is preferred, but meditation can also be done walking in nature or doing any task that takes our mind to another place, or to a state of being lost in our reveries. YouTube has guided meditations and other types of meditations available to choose from.

🧘 *Basic Breathing Meditation* involves closing the eyes and taking in a deep, slow breath through the nose. Hold for a moment and breathe out slowly through the mouth. Like a balloon, inflate the stomach while breathing in and deflate while breathing out. Allow thoughts to come and go, bringing focus back to the breath. Try and fit six breathing repetitions into one minute.

🧘 *Candlelight Meditation* involves staring into the flickering flame of a candle to induce alpha brain states.

🧘 *Chakra Meditation*, or Color Ball Meditation, is visualizing sending colored balls of energy to our chakras according to their corresponding colors.

🧘 *Counting Meditation* starts with the number 100, 50, or 25 and slowly counts backwards to one. When thoughts enter, attention is brought back to the rhythm of our breathing.

🧘 *Guided Meditation* uses a teacher or app to guide us through the meditation process. A combo of breathing and visualizing techniques brings us to a state of relaxation.

🧘 *Mala Meditation* uses a 108-beaded mala necklace to keep track of spoken mantras during meditation.

🧘 *Mantra Meditation* focuses attention on a mantra sound like "Om" or phrase like *Sat Nam*—meaning, essentially, I am truth.

🧘 *Mindfulness Meditation* requires being in the Now and being acutely aware of our body sensations by using the body scanning technique without judgment or interpretation.

🧘 *Movement Meditation* is physically active forms of meditation like yoga, mindful dancing, Tai Chi, walking through nature, and Zen gardens.

🧘 *Muhla Bandha Meditation* is used for kundalini activation (also called the Energy Orgasm) which involves sending energy through the spinal column to activate the pineal gland.

🧘 *Progressive Meditation* focuses on tensing and holding different muscle groups, then relaxing before moving on and tensing the next group of muscles.

🧘 *Sacred Geometry Meditation* focuses on geometric shapes such as the Merkabah or Flower of Life to activate inner states of calmness.

🧘 *Transcendental Meditation* uses silent mantras to ease the mind into peacefulness.

🧘 *Visual Meditation* uses the imagination to visualize peaceful scenes to bring the brain to alpha. Images like a tranquil lake nestled in the mountains, green meadows full of wildflowers, or waves gently crashing on a beach, help induce a state of relaxation.

> Bee watching is a secretly miraculous meditation. As bees dance from flower to flower absorbing the Sun and distributing pollen along the way, they emit a healing frequency that reverses disease and promotes soul and emotional restoration. Our brain may not comprehend this, but our cells do. This is believed to be the reason why beekeepers have one of the longest life expectancies out of all professions.

Meditation clears the noise and gives us the solitude needed to hear the wisdom of our inner voice. Without the intrusion of overactive thinking and outside interference, meditating instills a sense of calmness and peacefulness that helps us lose the limitations our thinking mind creates.

Mental Rehearsal is a visualization technique where we imagine the outcome of an event ahead of time to improve our chance of success.

> By imagining the best-case scenario for every situation, our mind will begin to attract solutions.

Mindful Movement uses easeful motion and flowing movement like dance that can put us in a trance state.

Prayer is Western's version of voice meditation. Prayer's effectiveness comes from its use of mantra words, the vibrations from our voice, being in the present, and gratitude.

Qigong (also *Chi Kung*) is the practice of using qi energy that combines posture, breathing, and focused intention. Qigong's ability to access the subconscious reconnects the body, mind, and soul. As a form of martial arts, Qigong varies from gentle Tai Chi to vigorous Kung Fu. Both can inspire a creative burst or may leave us feeling consumed, either of which helps release limiting beliefs held in the subconscious.

Remote Viewing is the process of projecting a part of our consciousness/mind outside of ourselves to "see" information in another location. This is the underlying tool for out-of-body experiences, and can be practiced during meditation, alpha brain states, or hypnosis.

✦ DIY Remote Viewing Exercise: *The next time we visit a place that we've never been, imagine ahead of time what we think we'll "see" at this location. Draw images on a piece of paper of what we think it looks like and compare this to how the place actually looks when we get there.*

> One method to reprogram ourselves is to gaze at a black dot on a white piece of paper while repeating positive affirmations.

Reprogramming is a neuroscience technique of behavior modification. To reprogram ourselves, we should be in an alpha or theta brain state through self-hypnosis or meditation.

This state helps access limiting beliefs imprinted during childhood. To reprogram ourselves, we have to show our subconscious a new belief system:

Begin by calling forth the memory we are trying to change. If the damage occurred when we were a child, we can visualize the memory of our younger self. When the situation unfolds in our mind, this time, we will intervene and say what needs to be said to protect our boundaries. We can walk away, speak our mind, or whatever feels right for healing. This process works for current situations as well: Remember and visualize the incident. Imagine taking control and healing from the situation. When we feel a sense of release in the body, like a big sigh, or maybe tears or laughter, we know that we have reprogrammed a deeply ingrained belief from our subconscious.

★ DIY Mind Reprogram Exercise: *Think of three impactful words to describe wishes for ourselves such as charismatic, confident, and creative. When we have chosen our three words, close our eyes, and access our subconscious by instructing our wishes to come forward in the form of a picture or thought. Mentally rehearse these three words while picturing ourselves on a large screen TV behaving in this manner using as much detail as possible. Do this for three weeks to reprogram the mind.*

Sacred Geometry's symbols and shapes awaken our soul to help us understand our divine nature. Every geometric shape has a specific energy vibration, and when used with meditation, the images super-charge our intention and bring energy to our healing. Meditating with the sacred shapes reveals subconscious wisdom, such as our purpose in life, opens pathways to higher dimensions, and facilitates healing. Some consider sacred geometry essential to the education of our soul, being symbolic or a catalyst to reaching higher levels of self-awareness and consciousness and enabling us to heal and rebalance by connecting our inner self with our outer self.

Satori is a state of non-thinking, the space between perception and thought where answers lie. Satori is found between the inhales and exhales of breathing during meditation.

Sensory Deprivation is deliberately removing stimuli from our senses using blindfolds, earmuffs, pink noise, virtual reality headsets, or flotation/isolation tanks to help us achieve a trance-like state to access the subconscious.

The Source or "Creator Source" is a frequency of energy that exists within each of us. As souls, we are made from the fragmented energy of All that exists; everyone's Source energy combined into One makes the collective consciousness of the Universe. Accessing internal Source power gives us unlimited ability to create and manifest our destiny.

Symbols are signs of synchronicity that grant access to the subconscious mind. Symbols show up as animals, feathers, repetitive numbers such as 11:11, in the form of words such as "Go," or as characters in a dream. Besides giving access, symbols can control the subconscious mind. Mandalas, alphabets, languages, and binary codes are forms of symbols used for subconscious control. Businesses and companies use symbols to entice us into believing they're the best. The widely used sun symbol represents happiness and goodness in our minds, whereas the symbol 666 reminds us of a corrupted mindset. It's best to use intuition when interpreting what symbols mean to us.

Synchronicities are those occurrences when something happens randomly but feels meaningful. However, no events occur by chance; synchronicities are messages from the subconscious as signs of universal guidance. When we're thinking of a friend and then they call, or we have a question on our mind and a sign shows up, it's the Universe's way of assuring us that we're on the right path. It may feel like intuition, but synchronicities come from outside us, whereas intuition is more of an inner knowing. Synchronicities, like spiritual awakening, are preprogrammed into our DNA and are activated by thoughts that have matching frequencies and vibrations. Synchronicity is reality confirming our thoughts.

Trance is a level of consciousness that brings relaxing, healing, intuitive, and inspirational states.

Trance can be induced through meditation, hypnosis, zoning out, breathwork, mantras, prayer, fasting, visualization, staring, [staring at a fire (good, staring at a TV (bad)], hypnosis, primal music, binaural beats, yoga, sacred geometry, looking at Platonic images in kaleidoscope form, or doing any activity that takes little thought and brings the mind to a state of reverie.

Signs and messages from the subconscious come when we least expect them and let us know that we're on the right path even if it's not always apparent. Doors open when we are quiet, listen, and are receptive. Even if information we receive seems counterintuitive, we're always in a better position to better understand our purpose when we have access to higher truths and awareness. When we're able to access the subconscious mind to revise and reprogram old beliefs stored in the body, then we have the ability to reprogram our DNA, because DNA, chakras, and levels of the mind are synonymous.

CHAPTER 16

The Deactivation of DNA

"There is a price to be paid for every increase in consciousness. We cannot be more sensitive to pleasure without being more sensitive to pain." — ALAN WATTS

Most of us know DNA as the spiraling two-strand double helix that holds our genetic blueprint from our mother and father. As the long-term storage of information, our DNA blueprint carries the genetic history of our ancestors and our past lives as well.

Science acknowledges two strands of DNA, however, the original model of our long-ago ancestors had a fully functioning twelve-strand DNA template with 144,000 chromosomes, implying that this is our natural birthright, not the present and commonly referred to double helix with 46 chromosomes. It is a bit of an anomaly that we have only 46 chromosomes instead of the 48 that we should have if we inherited two strands of DNA from each parent, or if we descended from apes.

The well-known fusion of chromosome two is what sets us apart from our closest predecessors, the Neanderthal, with whom we are not related; there is no genetic evolution between us, thereby discounting the theory of human evolution. If we were indeed related to the chimp, then we would expect primates to have 144,000 chromosomes as our ancient ancestors, but this is not the case since chimps have 48 and we currently have 46. Thus, in terms of more is better, humans must have de-evolutionized to reduce the number of chromosomes from that of a chimp.

Explanations have been given that the other ten strands of DNA became "lost" or "deactivated" from overuse of left-brain analytical thinking, causing our heart center to shut down and leaving us devoid of our innate DNA powers. However, another school of thought believes our DNA was intentionally deactivated by the Anunnaki to keep the Nephilim, the fallen angels, the giants, from having access to twelve-strand potential themselves. This reasoning explains for the mysterious genetic manipulation to chromosome 2 that occurred when Homo sapiens arrived with a genetic record unlike a chimp's.

As a side note, vitamin B_{12} is critical for DNA replication, but the gene on chromosome 22 has also been intentionally deactivated, causing the need for most humans to eat meat; chimps and apes don't have this need.

Some scientists of the Human Genome Project suggest that our extra DNA strands were created by an "extraterrestrial programmer" whose rush to colonize Earth left their humanoid project incomplete, suggesting that junk DNA is the genetic code of extraterrestrial life forms. Thus, Homo sapiens could be regarded as a hybrid being of an upgraded Homo erectus mixed with genes of extraterrestrials, making aliens our partial ancestors. (Stokes, 2007).

The twelve spiral strands of DNA are crystallized frequencies of light that activate and connect to chakra centers and provide light for the aura. Most of us have not evolved beyond the second chakra level, strand two of DNA, because the higher DNA strands haven't yet been activated. Two strands of available DNA indicate a third-dimensional reality, while twelve open strands signify a Fifth-Dimension reality. Although dubbed as "junk," 12-strand DNA is a memory bank of pre-encoded information whose activation leads to intuition, compassion, increasing levels of consciousness and spirituality, higher awareness, healing, anti-aging abilities, supernatural powers such as shape shifting and levitation, dormant psychic abilities, multidimensional travel, and more.

DNA Strand 1/ Root Chakra 1: Survival DNA Strand 2/ Sacral Chakra 2: Sexuality	Governs Genetic Profile Double Helix 1
DNA Strand 3/ Solar Plexus Chakra 3: Feeling DNA Strand 4/ Heart Chakra 4: Love & Compassion	Governs Emotional Profile Double Helix 2
DNA Strand 5/ Throat Chakra 5: Truth DNA Strand 6/ Third Eye Chakra 6: Psychic Knowledge	Governs Mental Profile Double Helix 3
DNA Strand 7/ Crown Chakra 7: Light Frequencies Enter DNA Strand 8/ Soul Star Chakra 8: Unity of Oneness	Governs Soul Profile Double Helix 4
DNA Strand 9/ Planetary Chakra 9: Planet Energies DNA Strand 10/ Solar Chakra 10: Solar Energies	Governs Soul Groups Double Helix 5
DNA Strand 11/ Galactic Chakra 11: Off-Planet Frequencies DNA Strand 12/ Universal Chakra 12: Source of Creation	Governs Creation Double Helix 6

Each strand of the 12-strand DNA template represents higher dimensional levels, or spheres of consciousness on the Tree of Life. The Tree illustrates our journey through this lifetime as well as the soul's journeys through different lifetimes of the paths taken to reach enlightenment. The interplay between chakras, DNA, kundalini, and the Tree of Life can be seen in the picture insert.

Because DNA acts as an antenna and receiver for light and sound vibrations, it absorbs vibrations from spoken words, internal dialogue, thoughts, vocal meditations, images, light language, and light codes, and changes and programs itself according to the frequency of the vibration it receives. Like a hypnotic suggestion, the frequency carried within thoughts and words such as mantras and affirmations activate the formation of new DNA strands. Since vibrational thoughts form mental images that are stored as memories in DNA, upgrading our inward thoughts will upgrade our DNA, and in turn, our outward reality.

> Your DNA is a multi-dimensional molecule which has within it everything known to the Universe. It carries the Akashic records, your karma, all past and future lifetimes, and your spiritual purpose. Everything is in your DNA.

Before we can activate the other ten strands of DNA, we need to first align the double helix. To do this, before going to bed at night and in the morning, simply *ask* that our DNA strands become aligned at the beginning of the meditation. Do this meditation once or twice daily for three days to ensure the alignment anchors. It should only take a few moments. Here is a short meditation to align and activate the DNA strands:

How To Align, Access & Activate DNA Meditation

Become quiet and take three deep breaths. Visualize the DNA helix rising up as pure energy through the contours of our spine, making it feel warm or tingly.

In our own way, ask our higher self to activate and anchor our strands of DNA. Mentally send energy from the base up to the top of the spine. Picture and feel this energy filling up our head and expanding until it overflows and surrounds the crown with golden light. Next, imagine the two-strand DNA helix growing from the base of the spine into the center of our head. Ask that the two-strand DNA become perfectly aligned and ready to receive the remaining strands of DNA. Remain in this energy until we sense that the alignment is complete. Then, slowly come back to awareness and give thanks.

Different Methods to Activate DNA

⚕ *Kundalini* energy activates DNA. Unlock kundalini energy located at the Root Chakra during meditation by "thinking the energy up the spine."

⚕ *Light Codes* reprogram DNA and activate kundalini, helping us realize our true potential. Bringing more light into our body from the Sun and light language raises our frequency and rebuilds DNA.

⚕ *Merkabah Activation* (8th chakra level) combined with thought and intention reverses ten-strand DNA mutation.

⚕ *Sacred Geometry* unlocks dormant DNA strands because reality is composed of binary codes such as 0101010 that awaken DNA consciousness.

⚕ *Sounds & Speech* reprogram DNA if our words are carrying the same frequency or higher as the DNA;

this is the vibrational power of affirmations, chanting, mantras, and singing.

🕱 *Vibrational Patterns* of high frequency positively affect DNA. Mudras and hand gestures in the shape of spirals and figure 8's can access DNA. ∞

> **What have you been up to lately?**
> Not much, just redesigning my DNA, freeing myself of ancestral trauma, mastering my soul lessons, giving gratitude, and cultivating space for the abundant flow coming my way.

Ancestral DNA that doesn't benefit us can be released using DNA clearing meditations. Begin by taking a few deep grounding breaths with the intention of identifying, locating, and clearing our genetic record. By plugging into our cells' mitochondria energy, we can rebuild and activate higher DNA strands. In our own words, here is an ancestral trauma-clearing meditation to try:

Ancestral Clearing Meditation

"Hello, soul self, please correct and heal all abusive programming and messaging in my mitochondria. I dedicate my mitochondria and cells to now receive only beneficial and positive messages so that I can express my highest divinity. With all my intent, I bless my mitochondria, tissues, and body parts healing through divine intelligence. I reclaim my higher DNA's abilities so that I may use its spiritual powers."

To reactivate light codes for manifesting and ascension, we must first raise our vibration, release energetic blockages, clear karma, and reassemble DNA strands one and two. Healing activates light codes. When we let go of trauma, it *makes room* for the evolutionary transmutation of carbon to crystal. Space is made for the cellular upgrade to turn our bodies into beings of light.

As we learn to look within and understand ourselves better, we can access all parts of our DNA as part of our personal path towards higher consciousness. As described throughout the book, our DNA Tree can be accessed through meditation, color, light, language, sound, aromatherapy, crystals and stones, sacred geometry, and other energy-based methods.

CHAPTER 17

Kundalini, the Stairway to Heaven

"When you succeed in awakening the Kundalini so that it starts to move out of its mere potentiality, you necessarily start a world which is totally different from our world. It is the world of eternity." — CARL JUNG

The name kundalini means 'coiled up' or 'serpentine' and has long been represented by two entwined serpents spiraling up the medical Staff of Hermes. This symbol is commonly used in medicine to represent healing. The staff is known as the magic wand carried by Hermes, or Mercury, the winged messenger of the gods. Symbolically, the staff symbolizes the spinal column, the serpents represent DNA and kundalini energy flowing up through the chakras, and the top of the staff is the pineal gland. Activating kundalini energy automatically activates DNA, as the energetic capacity of the 12-strand genetic code is stored in the kundalini.

Kundalini is life force energy that holds the power of all DNA strands not yet activated. These dormant DNA energies are stored in the kundalini area of the Root Chakra near the base of the spine. When activated, the biological feminine energy spirals its way from the Silver Cord, up the prana channel of the spine, to the pineal gland of the Third Eye Chakra, releasing blocked emotions, beliefs, and traumas on its journey. As kundalini energy works its way up the spine and through the chakras, it activates DNA to prepare the physical body to become a lightbody, necessary for ascension to the Fifth Dimension.

PERSONIFICATIONS OF ENERGY

Adam is an atom. Eve is an electron. The story is mythological, based on life beginning with the "splitting of the atom," as electrons are the "rib" of the atom. God is the "good" of your higher mind, the cerebrum. Devil is the "evil" of your lower mind, the cerebellum. Heaven is your "head," the highest, "heaved up" place of your body, your highest nature, and the Source within. Hell is your "heel," the lowest place of your body and lower nature. The snake is the spiraling electromagnetic energy of the Ida and Pingala circuits. The tree is your spine. The apple is consciousness. Kundalini energy means activating your pineal gland; hence, conquering your own dragon.

Kundalini can be accessed through root lock meditation, also known as *muhla bandha*, breathwork, mantras, mudras, and visualization techniques. Activating kundalini energy usually happens spontaneously but can be accomplished through evolved meditation practices and having cleared chakras that can handle the enormous electrical energy being transmitted through the Sushumna nadi, or spinal column. The energetic capacity of the chakras and our frame of mind must be able to handle the rising energy of kundalini. This should happen naturally, and rushing the process has potential to "blow the circuit." Often, karmic obligations must be met before kundalini ascension can occur. Kundalini awakening is the precursor to spiritual awakening and this rite-of-passage from transforming human consciousness into spiritual consciousness can sometimes be mistaken as psychosis or schizophrenia. Kundalini awakening is an evolutionary process that occurs naturally and spontaneously, and the psyche must be able to handle the energy going up the spine; hence, all chakras must be cleared and traumas released before awakening. Nonetheless, here is a method of inducing kundalini using the muhla bandha or "energy orgasm" meditation:

Muhla Bandha Meditation

1. Lie down on a firm surface like a carpet, bed, or grass, and bend the knees, or sit in a chair. Take a few deep breaths to ground ourselves to let go of tensions and let go of the ego.
2. Then take deeper breaths, inhaling through the nose and exhaling through the mouth, making the breath completely "circular" with no pauses between the inhales and exhales.
3. On an inhale, rock the pelvis while filling the belly with air like a balloon.
4. On the exhale, arch, then flatten the lower back while squeezing the Kegel muscles (the muscles you squeeze to stop the flow of urine). The squeezes pump energy (cerebrospinal fluid) up through the chakras. Continuously repeat breathing and squeezing. The legs may open and close like butterfly wings while doing this.
5. Visualize pulling in energy from the Universe into the Root and Sacral Chakra areas until it feels warm or tingly. Circulate the energy back and forth between the two chakras. Our hands can help guide, circulate, and create pathways for the energy to follow.
6. When the lower chakras are "activated," move the energy upward between the second and third, Solar Plexus Chakra areas. When this area feels "lit up," move to the fourth chakra level.

7. *Continue visualizing and circulating energy from our belly to the heart chakra, back and forth, again and again.*
8. *Then move the energy to the Throat Chakra area. Consciously make guttural sounds to release and open the fifth chakra. Continue circulating energy between the heart and throat until we feel it move to the Third Eye Chakra. Consciously keep energy circulating between the two chakras.*
9. *Continue the energy flow from the third eye to the top of the head, the Crown Chakra. With practice, this may feel like energy shooting out of the top of the head, like a mind-blowing energy orgasm, or the piezoelectric effect.*

It may take time and practice to activate kundalini. Although the experience usually happens spontaneously with ascension, it may take longer depending on karmic obligations and blockages that need to be cleared from the body first.

Ascension is "kundalini breakthrough," the process of activating DNA, awakening, and achieving Merkabah, or a lightbody. It's freedom from karma and full evolution for the soul, which means incarnations on this planet are no longer necessary. Ascension is the evolutionary path of consciousness on the Tree of Life to our ultimate destiny, the Source. The ascension path requires honesty, integrity, and fulfilling our purpose. It's breaking free of illusions and raising our vibration and consciousness from a Third to a Fifth-Dimension reality.

During the spiritual metamorphosis of ascension, as psychological crutches and toxic energies are released, "Dark Night of the Soul" symptoms can appear causing disorientation and mental confusion, where the ego gets ditched, and where we may experience symptoms akin to a spiritual depression. Here are a few methods for easing ascension and kundalini symptoms:

- Practice, slow, methodical breathwork.
- Relax, rest, take quiet time as needed, and remove negative influences.
- Stay present and neutral.
- Eat lighter, eat grounding foods, and keep the body well hydrated.
- Practice mindful movement, massage, toning, meditation, and keep the chakras clear.
- Soak in water and salt baths and sing in the shower.
- Use purple and clear crystals: auralite, amethyst, sodalite, quartz, and celestite.
- Use grounding essential oils: cedar, cilantro, vetiver, and patchouli.
- Engage with nature, pets, music, and motivational groups with others going through awakening.
- Seek a spiritual counselor if we continue having difficulty releasing trauma.

Awakening/Enlightenment occurs on the Fourth Dimension astral plane with the opening of the 4th, 5th, and 6th chakras, the Heart, Throat, and Third Eye, respectively. Awakening begins a disconnection from the ego which some consider to be the "Dark Night of the Soul" stage of spiritual ascension. Full awakening represents DNA activation and kundalini ascension.

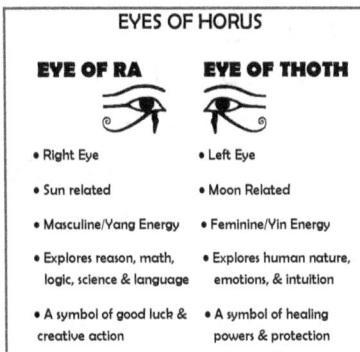

The Eyes of Horus are representations of the third eye of the pineal gland. The eyes symbolize someone who has "awoken." Like yin and yang, the Eyes of Horus is a concept meant to balance the left side of the body, the lunar Ida circuit, with the right solar Pingala circuit. When these two spiraling energy channels unify, it unleashes kundalini. The Eyes of Horus see the sun or *sol* [soul] within. The Eyes represent our true divine spark, our higher self, the Source within us all, that which we are.

Merkabah (also spelled Merkaba) means "lightbody," or "the spiritual light vehicle of consciousness." *Mer* means light, *Ka* means spirit, and *Ba* means body. Merkabah is Source energy consisting of light and consciousness surrounding the aura. The Merkabah shape consists of intersecting, counter-rotating star tetrahedron-

shaped energy fields located above the Crown Chakra. The opposite spins of the star energy fields are faster than light, giving it the ability to generate less dense matter, thereby creating light bodies from physical bodies. Through prana breathwork, meditation, visualization, or when DNA strands are fully activated, the Merkabah light energy encompasses our body and acts as a light vehicle, or a spiritual spaceship into higher frequencies for interdimensional travel between 5D and 12D. The Fifth Dimension is known as the Star Tetrahedron Dimension; Merkabah energy is a part of kundalini energy and meditating on the symbol can unlock our full potential as the upward point brings us closer to Source and the downward point grounds us with Earth.

The Pineal Gland is an organ in the brain that gets its name from its *pine*cone shape. It is one of the most heavily targeted and poisoned glands in the human body, due to its positive influence on human awareness. As a spiritual antenna, the pineal gland opens doors between the physical and the metaphysical, and its doors have long been locked in a targeted attempt to keep us docile and complacent due to its positive influence on spiritual awareness. A closed or calcified pineal gland means that the mind can easily be deceived, whereas an open pineal gland acts as a truth detector, able to see beyond fabrications and false intentions.

The pinecone has been a sacred shape throughout history and cultures and is considered a symbol for immortality. The design of the pinecone follows the

Fibonacci sequencing for growth, is engraved on Sumerian artwork, and is prolific in Vatican architecture, for reasons unknown, but possibly due their covert communication with aliens. (Haze, 2018).

"The infinite Wi-Fi signal for the ancients was a pineal gland modem hooked up to the Universe." — IAN HOWELL

The pineal gland links to the sixth, Third Eye Chakra, in the  middle of the forehead and is known for its intuitive capacity, ethereal powers, and ability to see beyond time and space. For this reason, it's commonly referred to as our "sixth sense" and "third eye" because just like the two eyes, it controls the action of light, has a lens, cornea, rods, cones, and retina like our real eyes do, giving the third eye the ability to see with intuitive, inner vision. As a transdimensional receiver, when the pineal is activated, we're able to perceive light frequencies outside the usual visible range, allowing for more ethereal, mystical, and spiritual experiences.

The pineal gland is part of the endocrine system of organs that correspond to the chakras along the spine. It produces the hormones serotonin and melatonin, which are responsible for our sleep/wake cycles, moods, energy levels, and helps us enter a meditative state. The pineal gland is our intended focus when doing muhla banda meditation and kundalini practices.

Unfortunately, fluoride poisoning and other toxins have calcified the pineal gland making it difficult to access our spiritual powers. Fluoride is the basic ingredient in Prozac, rat poison, and nerve gas, and it's added to our drinking water and toothpaste. Fluoride makes us submissive, compliant, and disconnected. Decalcifying the pineal gland will restore our intuitive capacities and open our minds to being the creators that we truly are.

Ways to Decalcify the Pineal Gland
- ◊ Activate and balance the Third-Eye Chakra through daily introspection by meditating, journaling, mindful movement, or kundalini yoga.
- ◊ Incorporate the color indigo around the home and in foods we eat. Meditate, carry, or wear healing crystals, such as amethyst or labradorite, to help with decalcification.
- ◊ Holotropic breathwork, chanting om, and using the gyan wisdom mudra help open the third eye.
- ◊ Using lavender or frankincense essential oils activate the third eye/pineal gland.
- ◊ Boron is a mineral found in beets, dried plums, and in the supplemental form of borax decahydrate, all of which help reduce calcification of the pineal gland.
- ◊ Chlorophyll-rich superfoods like spirulina, chlorella, barley grass, wheatgrass, kamut, and blue-green algae are like intensified leafy greens that decalcify the pineal.

- Fluoride-free toothpastes contain silica which draw out heavy metals like fluoride.
- Iodine can be found in seaweed and in supplemental form and helps remove fluoride. It's recommended to take additional calcium and lecithin if we're iodine supplementing.
- Melatonin comes in supplemental form. It helps with wake/sleep cycles, visualization, and pineal functioning.
- Oregano oil and neem extract help with pineal gland decalcification and endocrine system purification.
- Raw apple cider vinegar is a natural pineal detoxifier due to its malic acid properties, the compound that gives fruit its sour taste.
- Raw organic cacao is chocolate in its purest form; its high antioxidant content detoxifies the pineal gland and stimulates the third eye.
- Skate liver oil contains a compound known as Activator X (Vitamins K_1 and K_2), which removes calcium deposits in the pineal gland and arteries. It also helps reverse teeth decay.
- Sun gazing at sunrise or sunset helps decalcify the pineal gland.
- Turmeric is a spice that removes fluoride. Besides consumption, making a turmeric paste with water and placing it on the forehead overnight aids in detoxification.

◊ Visualize a little miner in the brain with a pickax, chipping away at the calcified shell around the pineal, and carting off the shattered shell in a wheel barrel until the gland is fluoride-free.
◊ Zeolites are mineral-based and water-soluble compounds that help remove calcification and heavy metals from the pineal gland.

Other foods that help decalcify and improve the function of the pineal gland, while also detoxifying other parts of the body, include cilantro, Goji berries, bananas, honey, watermelon, coconut oil, hemp seeds, noni juice, garlic, Chaga mushrooms, raw lemon juice, and tamarind. Pineal gland decalcification can be assisted by eating more alkaline, energy-promoting foods such as fresh fruits, vegetables, nuts, seeds, whole grains, and root vegetables. Alkaline foods increase our pH levels to reduce body acidity, helping to increase intuition, psychic powers, dreams, creativity, peace of mind, and overall energy levels.

Magnetite is magnetic crystals found in the pineal gland and DNA. These dormant crystals could be related to homing birds or swallows' magnetic sense of direction. Although we can detect and use the Earth's magnetic field and have the crystal brain hardware, we haven't yet developed our abilities for magnetoreception, or other abilities related to full DNA activation.

T. S. Martin

The Piezoelectric Effect occurs when electromagnetic energies stimulate microcrystals in the brain causing activation of the pineal gland. The piezoelectric effect transforms energy in the body, causing a multitude of reactions from what feels like an orgasm in the brain, to healing, to mystical encounters, to being able to transcend to higher dimensions of consciousness. The effect is the result of the ascension of cerebrospinal fluid through the chakras and prana channel of the spine until it reaches the pineal gland for full activation of kundalini energy. Holding calcite quartz crystals and focusing on the pineal gland during muhla bandha meditation activates microcrystals in the brain to increase our vibrational energy. Singing bowls also help activate the mind-blowing piezoelectric effect.

The kundalini path leads to awakening and connection with our higher self. When we have experienced kundalini, we may notice health upgrades, Oneness with all, or uncommon mystical and spiritual experiences as we move into higher dimensions of consciousness. Full activation of our DNA and kundalini powers leads to new paths for the future, one in which we can use our innate abilities to rise to be our best energetic selves.

CHAPTER 18

Psychic Potentiality

"Spirituology"

There is nothing we cannot be.
There is nothing we cannot do.
There is nothing we cannot have.
Our greatest potential is our unlimited potential.

Most of us probably believe we have no intuitive skills or psychic abilities at all. The truth is, we all have psychic potential hidden away in undeveloped DNA. Now is the time to reactivate and reopen this avenue of innate knowledge. Developing psychic abilities is essential to enlightenment and can be our way to help others when governments, religions, and even education as we know it, become obsolete in the Fifth Dimension.

Knowing that we all have our own unique, innate psychic potential makes it easier to tap into and develop these strengths. It isn't a mysterious science; psychic abilities are developed by having an open pineal gland, and through paying attention, introspection, observation, and trusting our intuition.

Quantum physics is the underlying basis for paranormal, remote healing, and mystical experiences being that telepathic communication is merely accessing different holographic levels or dimensions of reality.

Extra Sensory Perception (ESP) is also known as psi or hyper communication. These are all-encompassing terms for how we channel mental energy to access clairvoyance, psychokinesis, telepathy, precognition, intuition, remote viewing, and other inner knowledge for making decisions, self-healing, and self-awareness.

Intuitiveness is considered the ability to know things without being told, and intuition is at the cornerstone of psychic abilities. Developing daily intuitive practices enhance and increase other extrasensory powers that we may be unaware of. One way to cultivate a relationship with our intuition is to assign a color to an experience that has straightforward and strong feelings attached to it. For example, an argument that made us mad is assigned a random color such as red to symbolize that feeling. Another experience that made us feel loving and romantic can be assigned a random color such as pink to unify the color with the emotion, and so forth. Once the energy of the color and emotion have fused, seeing the color will non-verbally epitomize the emotion we are intuitively feeling. So, the next time we're feeling pink, it may be time for date night.

Observing and narrating our actions to ourselves as we're doing them helps us perceive their meaning and develops psi ability. Developing awareness allows us to perceive subtle nuances in others' behavior with more clarity than someone with no attention skills. The more aware we are of what's going on around us, the better we will be at sensing and interpreting different energies.

Here are some mindset guidelines for beginning development of psychic potentiality:

- *Be Open to Tapping into Psychic Skills* by not being intimidated by our natural spiritual abilities. They are here to lead and guide us towards our highest path. Declare to the Universe that we're ready, willing, and open to exploring these gifts and we won't let fear shut us down.
- *Develop Conscious Clarity* by training ourselves to be aware of everything around us. Notice, be aware, and sense the changes in sunlight and shadows, shifts in the wind, someone who has walked into a room, or someone who has walked out, or the subtle change in someone's demeanor.
- *Practice Reading Others' Energy* to understand others' vibes. Getting a bad vibe from someone is intuition shining through, and a skill that can be strengthened. We can tune into and interpret others' energy by going beyond how they look or how they speak and by paying attention to how their actions make us *feel* about them.

- *Listen to What's Being Said* and what's not when others are speaking. Often, we say one thing but mean something entirely different. When we ask a friend, "How's life?" and their answer relates to the kids but there's no mention of the spouse, then we can use intuitive deduction. Omission is communication, and understanding between what's being said and what's not, is information that develops our psychic ability. This is one way of just "knowing."
- *Meditation* is of the best ways to develop intuition and psychic abilities because it allows us to tap into the subconscious. When we wander into the depths of our subconscious, we create an open door for messages to come through. Meditating clears the mind of clutter and allows us to better focus on our intuitive sixth sense.
- *Get in Touch with Our Spirit/Angel Guides* by calling them for support when we need it. These advanced soul mentors reside in the angelic realm of the Tenth Dimension and help guide and teach us through intuition, signs, and synchronicities. We can connect to our spirit and angel guides by mentally thinking or asking aloud a question we have in mind and calling upon them for guidance.
- *Develop the Third Eye Chakra* by opening our sixth chakra which better connects us to our intuition and subconscious. This can be done through meditation, breathwork, yoga, clearing the other chakras,

incorporating purple crystals and foods, using essential oils, and mudras.
- *Practice Environmental Scans* to cultivate psychic abilities. To do this, stand in the middle of a room and scan and explore the space with our eyes noting as many sights, sounds, and scents as possible. Pay attention to the way different energies make us feel. The more we become aware of our surroundings, the easier it is to pick up on subtle shifts in energy. Eventually, this skill can extrapolate to memories, future events, remote viewing, and astral projection.
- *Test Ourselves* by trying to confirm a hunch. Give ourselves fun games like try and guess who's calling on the phone before we look, the outfit a friend might be wearing before we meet them, or the next band playing on Pandora. Like using a muscle, easy exercises like these help develop innate abilities.
- *Trust Our Gut* when an intuitive "hit" comes. Feelings that something "isn't quite right" or "this is 'uh-mazing'" are intuitive messages that we should pay attention to.

The "clairs" is a group term for psi capabilities. These intuitive senses are commonly used for understanding hidden meanings via the Third Eye Chakra. When sensing these different intuitive capacities, which one do we resonate with and feel that the strength lies within us to develop further?

- *Clairalience – Clear Smelling* is the ability to smell something that has symbolic meaning or being able to smell something that isn't there.
- *Clairaudience – Clear Hearing* is the ability to hear sounds from the spirit world without using the ears. Clairaudience is messages and unfiltered words that pop in our head that sound like thoughts but are louder and more pronounced.
- *Claircognition – Clear Knowing* or "precognition," is an intuitive inner knowing. Thoughts of knowing that just occur, being able to predict future events, and gut instincts impart this type of intuition.
- *Clairgustance – Clear Taste* is the ability to taste without putting anything in the mouth.
- *Clairkinesthesia – Clear Touch* is the ability to sense someone's physical symptoms.
- *Clairsentience – Clear Feeling or Clear Sensing* is the ability to sense the vibes and emotions of a room and the ability to absorb the feelings of others and the environment such as "getting goosebumps," or "feeling sparks." Clairsentience's emotions arise for no apparent reason.
- *Clairtangency – Clear Touch* (psychometry) is the ability to obtain information from the vibrations and energetic memory of objects.
- *Clairvoyance – Clear Seeing* is the ability to see visions and images beyond the normal range of the visual spectrum. Clairvoyance is the ability to "see the

signs" even though they're hidden. Sometimes used in remote viewing, clairvoyance has been credited for people finding missing children and in locating lost objects.

It wouldn't be too much of a stretch to assume that aliens' and Marvel characters' superpowers are based on full DNA activation. If this were true, we could potentially have abilities of X-ray and laser vision, time travel, pyrokinesis, teleportation, invisibility, shapeshifting, extended life, and much more. In the Fifth Dimension, all powers are used for the good of humanity. Skills and jobs in the 5th Dimension also have the underlying foundation of assisting, serving, and helping Earth and others, such as:

☿ *Lithomancy* is the practice of divination by reading stones. In some cultures, the casting of stones was believed to be common, like checking the daily horoscope. However, because very little information was left by our ancestors about how to read stones, many aspects of this practice have been lost. Dedicating the time to uncover this lost art could inspire someone's life purpose.

☿ *Mediumship* is the ability to establish or receive messages from the spirit world. This psychic skill can take many forms, such as being able to see or hear actual spirits or get messages through dreams or visions. Some mediums "channel" the spirit who may speak or write through them.

☿*Numerology* is a method of interpreting what numbers mean in our lives. Chaldean numerology's emphasis relates to numbers' meanings from our name, whereas Pythagorean numerology discerns numbers' relationship to our birthdate.

☺*Angel Numbers* work under the tenets of numerology in that every number is connected to certain vibrational frequencies that symbolize and encompass meaning. They are signs of synchronicity from the Universe that signify we're on the right path. Here are some interpretations:

111 – Gateway to intuition, the subconscious, and trusting our heart

222 – Confirmation that we're on the right path, duality of life

333 – Spiritual guidance, prayers are coming true, and closure of 3D reality

444 – Spiritual protection and 4D mastery of thought

555 – Exciting changes are coming representative of 5D, freedom, and adventure

666 – Creation of Merkabah, overfocus on materialism and ego, and the composition of DNA consisting of 6 protons, 6 electrons, and 6 neutrons

777 – Luck is coming our way, spiritual connection to the Crown Chakra

888 – Balance, rebirth, infinity

999 – Humanitarianism, a complete life cycle from beginning to end, a triad signifying completion, fulfillment, and attainment

911 – 9 (endings) and 11 (DNA) means the end of double strand DNA

1010 – Self-realization, reality is a biogenetic experiment created from numbers

0 – The Tree of Life, zero point, the void, the eternal, the nothingness of death and the totality of life

Some consider these "Angel Numbers" as signs from above; however, these numbers correspond to the symbolic history of sacred geometry and to dimensional planes on the Tree of Life, triggering the subconscious memory to alter our DNA. Since reality is composed of sequential numerical codes such as 0101010, number patterns access the subconscious to unlock dormant DNA.

☼ *Tarot Card Reading* is a pictorial representation of the Tree of Life and serves as an intuitive depiction of life events.

☼ *Telekinesis and Psychokinesis* are the abilities to move objects through the power of the mind without using hands to physically move the object. Many people currently possess this skill.

☼ *Telepathy* is being able to communicate with those in the afterlife; Indigo children are naturally born telepathic. This skill has many implications, including healing from past-life trauma.

MIND BLOWN

Possible Future Occupations

- ⚡ All Energy-Healing Techniques (color, crystals, essential oils, light, sound, and water)
- ⚡ Affirmation, Breathing, Meditation, and Visualization Techniques Teachings
- ⚡ Aura and Tarot Readings
- ⚡ Botanical Medicines
- ⚡ Crystallography
- ⚡ DNA Activation
- ⚡ Earth Grid Repair & Restoration
- ⚡ Energy Management & Manipulation Classes
- ⚡ Levitation, Teleportation, and Shapeshifting 101
- ⚡ Magus (Immortality) Practitioner
- ⚡ Mind Control Weather Patterning
- ⚡ Opening the Clairs and Chakras Classes
- ⚡ Past-Life Regression Hypnosis
- ⚡ Psi Classes and Telepathic Teachings
- ⚡ Self-Healing, Distance Healing, and Holistic Healing

T. S. Martin

For Fun, a Future Business Card

> ### Evolutionary Light Worker – Pure Love Life Coach
> Available for Altering Systems of Consciousness within the Free-Will Universe
>
> *As a Pure Love Light Life Coach, I help integrate spiritual guidance and knowledge for consciousness expansion and DNA upgrades to help you connect to your Higher Self.*
>
>
>
> ∞ Reiki, Reflexology, Realignment & Regression Readings ∞
> Currently Training & Hiring Energy and Light Worker Professionals

The future of the Fifth Dimension will call on those with healing powers to help and teach others to do the same. As some professions become obsolete, training will be needed to teach new spiritual attainment skills to others. Finding a job within the spiritual industry may be a calling that provides answers for our life's purpose. One goal of this book was to point the way to higher consciousness using energy-based techniques such as thought, meditation, and visualization. Another was to shift our minds from 3D to 5D thinking to make way for the celestial shift in ages. By connecting to our subconscious mind, we can create and manifest enlightenment, health, and happiness. With every door we open, every person we meet, every skill we learn, and every idea we create, we continually become a better energetic version of ourselves.

CONCLUSION

The Evolution from Carbon to Crystal - from Compliance to Cognizance

"You must be the change you want to see in the world."
— MAHATMA GANDHI

We're in a time of transition—a galactic kundalini, considered to be the greatest evolutionary event in human history. As star systems of the Universe align, we awaken from the Piscean Age of power to the Age of Aquarius where humanity takes back the powers of its birthright. As we shift from 3D to 5D, we move from a dimension of "survival of the fittest," an old belief system of evolution and separation where every man fends for himself, to that of 5D, a dimension filled with love, compassion, and Oneness of All. The Age of Aquarius can be compared to the golden days of Atlantis.

The Great Awakening into One Consciousness

As the Fifth Dimension changes us from two-strand carbon bodies to 12-strand crystal beings, Third-Dimension belief systems will be left behind as more become aware of religion's fear-based ideology and corporations that don't have the best interests of All in mind. More of us are awakening and unplugging from the matrix because we realize we don't need an outside force to dictate the limits of our potential. As consciousness shifts from compliance to cognizance, the shift will enable us to create health, healing, happiness, and harmony for ourselves, others, and the planet.

The continual rise in the Schumann Resonance, the vibration of Earth, indicates that the collective consciousnesses of All are increasing, and we must keep the vibrations rising to help Planet Earth. The global shift in everyone's consciousness will help us focus on what we really want and need to create for our planet.

One suggestion for a new planet consciousness is to turn the overabundant grassy fields of schools and churches into vegetable and botanical herb gardens. These community gardens would be available to everyone, including the homeless, at no charge, for donations or in exchange for garden maintenance. Members of the church, schools, or anyone in the community willingly take care of the gardens in exchange for food. Anyone can go in, pull a few weeds, and come out with fresh vegetables for the evening's meal.

It is hard to say if churches will still be viable institutions in the Fifth Dimension; however, their buildings need not go unused. As well as having the grounds serve as community gardens, churches can be converted into 'spirituology' retreats, again, available for everyone's use. Sunday mass becomes Sunday meditation. Individual rooms within the once-religious buildings can be used for spiritual and energy-based healing businesses.

How Can I Raise My Consciousness to Raise Global Consciousness?

- Live a life with intention and awareness.
- Cultivate a spirituology practice that suits our needs.
- Align our actions and raise our vibration to the emotion and frequency of love.
- Integrate our shadows, ditch old beliefs, and mend our karmic history.
- Understand our life's purpose through self-reflection and doing what we love.
- Find peace and purpose by quieting our mind and listening to our heart.
- Be kind, caring, and compassionate to everyone and everything.
- Trust our innate wisdom to guide our soul's journey of growth.
- Find forgiveness for ourselves and others.
- Live without limitation.

MIND BLOWN

Inner peace creates peace for the world.

To reach our true potential, we must consciously design our days with intention and purpose. With newfound knowledge that we are creators of our reality and masters our mind, there are no limits to our heart's desires. Compassionate thinking and love are the energies that can make anything happen. It's now our time to vibrationally rise to the occasion and create a beautiful future for us, humanity, and Earth.

According to numerology, we're at the end of a cycle. If history is to repeat itself, we could end up at the bottom of an ocean, or we could save the planet depending on the integrity of our actions. As members of the family of light, our job is to carry higher frequencies into the next dimension. In the Fifth Dimension, the meaning of "love and light" will evolve to a new understanding of what truly makes us human living on Planet Earth.

The Fifth Dimension is ultimate consciousness. It's about new and expanded ways to live, think, and feel. It's about making better choices and shedding layers of the matrix illusion. It's knowing that peace and joy come from living in the present moment and love for One is love for All.

Not knowing all the answers helps keep the humility in humanity.
With joy, safety, and harmony, I step into the unknown.

"Man, the beautiful creation of endless possibilities as a result of the one mind, crafted through the quadromillions of molecular possibilities and Universal shifting. Never have I realized that so well until now. The Universe's repetition of the law that's most important – what keeps us together – is the most noticeable of its kind. As magnets attract, as gravity holds planets, and as a kiss to your love brings you closer, our Universe christens us within its warm arms.

Sometimes I look at the many things around me and cry with happiness, and sometimes I leave offerings to the Earth, and thank the Great Mother for such a wonderful gift she allows us to have. As we reside in her womb, I've always wondered, after we've outgrown this world, what beautiful thing shall we receive next?"

Yoshimitsu, age 13
Virginia, USA

BIBLIOGRAPHY

Adler, V. (2022, February 24). *The Fifth Dimension and the Future of Mankind.* Retrieved from https://en.wikiquote.org/wiki/The_Fifth_Dimension_and_the_Future_of_Mankind

Aliff, A. (n.d.). Numerology. *The Awakened State.* Retrieved from https://www.theawakenedstate.net/numerology/

Amen, D. (2019, October 17). How negative thoughts affect brain health + what to do about them. *MindBodyGreen.* Retrieved from https://www.mindbodygreen.com/articles/how-negative-thoughts-affect-brain-health-what-to-do-about-them

The American Cancer Society Medical and Editorial Content Team. (2021, November 19). Getting photodynamic therapy. *American Cancer Society.* Retrieved from https://www.cancer.org/treatment/treatments-and-side-effects/treatment-types/radiation/photodynamic-therapy.html

Anodea, J., and White, A. (2021). The complete guide to the 7 chakras—for beginners. *Mindvalley.* Retrieved from https://blog.mindvalley.com/7-chakras/

As above, so below [Digital Image]. (2022, February 16). *The Law of Awareness.* Retrieved from https://www.instagram.com/p/CaC7w-6sDNi/?hl=en

Austin, V. (2015). *Self-Hypnosis. Reach Your Full Potential Using All of Your Mind.* London, UK: Hay House, Inc.

Backman, L. (2014). *The Evolving Soul: Spiritual Healing Through Past Life Exploration.* Woodbury, MN: Llewellyn Publications.

Baldwin, A., and Trent, N. (2017, August). An integrative review of scientific evidence for reconnective healing. *MaryAnn Liebert, Inc. Publishers.* Retrieved from https://www.liebertpub.com/doi/10.1089/acm.2015.0218

Bernard, R. W. (n.d.). Agharta, the subterranean world. The hollow earth. Chapter 7.2. *Bibliotecapleyades.* Retrieved from https://www.bibliotecapleyades.net/tierra_hueca/tierrahueca/Chapter7-2.htm

Bhaumik, G. (n.d.). Sound healing—how it works and its health benefits. *Destination Deluxe.* Retrieved from https://destinationdeluxe.com/sound-healing-health-benefits/

Bhaumik. G. (n.d.). The new energy healing: how science is making traditional practices mainstream. *Destination Deluxe.* Retrieved from https://destinationdeluxe.com/energy-healing-science-shamanism/

Bien, J. (2018). On the verge with violet. *Lumalight by Spectrahue™.* Retrieved from https://spectrahue.com/color-violet-meaning/

Black, W. (2018, December 7). Fire letters—history behind it and activating them to help you manifest. *The Awakening Within.* Retrieved from https://theawakeningwithin.net/blog/fire-letters/

Blair, E., and Galland, L. (n.d.). 8 surprising effects of black cumin seed. *Atlanova.* Retrieved from https://atlanova.com/8-surprising-benefits-of-black-cumin-seed/

Blakeway, J. (2019). *Energy Healing.* The Science and Mystery of Healing. New York, NY: HarperCollins Publishers.

Blueprint. (2021, August 5). *Ascension Glossary.* Retrieved from https://ascensionglossary.com/index.php/Blueprint

Braden, G. (2017). *Human By Design. From Evolution by Chance to Transformation by Choice.* Carlsbad, CA: Hay House, Inc.

Cannon, D. (2001). *The Convoluted Universe, Book One.* Huntsville, AR: Ozark Mountain Publishing.

Caron, M. (n.d.). The Taoist rejuvenation technique of 'bone breathing.' *SivanaEast*. Retrieved from https://blog.sivanaspirit.com/md-sp-taoist-technique-bone-breathing/

Cascella, N. (n.d.). The science behind aromatherapy. *NuWorld Botanicals*. Retrieved from https://nuworldbotanicals.com/miscellaneous/science-behind-aromatherapy/

Chakra locations on the head [Digital Image]. *The Chakra Collective.* (2022). Retrieved from https://www.reddit.com/r/TheChakraCollective/comments/wx1c2h/chakras_and_points_on_the_head/

Chamness, R. (n.d.). What is light language? *Sound Waves Heal.* Retrieved from https://www.soundwavesheal.com/light-language/

Cherubim, L. (2018, July 29). Fire letters, DNA, and more. *Xen Qabbalah Wiki.* Retrieved from https://xenqabbalah.fandom.com/wiki/User_blog:Dimensional_consciousness/Fire_letters,_DNA_and_more

Cherubim, L. (n.d.). Zero-point energy. *Xen Qabbalah Wiki.* Retrieved from https://xenqabbalah.fandom.com/wiki/Zero-point_energy

Chittaranjan, A., and Radhakrishnan, R. (2009). Prayer and healing: A medical and scientific perspective on randomized controlled trials. *National Library of Medicine.* Retrieved from https://www.ncbi.nlm.nih.gov/pmc/articles/PMC2802370/

Chmelik, S. (2019, April 30). How the vagus nerve positively boosts your well-being. *Sensate*. Retrieved from https://www.getsensate.com/blogs/news/everything-vagus-nerve

Color meanings and symbolism. (2022). *Art Therapy*. Retrieved from http://www.arttherapyblog.com/online/color-meanings-symbolism/#

Craig, S. (2014, March 4). Martyr syndrome/compassion fatigue part 2: Can hypnotherapy help? *Hypnolight*. Retrieved from https://hypnolight.co.uk/martyr-syndrome-compassion-part-2-can-hypnotherapy-help/

Croft, W. (n.d.). Geometric Information Field Technology (GIFT). *LightfieldSystems*. Retrieved from http://www.lightfield.com/gift.htm

Croke, M. (n.d.). What is colorpuncture? *U.S. Esogetic Colorpuncture Institute*. Retrieved from https://colorpuncture.org/about/

Cross, A. (2018, May 13). The great 440 Hz conspiracy, and why all of our music is wrong: Alan Cross. *Global News*. Retrieved from https://globalnews.ca/news/4194106/440-hz-conspiracy-music/

Dadabhay, Y. (2022, May 23). How to manifest money with the amazing power of visualization. *Subconscious Servant*. Retrieved from https://subconsciousservant.com/manifest-money-visualization/

Davidson, K. (2020, August 5). What are the Ayurveda doshas? Vata, kapha, and pitta explained. *Healthline*. Retrieved from https://www.healthline.com/nutrition/vata-dosha-pitta-dosha-kapha-dosha

Davies, P. (n.d.). 6 tips on how to balance your chakras. *Destination Deluxe*. Retrieved from https://destinationdeluxe.com/balance-chakras/

Davis, S. (2020, July 28). 5 easy houseplants to love based on your mental health needs. *Healthline*. Retrieved from https://www.healthline.com/health/mental-health/plants-self-care

Dawson, D., Neville, H., Adames, H., Chavez-Dueñas, N., French, B., Lewis, J., Chen, G., & Mosley, D. (2021, August 2). Curating Radical Healing communication technologies. *Psychology Today*. Retrieved from https://www.psychologytoday.com/us/blog/healing-through-social-justice/202108/curating-radical-healing-communication-technologies

Day, N. (2022, February 21). [Digital Image]. Emotion wheel printable for kids. *He's Extraordinary. Tools for Raising an Extraordinary Person*. Retrieved from https://hes-extraordinary.com/emotion-wheel-for-kids

Delafield, M. (n.d.). *The Energetic Repatterning Technique*. Retrieved from http://marthadelafield.com/energy-psychotherapy-2/spinal-release/

Discard ego [Digital Image]. (2022, February 7). *Cherry Bomb 8888*. Retrieved from https://www.instagram.com/p/CZrAJgJBV-I/?hl=en

Discover the Energy Enhancement System! (n.d.). *Emerge Integrative Wellness*. Retrieved from https://emergeyogawellness.com/eesystem/

Dispenza, J. (2017). *Becoming Supernatural. How Common People are Doing the Uncommon*. Carlsbad, CA: Hay House, Inc.

Doctor, I don't feel well [Digital Image]. (2018, October 1). *Spiritual Science Official*. Retrieved from https://www.instagram.com/p/BoYwwxJgBOC/?hl=en

Dr. Gerald Pollack. The most important scientist you've never heard about. (2020, December 4). *The Wellness Enterprise*. Retrieved from https://thewellnessenterprise.com/dr-gerald-pollack/

Dr. Masaru Emoto and water consciousness. (2017, March 23). *The Wellness Enterprise*. Retrieved from https://thewellnessenterprise.com/emoto/

Ear heart [Digital Image]. (2022, April 7). *The Law of Awareness*. Retrieved from https://www.instagram.com/p/CcDlLP2KHf4/?hl=en

Earthing [Digital Image]. (2021, June 13). *The Law of Awareness*. Retrieved from https://www.instagram.com/p/CQEPjQ7lPsK/?hl=en

Ebner, K. (2005). *Health and Healing through Water*. Retrieved from https://scholarsbank.uoregon.edu/xmlui/bitstream/handle/1794/1916/ARM_Ebner.pdf;sequence=1

Eden, D. (2022, March 14). *Radiant Circuits: The Pathways to Joy, Bliss & Wonder!* Retrieved from https://edenmethod.easywebinar.live/registration-12-login?key=8a65db5f1c2c116021b9e41579442ccb

Edwards, D. (2012, October 1). The piezoelectric effect and the pineal gland in the human body. *The Awakened State*. Retrieved from https://theawakenedstate.tumblr.com/post/32678761714/the-piezoelectric-effect-and-the-pineal-gland-in

Elevate your energy with high frequency foods. (n.d.). *Royal Fruits*. Retrieved from https://www.royalfruits.com.au/how-to-increase-vibrational-frequency/

EMDR Healing Team. (2022, July 18). How to self-administer EMDR therapy from home. *EMDR Healing*. Retrieved from https://emdrhealing.com/how-to-self-administer-emdr-therapy/

Emoto's water crystals [Digital Image]. (2021, October 27). *The Law of Awareness*. Retrieved from https://www.instagram.com/p/CVibsk4pOoF/?hl=en

Estrada, J. (2020, February 25). We're all a little psychic—here are 4 ways to develop that intuitive muscle. *Well + Good.* Retrieved from https://www.wellandgood.com/how-to-develop-psychic-abilities/

Fallis, J. (2022, April 24). How to stimulate your vagus nerve for better mental health. *Optimal Living Dynamics.* Retrieved from https://www.optimallivingdynamics.com/blog/how-to-stimulate-your-vagus-nerve-for-better-mental-health-brain-vns-ways-treatment-activate-natural-foods-depression-anxiety-stress-heart-rate-variability-yoga-massage-vagal-tone-dysfunction

Fiolet, S. (2020, September 6). The spiritual meaning of the Platonic solids. *Sacred Creation.* Retrieved from https://www.sacredgeometryshop.com/spirituality/the-spiritual-meaning-platonic-solids/

5 ways to stimulate your vagus nerve. (2022, March 10). *Cleveland Clinic.* Retrieved from https://health.clevelandclinic.org/vagus-nerve-stimulation/

Forrester, M. (2013, August 5). How DNA is reprogrammed by words and frequencies. *Bibliotecapleyades.* Retrieved from https://bibliotecapleyades.net/ciencia/ciencia_genoma73.htm

Fosu, K. (2020, August 25). These things were keeping me in a low vibration. *Mystic Minds.* Retrieved from https://medium.com/mystic-minds/these-things-were-keeping-me-in-a-low-vibration-9ae4f5b2b882

Gadbois, L. (2018, January 29). DNA—the phantom effect, quantum hologram and the etheric body. *MedCrave*. Retrieved from https://medcraveonline.com/MOJPB/dna-the-phantom-effect-quantum-hologram-and-the-etheric-body.html

Garis, M. (2020, July 28). How to use each of the 4 'clair' senses to receive informational psychically. *Well + Good*. Retrieved from https://www.wellandgood.com/psychic-clair-senses/

Gillihan, S. (2016, November 1). Discovering new options: Self-help Cognitive Behavioral Therapy. *National Alliance on Mental Illness*. Retrieved from https://www.nami.org/Blogs/NAMI-Blog/November-2016/Discovering-New-Options-Self-Help-Cognitive-Behav

Glass, J., McKusick, E., & Wooten, V. (2022, March 2). *Science of Healing Summit*. Sound: A safe space for emotional healing. Retrieved from https://scienceofhealingsummit.com/program/47024

Golden Merkabah [Digital Image]. (2022, November 3). *Higher Dimensions*. Retrieved from https://www.facebook.com/photo/?fbid=211471121223390&set=g.2454207508135615

Goldsmith, M. (2009, May 19). Are you full of mojo or nojo? *Bloomberg*. Retrieved from https://www.bloomberg.com/news/articles/2009-05-19/are-you-full-of-mojo-or-nojo

Gowmon, V. (n.d.). Activating light codes—The genetic seeds of your soul's cosmic garden. *Vince Gowmon Healing for a New World.* Retrieved from https://www.vincegowmon.com/activating-light-codes/

Guenther, B. (2022, May 24). Covid vaccines—consequences on the soul, spirit, and life after death. *Bibliotecapleyades.* Retrieved from https://www.bibliotecapleyades.net/ciencia3/ciencia_conscioushumanenergy616.htm?

Guenther, B. (n.d.). Holographic Kinetics. An advanced Aboriginal healing modality. *Veil of Reality.* Retrieved from https://veilofreality.com/holographic-kinetics/

Hand, E. (2016, June 23). Maverick scientist thinks he has discovered a magnetic sixth sense in humans. *Science.* Retrieved from https://www.science.org/content/article/maverick-scientist-thinks-he-has-discovered-magnetic-sixth-sense-humans

Harris, M. (n.d.). A beginner's guide to crystal healing. *Destination Deluxe.* Retrieved from https://destinationdeluxe.com/crystal-healing/

Hartenstein, M. (2010, July 20). Botox improves happiness, says new study: injections stop frowns and trick brain into feeling better. *NY Daily News.* Retrieved from https://www.nydailynews.com/life-style/botox-improves-happiness-new-study-injections-stop-frowns-trick-brain-feeling-better-article-1.467026

Hartsfield, C. (2021, September 3). Hidden symbolism of the pinecone. *Medium*. Retrieved from https://medium.com/@chad.hartsfield84/stroking-your-interest-in-the-hidden-symbolism-of-the-pinecone-2813fc329953

Hart, W. (2017). *Ancient Alien Ancestors. Advanced Technologies that Terraformed Our World.* Rochester, VT: Bear & Company.

Hattangadi, V. (2022, September 26). *What is Chromotherapy?* Retrieved from https://drvidyahattangadi.com/what-is-chromotherapy/

Hay, L. (1984). *Heal Your Body.* Carlsbad, CA: Hay House, Inc.

Hay, L. (n.d.). What is mirror work? *Louise Hay.* Retrieved from https://www.louisehay.com/what-is-mirror-work/

Haze, X. (2018). *Ancient Aliens in the Bible. Evidence of UFO's, Nephilim, and the True Face of Angels in Ancient Scriptures.* Wayne, NJ: The Career Press, Inc.

Hicks, E., and Hicks, J. (2004). *Ask and It Is Given. Learning to Manifest Your Desires.* Carlsbad, CA: Hay House, Inc.

Hoodah, T. (2015, July 28). What is color light therapy? *Natural Awakenings Tampa.* Retrieved from https://www.natampa.com/2015/07/28/242419/what-is-color-light-therapy-

Hopler, W. (2019, May 23). Archangel Metatron's cube in sacred geometry. The geometry and patterns of creation. *Learn Religions.* Retrieved from https://www.learnreligions.com/archangel-metatrons-cube-in-sacred-geometry-124293

Horeis, M. (2020, June 23). The vagus nerve: Your secret weapon in fighting stress. *Allied Health Services Integrated Health System.* Retrieved from https://www.allied-services.org/news/2020/june/the-vagus-nerve-your-secret-weapon-in-fighting- r

The human-animal bond for mental health. (2020, May 18). *Habri.* Retrieved from https://habri.org/blog/the-human-animal-bond-for-mental-health/

Hunt, A. (2014, November 16). Top 8 supplements to boost your pineal gland function. *Waking Times.* Retrieved from http://www.wakingtimes.com/top-8-supplements-boost-pineal-gland-function/

Iachia, J. (2019, February 6). Learn to live on higher vibrations. *Food for Soul.* Retrieved from https://medium.com/food-for-soul/learn-to-live-on-higher-vibrations-e67ea515e5f

Ijaz, R. (2021, September 17). What is quantum healing? How does it work? *Health Works Collective.* Retrieved from https://www.healthworkscollective.com/what-is-quantum-healing-how-does-it-work/

Inglis-Arkell, E. (2011, February 24). The Fibonacci series: When math turns golden. *Gizmodo*. Retrieved from https://gizmodo.com/the-fibonacci-series-when-math-turns-golden-5768696

Inner child wounds [Digital Image]. (2021, April 9). *We the Aether*. Retrieved from https://www.instagram.com/p/CNc6KfSLMIr/?hl=en

Internal Family Systems Therapy. (2022, May 20). *Psychology Today*. Retrieved from https://www.psychologytoday.com/us/therapy-types/internal-family-systems-therapy

Jacques, E. (2022, March 17). Ultrasound therapy treatment for chronic pain. *Very Well Health*. Retrieved from https://www.verywellhealth.com/what-is-ultrasound-therapy-2564506

Jarrell, J., and Farmer, S. (2017, November). Anunnaki revealed. *Bibliotecapleyades*. Retrieved from https://www.bibliotecapleyades.net/sumer_anunnaki/anunnaki/anu_102.htm

Julson, E. (2022, January 26). The 14 best nootropics and smart drugs reviewed. *Healthline*. Retrieved from https://www.healthline.com/nutrition/nootropics

Judith, A. (2016). *Chakras. Seven Keys to Awakening and Healing the Energy Body*. Carlsbad, CA: Hay House.

Kelly, A. (2018, July 2). Am I psychic? How to tap into your own psychic abilities. *Allure*. Retrieved from https://www.allure.com/story/am-i-psychic-how-to-tap-into-psychic-abilities

Langlois, O. (n.d.). Egyptian third eye (pineal gland) secret: The eye of Horus. *Olivier Health Tips*. Retrieved from https://olivierhealthtips.com/egyptian-third-eye-of-horus/

Lee, C. (n.d.). Intermittent fasting 101—what, how & why? *Destination Deluxe*. Retrieved from https://destinationdeluxe.com/intermittent-fasting-diet/

Levy, P. (2014). Dispelling wetiko: Breaking the curse of evil. *The Theosophical Society in America*. Retrieved from https://www.theosophical.org/publications/quest-magazine/3472-dispelling-wetiko-breaking-the-curse-of-evil

Liana, L. (n.d.). Hapé medicine—the sacred Amazonian snuff you blow up your nose. *EntheoNation*. Retrieved from https://entheonation.com/blog/hape-amazonian-snuff/

Licalzi, D. (2022, April 8). Autophagy: What you should know before starting your fast. *Inside Tracker*. Retrieved from https://blog.insidetracker.com/autophagy-know-before-starting-fast

Likhov, M. (2022, March 31). The Golden ratio. Alignment to the Universe's frequency through sacred geometry. *Modern Ōm*.

Retrieved from https://www.modernom.co/blogs/blog/the-magic-of-fibonacci-sequence-the-golden-ratio

Life, D. (2007, August 28). Mula bandha: Your ticket to infinity and beyond. *Yoga Journal.* Retrieved from https://www.yogajournal.com/practice/beginners/how-to/to-infinity-and-beyond/

Light Therapy Medical Affairs. (2022, March 12). Blue light therapy: Benefits, uses, and science. *Light Therapy.* Retrieved from https://lighttherapy.org/blue-light-therapy/

Little, D. (n.d.). Miasms in classical homeopathy. *Whole Health Now.* Retrieved from https://www.wholehealthnow.com/homeopathy_pro/miasms-03.html

Liu, L. (2021, July 20). Learn more about the benefits of the terahertz stone. *Laurel Liu.* Retrieved from https://www.laurelliu.com/blogs/learn-more-about-the-benefits-of-the-terahertz-

Lombardo, A. (2019, April 18). 4 steps to eliminating self-limiting beliefs & creating possibility. *MindBodyGreen.* Retrieved from https://www.mindbodygreen.com/articles/4-steps-to-eliminating-self-limiting-beliefs-and-creating-possibility

Longdon, E. (2020). *Vibrational Sound Healing. Take Your Sonic Vitamins with Tuning Forks, Singing Bowls, Chakra Chants, Angelic Vibrations, and Other Sound Therapies.* Rochester, Vermont: Healing Arts Press.

Luna, A. (2022, January 13). How to use a dowsing pendulum for divination—A beginner's guide. *Loner Wolf.* Retrieved from https://lonerwolf.com/dowsing-pendulum/

Luna, A. (2022, January 28). Synchronicity: 7 ways to interpret and manifest it. *Loner Wolf.* Retrieved from https://lonerwolf.com/synchronicity/

The lungs produce the most DMT [Digital Image]. (2019, April 23). *Breathing God.* Retrieved from https://www.instagram.com/p/BwmSte6na8q/?hl=en

"Magic mushrooms," psilocybin and mental health. (2022, May 15). *University Hospitals. The Science of Health.* Retrieved from https://www.uhhospitals.org/blog/articles/2022/05/magic-mushrooms-psilocybin-and-mental-health

Marciniak, B. (1990, November 15). Genetic changes. *Bibliotecapleyades.* Retrieved from https://bibliotecapleyades.net/pleyades/esp_pleyades_15a.htm

Mattern, M. (2019, December 3). How to access your subconscious mind in 4 steps. *Gaia.* Retrieved from https://www.gaia.com/article/4-steps-access-your-subconscious

McClure, B., and Byrd, D. (2021, January 8). When will the Age of Aquarius begin? EarthSky. Retrieved from https://earthsky.org/human-world/when-will-the-age-of-aquarius-begin/

McTaggart, L. (2017). *The Power of Eight. Harnessing the Miraculous Energies of a Small Group to Heal Others, Your Life, and the World.* New York, NY: Atria Books.

Me in a crystal shop [Digital Image]. (2022, October 26). *Loving Thyself Rocks.* Retrieved from https://www.instagram.com/p/CkJAdSnukxm/?hl=en

Messelbeck, L. (2020). Ear seeds: Do they really work? *Life Point Acupuncture.* Retrieved from https://lifepointacupuncture.com/blog/2020/4/13/ear-seeds

Me trying to explain to toxic people why I can't be around them [Digital Image]. *blue.marble.mentor.* (2020, October 25). Retrieved from https://www.instagram.com/p/CGxQUS3niNr/?hl=en

Mishra, S. (2014, April 28). DNA and chakra activation the gateway to higher consciousness. *Speaking Tree.* Retrieved from https://www.speakingtree.in/blog/dna-and-chakra-activation-the-gateway-to-higher-consciousness

Mishra, S. (2017, October). Electroceuticals in medicine—the brave new future. *Science Direct.* Retrieved from https://www.sciencedirect.com/science/article/pii/S0019483217308131#:~:text=Electroceuticals

Molnar, B (2017, June 6). 5 ways to raise your vibration and have more positive energy (part 1). *Follow Your Own Rhythm.* Retrieved from https://www.followyourownrhythm.com/blog-1/2017/6/18/5-ways-to-raise-your-vibration-and-have-more-positive-energy

Molnar, B. (2017, July 10). 10 toxic habits that are lowering your vibration (part 2). *Follow Your Own Rhythm.* Retrieved from https://www.followyourownrhythm.com/blog-1/2017/6/18/5bsh1ry hitjsknubf47tnv1grtc6nq

Morphogenetic field. (2019, February 18). *Ascension Glossary.* Retrieved from https://ascensionglossary.com/index.php/Morphogenetic_Field

Murray, P. (n.d.). *From two to twelve strand DNA.* Retrieved from https://pammurray.tripod.com/DNA1and2.html

Murray, P. (n.d.). *What is Spiritual Response Therapy (SRT)?* Retrieved from https://pammurray.tripod.com/srt.html

Myers, S. (2013, February 14). Alkaline foods to help decalcify the pineal gland. *Waking Times.* Retrieved from https://www.wakingtimes.com/alkaline-foods-to-help-decalcify-the-pineal-gland/

Neville, H., Adames, H., Chavez-Dueñas, N., Chen, G., French, B., Lewis, J., & Mosley, D. (2019, March 5). The psychology of radical healing. What can psychology tell us about healing from racial and ethnic trauma? *Psychology Today.* Retrieved from https://www.psychologytoday.com/us/blog/healing-through-social-justice/201903/the-psychology-radical-healing

Newton, M. (2000). *Destiny of Souls: New Case Studies of Life Between Lives*. Woodbury, MN: Llewellyn Publications.

Nikolai, M. (2016). LifeLine Technique. *LifeLine Healing*. Retrieved from https://www.lifelinehealing.com/

O'Conner, S. (2020, January 13). [Digital Image]. Brainwave chart. *Psychedelic Science Review*. Retrieved from https://psychedelicreview.com/altered-oscillations-the-modulatory-effect-of-dmt-on-brain-waves/

Perrakis, A. (2019). *The Chakras Handbook*. Quarto Publishing Group USA Inc.: FairWinds.

Perry, M. (2017, November 9). What is Seraphim Blueprint? *Wings Unfurled*. Retrieved from https://wings-unfurled.com/what-is-seraphim-blueprint/

Phillips, K. (2019, June 2). How do you know if you have a miasm? *Thrive with Wellness*. Retrieved from https://www.thrivewithwellness.us/blog/miasm

Phillips, L. (2017, January 9). Five manifestation hacks. *To Be Magnetic*. Retrieved from https://tobemagnetic.com/tbm-blog/2017/1/9/five-manifestation-hacks-manifestation

Phillips, L. (2016, April 18). Negative thoughts. *To Be Magnetic.* Retrieved from https://tobemagnetic.com/tbm-blog/2016/4/18/negative-thoughts

Pinchbeck, D. (2003, September 19). Ten years of therapy in one night. *The Guardian.* Retrieved from https://www.theguardian.com/books/2003/sep/20/booksonhealth.lifeandhealth

The power of healing with water and energy. (2021, October 20). *The Qi.* Retrieved from https://the-qi.com/blogs/journal/the-power-of-healing-with-water-and-energy

The power of water [Digital Image]. (2022, September 29). *Billion Million Business.* Retrieved from https://www.instagram.com/p/CjFtWY3Pmus/?hl=en

Prath, S, (n.d.). How to get rid of limiting beliefs using qi gong. *Tai Chi Basics.* Retrieved from https://taichibasics.com/how-to-get-rid-of-limiting-beliefs-using-qi-gong/

Prescott, G. (2017, October 9). 30 astral projection techniques. *In5D.* Retrieved from https://in5d.com/30-astral-projection-techniques/

Prescott, G. (2015, February 25). Symbolism for a type 1 civilization; breaking out of the 3D symbolism. *In5D.* Retrieved from https://in5d.com/symbolism-for-a-type-1-civilization-breaking-out-of-the-3d-symbolism/

Prescott, G. (2015, March 20). Your graduation into The Age of Aquarius. *In5D*. Retrieved from https://in5d.com/your-graduation-into-the-age-of-aquarius/

Quantum apometry: the deep healing encounter. (2022). *Supergirl*. Retrieved from https://supergirl.life/quantum-apometry-the-deep-healing-encounter/

Raby, J. (2022, May 16). The 12 chakras system and how to activate each energy center. *The Yoga Nomads*. Retrieved from https://www.theyoganomads.com/12-chakras-system/

Rajan, S. (2020, October 16). Platonic solids and sacred shapes for healing. *The Sacred Being*. Retrieved from https://thesacredbeing.com/platonic-solids-and-sacred-shapes-for-healing/

Raphael, D. and Charles, D. (2014, January 24). Iboga, the matrix, and pineal gland decalcification. *Bibliotecapleyades*. Retrieved from https://bibliotecapleyades.net/ciencia/ciencia_brain63.htm

Red light therapy: benefits, side effects, & uses. (2021, December 1). *Cleveland Clinic*. Retrieved from https://my.clevelandclinic.org/health/articles/22114-red-light-therapy

ReGain Editorial Team. (2022, June 23). What is color therapy, what is it for, and is it right for me? *ReGain*. Retrieved from https://www.regain.us/advice/therapist/what-is-color-therapy-what-is-it-for-and-is-it-right-for-me/

Regan, S. (2022, April 27). Manifestation 101: What it is & how to use it for love, money, & more. *MindBodyGreen*. Retrieved from https://www.mindbodygreen.com/articles/manifestation

Regan, S. (2021, June 16). Self-fulfilling prophecies & how to overcome negative ones, from experts. *MindBodyGreen*. Retrieved from https://www.mindbodygreen.com/articles/guide-to-self-fulfilling-prophecies-pygmalion-effect

Renier, N. (2011). *The Practical Psychic.* Avon, MA: Adams Media.

Richards, S. (2018, November). Aboriginal Dreamtime Healing using Holographic Kinetics. *Holographic Kinetics*. Retrieved from https://www.holographickinetics.com/

Rodrigo, A. (2017, July 7). Light symbol codes. *Ascension Dictionary.* Retrieved from https://www.ascensiondictionary.com/2017/07/light-symbol-codes.html

Ruscio, M. (2021, December 31). Does vagus nerve tapping live up to the hype? Your guide to vagus nerve stimulation. *Dr. Ruscio Blog.* Retrieved from https://drruscio.com/vagus-nerve-tapping/

Sacco, R. (2017, April 17). The purpose of life and golden ratio explained. *Fibonacci Lifechart.* Retrieved from http://www.fibonaccilifechart.com/blog/the-purpose-of-life-and-golden-ratio-explained

Sacred geometry symbols [Digital Images]. (2021, July 26). *7 Chakras Store.* Retrieved from https://7chakrastore.com/blogs/news/sacred-geometry

Saha, M. (2022, June 29). Forget Flat-Earth, Donut Earth theory is gaining popularity. *Truth Theory.* Retrieved from https://truththeory.com/donut-earth-theory-is-gaining-popularity/

Sarich, C. (2013, March 29). Ways to cleanse the body…from chemtrails, GMOs, fluoridated water, and other environmental toxins. *Bibliotecapleyades.* Retrieved from https://www.bibliotecapleyades.net/ciencia/ciencia_industryhealthiermedica152.htm

Scher, Amy. (2022, July 13). 7 ridiculously simple tapping techniques to unblock your chakras. *Soul & Spirit.* Retrieved from https://www.soulandspiritmagazine.com/13951-2/

Science the torus. (2022). *Monatomic Orme.* Retrieved from https://monatomic-orme.com/monatomic-gold-science/the-torus/

Sebastiano, J. (2022, August 12). Ego self, higher self [Digital Image]. *James.Sebastiano.* Retrieved from https://www.instagram.com/p/ChKcX1fMymW/?hl=en

The 7 chakras. Their colors, symbols, meanings, and glands explained. (n.d.). *Voltlin.* Retrieved from https://www.voltlin.com/pages/chakras

Shipman, D. (2018, August 6). Holographic medical pods (Med Beds). *Blissful Visions*. Retrieved from http://www.blissfulvisions.com/articles/med-beds.html

Sinclair, G. (2021, January 24). The 12 archetypes of the human soul. *Awareness Act*. Retrieved from https://awarenessact.com/the-12-archetypes-of-the-human-soul/

6 types of kriyas to ultimate purification. (2020, October 6). *Rishikesh Yogis Yogshala*. Retrieved from https://www.rishikeshyogisyogshala.org/6-types-kriyas-ultimate-purification/

Smart, A. (2020). *Breathwork. How to Use Your Breath to Change Your Life*. San Francisco, CA: Chronicle Books.

Solfeggio frequencies and the chakras. (n.d.). *West Coast Yoga*. Retrieved from https://www.westcoastyogaperth.com/2020/06/30/solfeggio-frequencies-and-the-chakras/

Sprinkle, A., and Jwala. (2018, February 27). How to have energy orgasms. *Ra-Hoor-Khuit Network*. Retrieved from http://www.rahoorkhuit.net/library/yoga/tantra/techniques/how_to_have_energy_orgasms.html

Staff of Hermes [Digital Image]. (2022, July 6). *Hermes the Alchemist*. Retrieved from https://www.instagram.com/p/Cfrkz_QsZwb/?hl=en

Stanton, A. (2022, July 6). How does the color of your clothing affect your mood? *The Good Trade*. Retrieved from https://www.thegoodtrade.com/features/clothing-color-psychology

Stokes J. (2007, August 1). Scientists find extraterrestrial genes in human DNA. *Bibliotecapleyades*. Retrieved from https://bibliotecapleyades.net/vida_alien/esp_vida_alien_18n.htm

Strong, R. (2022, June 24). 5 ways to stimulate your vagus nerve and regain control from stress faster. *Insider*. Retrieved from https://www.insider.com/guides/health/mental-health/vagus-nerve-exercises

Synctuality. (2014, June 21). Activation of the chakras and forming the auric shield. *Mission Earth Home*. Retrieved from http://missionearthhome.blogspot.com/

Tang, V. (2022, July 8). Healing with sacred geometry. *Destination Deluxe*. Retrieved from https://destinationdeluxe.com/healing-with-sacred-geometry/

Tang, V. (n.d.). Wim Hof: The Iceman on breathwork, ice baths, and how to reset and control your immune system. *Destination Deluxe*. Retrieved from https://destinationdeluxe.com/wim-hof-method-iceman-breathwork/

Tracy, J. (2021, July 26). Sacred geometry: symbols, patterns, and meanings explained. *7 Chakra Store*. Retrieved from https://7chakrastore.com/blogs/news/sacred-geometry

True currency [Digital Image]. (2021, December 2). *The Law of Awareness*. Retrieved from https://www.instagram.com/p/CW_PJY2MZqR/?hl=en

Turner, J. (n.d.). QNRT therapy. *QNRT™ Professional Association*. Retrieved from https://www.qnrt.com/

Tuttle, C. (2019). *The Modern Chakra Guide. 7 Steps to Awaken Your Energy in Today's World*. Draper, UT: Live Your Truth Press.

The 12 layers of the auric field. (2022, March 23). *Lalulutres*. Retrieved from https://lalulutres.tumblr.com/post/19773541570/the-12-layers-of-the-auric-field

Ullman, D. (1995). *The Consumer's Guide to Homeopathy*. The Definitive Resource for Understanding Homeopathic Medicine and Making It Work for You. New York, NY: The Putnam Publishing Group.

Unani. (2020, February 20). *Vikaspedia*. Retrieved from https://vikaspedia.in/health/ayush/unani

Uses and benefits of Epsom salt baths. (n.d.). *SaltWorks*. Retrieved from https://seasalt.com/salt-101/about-bath-salt/epsom-salt-uses-and-benefits

Vince, G. (2015, May 25). Hacking the nervous system. *Mosaic Science*. Retrieved from https://mosaicscience.com/story/hacking-nervous-system/

Vishwavidyalay, A. (n.d.). Universal thermal scanner shows positive effect of Box Treatment. *Maharshi University of Spirituality.* Retrieved from https://www.spiritual.university/spiritual-research/universal-thermo-scanner-shows-positive-effect-of-box-treatment/

Walia, A. (2014, September 27). Nothing is solid and everything is energy. *Bibliotecapleyades.* Retrieved from https://bibliotecapleyades.net/ciencia/ciencia_quantum29.htm

Walsch, N. (2005). *The Complete Conversations with God. An Uncommon Dialogue.* New York, NY: TarcherPerigee.

Water: elixir of life. (2017, December 6). *The Wellness Enterprise.* Retrieved from https://thewellnessenterprise.com/water-elixir-of-life/

Weingus, L. (2022, April 27). How to open your third eye with 15 tips from experts. *Well + Good.* Retrieved from https://www.wellandgood.com/how-to-open-your-third-eye/

What aliens do on Earth (n.d.) [Digital Image]. *Memegine.* Retrieved from https://memegine.com/m/memes-dsdded/what-aliens-do-on-earth-what-h

What are you throwing away? [Digital Image]. (2021, September 23). *Living 5D in a 3D World.* Retrieved from https://www.facebook.com/

photo/?fbid=10226148868527417&set=g.773364133155150

What is 'manifestation journaling?' Here's everything you need to know. (2022, May 6). *Silk and Sonder.* Retrieved from https://www.silkandsonder.com/blogs/news/what-is-manifestation-journaling-heres-everything-you-need-to-know

When you've experienced a soul lesson for the 1500 lifetime [Digital Image]. (2021, April 27). *Living 5D in a 3D world.* Retrieved from https://www.facebook.com/photo/?fbid=10226405416300951&set=g.773364133155150

Where did you find that? [Digital Image] (2021, April 6). *The Three Waves of Volunteers with Sandy.* Retrieved from https://www.facebook.com/photo/?fbid=10161506620461840&set=g.252320189669740

Where energy gets stuck [Digital Image]. (2021, September 2). *We the Aether.* Retrieved from https://www.instagram.com/p/CTUnwRCLj2V/?hl=en

Wigington, P. (2019, November 27). Methods of Divination. *Learn Religions.* Retrieved from https://www.learnreligions.com/methods-of-divination-2561764

Wigington, P. (2019, April 26). 7 Ways to Develop Your Psychic Abilities. *Learn Religions.* Retrieved from https://www.learnreligions.com/ways-to-develop-your-psychic-abilities-2561759

Wooll, M. (2022, June 13). *The Benefits of Shadow Work and How to Use it in Your Journey*. Retrieved from https://www.betterup.com/blog/shadow-work

Yesun. (2020, November 25). The twelve auric layers explained. *Holistic Healing by Dani*. Retrieved from https://healingsydney.com.au/the-twelve-auric-layers-explained/

Yoshimitsu poem. Harrington, P. (2009). *The Secret to Teen Power*. Luxembourg Branch: Simon Pulse.

Thank You for Reading My Book!

I truly appreciate all of your feedback and I love hearing what you have to say.

I really need your input to help make the next version of this book and my future books better.

If you could please take a couple of minutes to leave a helpful review on Amazon letting me know what you thought of *Mind Blown:*

Thank you so much!!!

Teresa

www.ingramcontent.com/pod-product-compliance
Lightning Source LLC
Chambersburg PA
CBHW050245010526
44107CB00003B/193